THE H

OF ST JOHN BAPTIST CHURCH,

BROUGHTON-IN-AMOUNDERNESS

by

Brendan Hurley

Neice daughter of Half Sister Chris met in 2001 same time I met my Biological mother! They were very warm & welcomed us my Diana & Self. An amazing meeting. Diana Crane Welsh.

i

First published 2012.

© Brendan Hurley

The photograph reproduced above of the church interior will evoke affectionate memories among older parishioners. In many respects there is a comforting familiarity about the scene. However there are some interesting changes, notably in the lighting; the north and south curtained doorways, now blocked up; the curtained organ chamber and the carpeted aisles. Notable too are the damp-ridden walls before restoration and redecoration.

ACKNOWLEDGEMENTS

Many people have contributed to this book but I would especially like to thank the following for their support, their help and their knowledge so readily shared: Mr Michael Anson; Reverend Sidney Fox; Mr John Catterall M.B.E. and Mr Chris Couper.

DEDICATION

This book is dedicated to the memory of the late Joyce Rawlinson, a devout and dedicated parishioner, whose initial research into the history of Broughton Church inspired me to dig deeper.

CONTENTS

CHAPTER 9: TOWARDS THE NEW MILLENNIUM
Pages 79-87

CHAPTER 13: BELLS AND BELL RINGERS
Pages 150-157

INTRODUCTION

An English village church is much more than a building, more even than a place of community worship, it is a construct established firmly within our national cultural psyche. Whether it resembles a small cathedral or a stone-built dog kennel; whether in the heart of a village or perched on a hillside or isolated in a secluded valley; whether we view it as a sacred place, or take a more secular view, and consider only its architectural merits or lack of them, it is a place to which many of us are almost irresistibly drawn. Philip Larkin captures this peculiar magnetism and reverence, even for those living in what is sometimes deemed a secular, post-Christian society, in the lines:

> Once I am sure there's nothing going on
> I step inside, letting the door thud shut.
> Another church, matting, seats and stone,
> And little books; sprawlings of flowers, cut
> For Sunday, brownish now; some brass and stuff
> Up at the holy end; the small neat organ;
> And a tense, musty, unignorable silence
> Brewed God knows how long ago. Hatless, I take off
> My cycle-clips in awkward reverence.

(Church Going)

There is however another dimension to these holy buildings, one which I would like to consider in this book. A church, along with the land that surrounds it, is in its very essence, a sacred space but more than that, it forms what Roy Strong calls an *historic microcosm*. He explains:

Their very fabric tells us of prosperity and depression, of war and peace; extensions in size reflect rise in population; the names of the headstones reveal the families who for generations moulded the life pattern of the land around.

It is my considered view that Broughton Church has existed for close to a thousand years but what truly fascinates me is the way that its long history and that of the people who have worshipped there, are inextricably entwined, preserved and recorded in its very stones. I hope that this book helps all who are interested to read the building and to explore the history it records.

CHAPTER 1

THE ORIGINS OF A SACRED SPACE

If history deals with solid facts then few can be literally as solid as the date 1533 carved into the millstone grit of the tower of Broughton Church. In the same way that the building of many houses of that period and later, was commemorated by

a date carved into the lintel stone over the doorway, so the building of the tower and the church of which it was a part, was recorded in the stone mason's carving, whose own mark is illustrated below.

History however is also a matter of reasonable conjecture, stemming from those converging lines of probability that originate in variety of different sources and which come together to describe, with some degree of clarity and certainty, what is very likely to be true.

We can be certain then that a stone church existed on the site in the early part of the C16th. However, as I hope that this book proves, it is my considered view that a place of worship existed on the site long before that date.

DOMESDAY

It is asserted by some sources that a sacred place existed on the site of the present Broughton Church sometime in the early C12th, possibly about 1110 A.D. However no church or chapel is recorded there in the Domesday Book, compiled some twenty-five years earlier, possibly because this area, north of the Ribble, was inadequately surveyed.

Lancashire as a county or indeed a geographical area, did not exist at the time the Domesday survey was commissioned in December 1085 by William the Conqueror. The area in the southern part of what was to become Lancashire in

2

1182, was, sixteen years earlier, designated *Inter Ripam et Mersam*, in other words the land between the Rivers Ribble and Mersey, and formed part of the survey's return for Cheshire.

Land north of the Ribble was divided into six *hundreds*, one of which was Amounderness. This whole area, surveyed and reported as an appendage to Yorkshire and gifted later to Roger de Poitou by William, occupied less than a folio (two pages), in the final publication produced in 1086. It is reported as being almost entirely denuded of population and resources – only the area around Preston having any substantial population. This area, centred on Preston, consisted of 62 *vills*, the smallest unit in the Norman administrative system, and part of a manor, equivalent perhaps to a township or parish. Of these only sixteen were occupied and even then by *but few inhabitants, but how many is not known*: the rest were deserted and are described as *waste*, that is they had no fiscal value and no animal resources. Such areas were largely uncultivated or uninhabited, either as a result of the devastation incurred during what has become known as the *Harrying of the North*, ordered by William in 1069, or because of the destruction suffered during the turbulent times of its previous master, Earl Tostig of Northumbria, and the intestine wars accentuated by the downfall of Roger de Poitou. Indeed it has been suggested that William's surveyors did not actually penetrate this region at all and instead based their accounts on earlier Saxon tax returns. Such returns were recorded in *geld books*, *geld* being the tax levied annually by the crown to support its various military campaigns. The vagueness of the recorded facts about this area particularly, is perhaps indicative not of the inadequate work of trained Norman surveyors but rather of the purely financial returns of some earlier official.

Broughton was assessed as one *ploughland* or *carucate*, owned by Earl Tostig and after the Conquest, held in *thegnage*, i.e. it was land owned by the crown and held by a member of the territorial nobility, a *thegn* or thane, a rank those familiar with *Macbeth* will recognise. In terms of area, a *carucate* (from the Medieval Latin *carrucata* meaning a wheeled plough) was the amount of land which a farmer with 8 oxen could till in a single season, roughly equivalent to between 80 and 120 acres. This area was further subdivided into *oxgangs* or *bovates* based on the land which could be ploughed by a single ox in the same period and so equivalent to one eighth of a carucate.

What then does all this have to do with the foundation of a church at Broughton? Simply that though there are only three churches identified in the Amounderness hundred and noted in the Domesday Book, at *Prestune*, *Chiceham* (Kirkham) and *Micheles-cherche* (St Michael's-on-Wyre), there may well have been smaller chapels, built by and for particular important families. These private chapels or chantries, perhaps because they did not themselves have tenure of any cultivated land and so had negligible or nil taxable value, were not included in Saxon tax assessments. By default therefore they were not included in the Domesday survey. Thus it is perfectly possible that a simple wooden chapel, with an earthen floor and no heating or lighting, did exist on the present site next to Blundel Brook in the late C11th but was *hidden* from the survey simply because it did not appear in earlier *geld books*.

BROUGHTON CHAPEL IN THE TWELFTH CENTURY

If the existence of a church or chapel in the C11th is mere conjecture, then a certified copy of a decree of the Archbishop of York, dated December 1630, and found in an old safe in the church vestry in the late 1940s, offers firm evidence that a chapel definitely existed a century later. This decree, made at the request of John Glave and Edmund Blakey, chapel wardens of Broughton, was for the Vicar of Preston *to perform the cure of Broughton by sufficient deputy as from time immemorial*. The request is simple enough: that the Vicar of Preston *perform* or carry out the *cure*, or spiritual welfare, of the people of Broughton through an adequate deputy or curate. The key words however are, *as from time immemorial.*

Nowadays we often use this phrase merely to indicate that something has existed or been the custom, for many years. However in an ecclesiastical document such as this, the term at that time and until 1832, had a much more precise meaning. In English law, in terms of precedents and property disputes for example, the phrase *since time immemorial*, rather like *time out of mind*, indicated a time before legal history was recorded or the limit of legal memory. In 1275, by the first Statute of Westminster, the *time of memory* was limited to the reign of Richard the Lionheart, more precisely to the 6th July 1189, the date of his accession. In other words the phrase *from time immemorial*, referred specifically to a date on or before 1189. If the chapel wardens, through the Bishop, were pressing the Vicar of Preston to continue to appoint a curate to minister to the spiritual needs of those who worshipped at Broughton Chapel, as he had from *time immemorial*, then **a chapel had existed there at some date before 1189**. How long before that date needs to be explored more closely.

In the hundred years between 1050 and 1150, many local lords built small churches for their families, tenants and serfs, in a period that has become known as the *Great Rebuilding*. Local churches increased in number as a response to the emergence of many more self-contained manors, presided over by a thegn. This word *rebuilding,* however, suggests that many such chapels or churches dated from an even earlier period. While it is possible that Broughton Chapel was constructed during this period, it is more likely that it was built in the later decades of the C12th.

Between 1153 and 1160 William, Count of Boulogne, the son of King Stephen, confirmed to Uctred, son of Huck, and his heirs, ancestors of the Singleton family, eight oxgangs of land in Broughton by dint of service due, namely eight shillings per year. Uctred and his family took their surname from Little Singleton, which they held by Serjeanty of the wapentake of Amounderness. Richard de Singleton, the son of Uctred, succeeded. At some point after 1189, Richard de Singleton was ejected by Theobald Walter, whose holdings, the whole of Amounderness, were confirmed by Richard I.

4

Walter was the son of Hervey Walter and his wife Maud de Valoignes, who was one of the daughters of Theobald de Valoignes. Theobald's father had been the hereditary holder of the office of Butler of England, and when Theobald accompanied Prince John to Ireland in 1185, he was named Butler of Ireland, as well as a large section of the north-eastern part of the kingdom of Limerick.

The king conferred upon him the Butlership of Ireland in 1177, whereby he and his successors were to attend the Kings of England at their coronation, and on that day, present them with the first cup of wine

In 1194 Theobald supported his brother during Hubert's actions against Prince John, with Theobald receiving the surrender of John's supporters in Lancaster. He was rewarded with the office of Sheriff of Lancaster, which he held until Christmas of 1198. He was again Sheriff after John took the throne in 1199.

Early in the year 1200, however, John deprived Theobald of all his offices and lands because of irregularities which had surfaced during his time as Sheriff. His lands were not restored until January 1202.

If the chapel at Broughton was constructed towards the end of the C12th, that wooden or wattle and daub structure would almost certainly have been a private foundation, established, built and operated by a local lord, who had the power to install a priest of his own choosing, change that priest at will and even dismantle the church if he so chose. Given its future endowments and financial support from the Singleton family, it is highly probable that a chapel at Broughton was built by them while they were lords of the manor and in control of the area and before they were deposed by Walter. **This narrows down the time of its original construction to the thirty years between 1160 and 1190**.

After Theobald Walter's death and forfeiture, King John detained the manor. It subsequently remained in the hands of King Henry III, the township at this time providing the Crown with increased revenue.

THE MIDDLE AGES

By the middle of the thirteenth century the Church in England had become an organised body containing about 9,500 parish churches. At the same time the church began to develop as a recognisable building. In 1261, Henry III, after inquiry, restored Amounderness as a matter of right, to William de Singleton, grandson of Richard, who paid three marks of gold. It seems highly likely that William would have rebuilt, or at least refurbished, the simple wooden church built some years earlier by his grandfather Richard.

In 1325 Gilbert de Singleton held a *messuage* in Broughton, a dwelling place including outbuildings and orchards for example. By this time, the earlier wooden church built and maintained by his ancestors, would almost certainly have been replaced, if it had not been already, by some form of simple stone structure, one that would survive until the rebuild or refurbishment of the late 1520s and early 1530s.

In 1348 Archbishop Zouche granted a licence to Thomas Singleton, the son of Gilbert, to hold divine service by a fit chaplain within the manors of Broughton, Fernyhalgh and Farmunholes, for three years, *without injury to the parish of Preston*.

In a deed of 1377 a man named Geoffrey is noted as *chaplain* of the *hermitage* at Broughton, suggesting once again that a small, simple building existed on the site, in some isolation and as a private place of worship for the Singleton family, and that the three-year licence had been extended.

Another old deed discovered in an oak chest in the church vestry and now lodged in the Lancashire County Record Office, records a grant made on the 28th September 1433 from Ralph, son of Roger Hyles of Goosnargh to Thomas of Ureswyke Esq., of all his property in that village. A transcript of the deed is reproduced on page 7.

Fishwick writing in his book *The History of the Parish of Preston*, published in 1900, claims that a church existed on the site in the C14th and was founded prior to the Oratory at Fernyhalgh, for which a licence was granted to Nicholas Singleton in 1454. Again this points to Broughton Church being a similar private place of worship built much earlier by another branch of the family.

A second document, dated 20th May 1464, is a quit claim by Richard Barton Esq. to Robert Cowell, Vicar of Preston, dealing with the rights of the Goosnargh property, which belonged to Henry Broughton, chaplain, deceased. This Henry was the first recorded Vicar of Broughton and the land in question was that later given by Lawrence Stadagh in 1527 upon trust, to pay the yearly rent and profits to the Churchwardens of Broughton.

One Thomas Barton was underage when his father died. When Thomas reached the age of majority in 1535, proof of his age was attested in Wigan before a jury, by William Singleton of Synglehall (Chingle Hall) who verified that he was *present at Broughton Church on the day the said Thomas was baptised, and further, that Anna his wife, was godmother to the said Thomas and took him up from the font on that day in 1514*.

However references within several other legal documents further support the existence of a stone church at least a hundred years prior to the early years of the sixteenth century. In 1530 a dispute about property in Broughton and Goosnargh, which was taken to the Duchy Court, saw several witnesses testify that: *Adam Fyshwyke, grandfather of the plaintiff in the suit, married Isabel Barton and that there was a dyvorce redde in Broughton Church in or about the year 1460 and afterwards he married Margaret, daughter of James Syngleton of Brockhall, in 1460*.

Know ye, both present and future, that I Ralph
de Hyles son of Roger de Hyles of Goosnargh, have
given, granted, and by this my present
Charter have confirmed to Thomas de Urswick
his heirs and assigns, all my Lands and
Tenements in the Village of Goosnargh. To
have and to hold all their appurtenances
in the aforesaid village to the aforesaid
Thomas his heirs and assigns, of the chief
lord of that Fee, by the service thence due
and accustomed with Turbary and common
Pasture for ever, and with all the liberties
and Easements belonging to the aforesaid
Village.

And I, truly, the aforesaid Ralph
and my heirs all the aforesaid Lands
and Tenements with all their appurtenances as is aforesaid, against all men,
will warrant and defend for ever. In
testimony whereof to this present Charter
I have affixed my seal before these
Witnesses:—
      Allan   de Singleton
    William de Wytinghame
   Christopher Singleton de Wytenase
(N.J. 193 Coucher) Thomas de Singleton Senior
    Robert de Singleton
            and many others
Dated at Goosnargh on Monday next
before the feast of St. Michael the
Archangel in the twelfth year of the
reign of King Henry the Sixth after
the conquest.

                         (1433)

If Broughton church in the fifteenth century followed the normal building pattern and the northern fashion, it would be, as has been every church on the site, aligned east – west, with the altar at the eastern end.

It would have been a narrow, tall, rectangular building, the exterior and interior walls of which were plastered, the latter being vividly painted with Biblical scenes. Statuary would have adorned the nave.

Such imagery and iconography was hugely important to the medieval congregation. In an age when we take reading, writing and daily bombardment by visual images very much for granted, it is hard to grasp that we experience more visual stimulation in a day than an illiterate medieval villager would have seen in an entire lifetime. Almost all the images he experienced would have been those in the stained glass, statues and wall paintings of his local church. Moreover such images of saints, angels and especially the Virgin, an array of mediators between Earth and Heaven, intercessors, to whom the congregation could pray, would have been enormously reassuring to the parishioners.

The church would have probably been built in a style adapted from the basilica design brought over by Augustine and his followers from the Byzantine Empire. This design would have consisted of a rectangular nave housing the congregation and semi-circular apse where the altar was located. The apse gradually disappeared and, at Broughton, would have been replaced by a rectangular chancel, probably curtained off from the nave to hide the sacred mysteries during Mass, but with an imposing east window. At the same time a transept was added to the design, giving the familiar cruciform plan of so many country churches.

Wooden rood screens, often elaborately carved and built to replace the curtain across the chancel arch, depicted Christ on the cross, (the Anglo Saxon word *rood* or *rode* means cross) flanked by the Virgin and St John. These screens, many of which were lost during the Reformation, marked the division of nave and chancel, of church and laity. Such screens were often carved in a latticework: the word *chancel* itself derives from the Latin word *cancelli*, meaning latticework. The chancel belonged to the priest: the nave to the congregation, effectively separating the religious from the secular, and creating a situation in which each was responsible for the upkeep of its respective domain. The nave, common to all, represented the visible world, while the chancel, the province of the priest, typified heaven. There is no evidence that Broughton Church had such a screen at the time but a rood loft was added some years later, in 1547, either above an existing screen or, more likely, complete with a screen to replace a simple curtain.

Interestingly there was still no seating in churches and the small congregation stood or knelt in the nave: fortunately it was only much later that long sermons became popular, at least among those who delivered them! Though the celebration of Matins and Mass could still last some three hours, this was not perhaps the ordeal it appears as the congregation was likely to come and go during the service. An early Tudor poem had to remind churchgoers that a church;

> Is a place of prayer
> Not of claterynge and talkynge
> Charge them also to keepe theyr sight
> In the chirche close upon theyr bokes
> Stande or syt
> And never to walk in the chirche

At Broughton, as in every other church, Communion at this time was taken only at Easter. On every other Sunday only the priest consumed the Host; the congregation was only invited to kiss the pyx (a container for the host, often made of precious metal) and then symbolically, at the end of Mass, to take a portion of the Holy Loaf, baked in turn by different parishioners and brought to church. Broughton parishioners would have received annual Communion at the rood-screen, a piece of fabric, the *houselling* cloth, being stretched across their hands to catch any crumbs that may fall accidentally from the host. Communion was taken in only one form and everyone over the age of fourteen was obliged by law to take it.

Parish life at Broughton would have been structured by the events of the liturgical year: the feast and fast days that shaped everyone's weeks and months. Starting with Candlemas, the 2nd of February, at the end of the Christmas season, the year was marked by processions; the beating of the parish bounds; candles, banners, singing and hand-bells. With Holy Week as its climax, this was religion with a strong sense of theatre, that permeated everyday life in the village, and which through its rituals, impinged on every single person from cradle to grave; from Baptism, through marriage to Extreme Unction and burial.

It is difficult for us to imagine the impact that the disappearance of many of these ceremonies, which had shaped lives for generations, would have had on the Broughton congregation with the coming of the Reformation.

CHAPTER 2

BROUGHTON CHURCH IN THE C16TH

RE-BUILDING AND REFORMATION

Despite all the evidence identified in the previous chapter, Hardwick in his *History of Preston* asserts that the actual date of the foundation of Broughton Church remains uncertain:

The origin of the church is not known. The older portion of the present edifice is evidently of the time of Henry VIII. Laurence Stadagh bequeathed his lands, in the event of a school not being founded, for the repair of Broughton Church and the Church bridges in the eighteenth year of the reign of that monarch (1526).

In his book *Northward* Hewiston comments:

The present Church is the successor of one which stood on the same site certainly in 1527. The tower contains in its masonry, towards the top, a stone which bears the date 1533, and that is conjectured to be the year in which it was erected.

While there may be little agreement of the date of the foundation of St John's, the building as it existed in the pre-Reformation days of the early C16th and for the following three centuries, is the first about which any definite and detailed information is known.

Certainly, and not perhaps surprisingly, it would appear that in impoverished Lancashire, reconstruction, financed by wealthy families, was more attractive than routine maintenance funded by congregations. Though we do not know how the new tower at Broughton Church was financed, *we can be sure that most of the money came from gentry families* (Haigh, 1975).

References to the church were made in several wills of local families, in which it was often referred to as the *Parish Church of Broughton* and rarely as a chapel. This would suggest that even at this early date, attempts were being made to gain some degree of independence from the mother church in Preston. As Haigh indicates:

When the people's allegiance was directed towards a chapel, that chapel acquired, in the eyes of those who frequented it, a certain independence, and there was resentment of any interference by the incumbent and wardens of the parish church.

He continues:

Curates of chapels had little choice but to follow the dictates of local opinion, and when governments were trying to alter the religious beliefs of the people, there would be no change unless local opinion desired it.

It might be added that curates had even less choice about following the dictates of the wealthy gentry who financed their livings and churches. This dominant influence was very likely to have been felt at Broughton and, as indicated later in this chapter, would certainly have had important consequences once ideas of reformation began to bite.

Richard Haydocke, the son of Gilbert Haydocke, gentleman, in his will dated the last day of February 1557, bequeathed 6s 8d to be spent on *the ornaments of Broghton Church.* Richard Barton Esq. of Barton in his will of 1569 expressed the wish that he be buried in the *parish church of Broughton;* while one Ellen Dilworth left instructions in 1586 that her burial should be *in the church of Broughton.* John Crosse of Barton, in his will of 1623, asked that *my body be buried in the Chapel of Broughton under the seat there standing belonging to me, so near the pillar as conveniently might be.* Despite this reference to a chapel, Broughton Church had now become recognised as a church and had been since as early as 1559, when in a deposition the wardens were referred to as *churchwardens.*

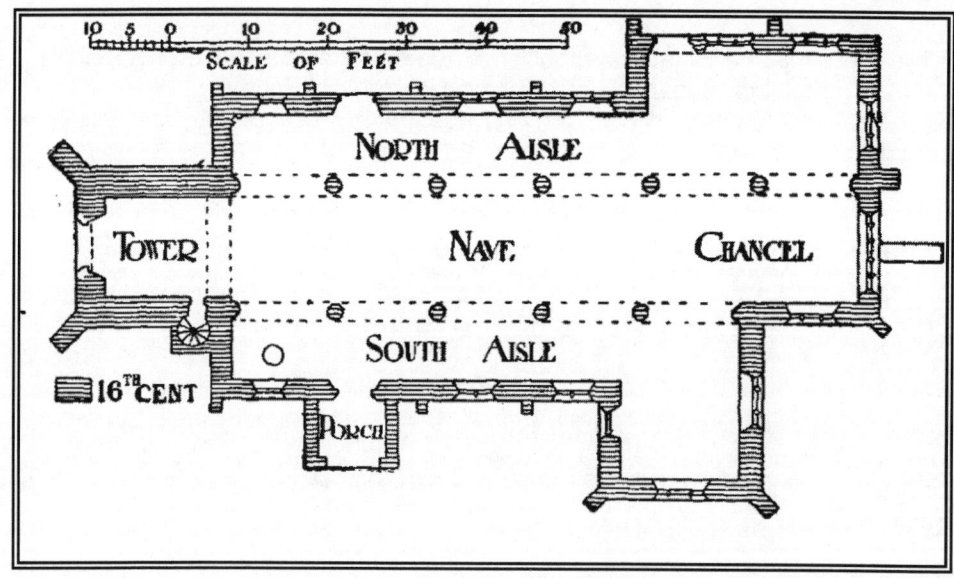

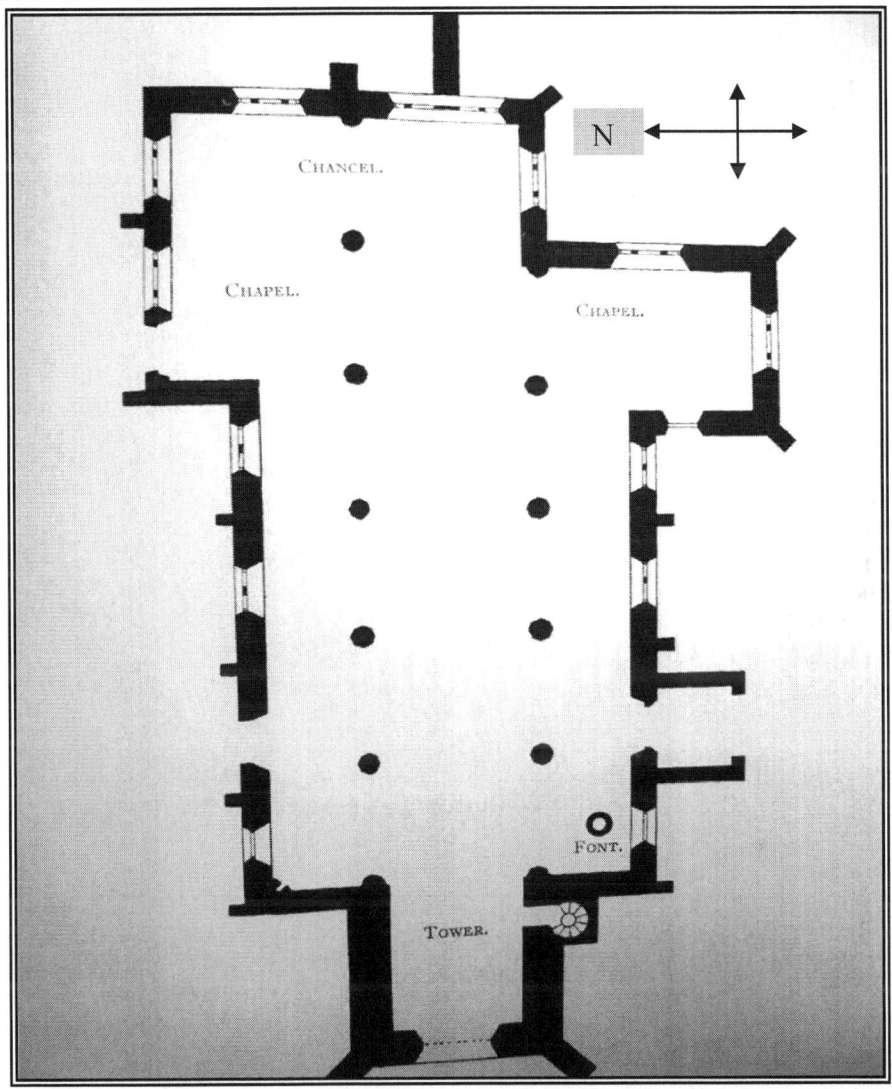

As can be seen from the diagrams of the pre-1823 building on the previous page and above, the church consisted of a nave and chancel, with a large chapel on the north side separated from it by an arcade of two arches and a smaller south chapel, open to the chancel through a single arch. The nave consisted of four bays and had north and south aisles, a south porch and a west tower. This was separated from the nave by walls some five feet wide. Both chapels projected beyond the line of the aisle walls and were separated from the nave by oak screens. There was no apparent structural division between the nave and chancel.

12

The roof was supported by two rows of four pillars down each side of the nave. Older Broughton inhabitants, in conversation with the vicar Samuel Collinson, described it as a plain, later type of Gothic building, with low, overhanging eaves and dormer windows.

Extrapolating from the marks of the old, pitched roof line, still visible on the east wall of the tower and pictured below, the old nave seems to have been some fifteen and a half feet wide (4.7m), with aisles possibly eight feet wide (2.4m). The total length of the nave and the chancel was approximately seventy-nine feet (24m).

The photograph above, shows the old roof line on the left-hand side of the tower's east wall

The interior of the building contained several images, repaired and repainted in 1512 through funding raised by a public collection. These paintings of St Katherine, St James, St Margaret, St Nicholas and St Syth, and their costly restoration, indicates perhaps that the cult of the saints and their images was strong and so attracted popular investment.

In 1547 a rood loft was added to Broughton chapel. While evidence of this structure no longer exists, the photograph on the following page of the one still to be found in Hubberholme Church, gives some idea of what it may have looked like.

THE CHAPELS

The Lady Chapel on the north side belonged to the Barton family of Barton and could be accessed through a private door. On the oak screen, which separated it from the chancel, there was carved an inscription, the arms and initials of Thomas Barton and his wife, Maud, (see below). This chapel also had associations with the Jacson and Shuttleworth families.

The south chapel or chantry was erected by the Singleton family, probably around 1537, when the church building prior to that date was rebuilt or enlarged. After that date it passed to other successive owners of Broughton Tower, the family home of that branch of the Singletons.

A chantry is the term for a fund established to pay for a priest to celebrate sung masses for a specified purpose, generally for the soul of the deceased donor. Chantries were endowed with lands given by donors, the income from which maintained the chantry priest. A chantry chapel was a building often dedicated to the donor's favourite saint, erected on private land or existing as an area within a greater church, as at Broughton, and set aside especially for and dedicated to the performance of the chantry duties by the priest. Many altars within them became richly endowed, often with gold furnishings and valuable vestments.

The degree of poverty in Lancashire in Tudor times had serious implications for the practice of religion. Congregations were generally not wealthy enough to maintain the fabric of their churches: in 1554-5 over half of the thirty-one churches visited by the Chancellor of the diocese were in need of repair. Clergy and churchwardens were often harried by officialdom to improve the condition of their churches and as a result were driven to sell church property. Broughton church, it would appear, enjoyed a more financially secure position, thanks mainly to the settled endowments and patronage of wealthy families such as the Singletons.

THE SINGLETON FAMILY

The Singleton family can be traced back to Huck or Hucca de Singleton, who was born c1100 in what we now know as Little Singleton. He married in or about 1124 and the couple had a son Uctred, probably born the following year. William Count of Boulogne and Earl of Warren gave Broughton to Uctred to hold upon payment of 8 shillings a year. Huck died in Broughton c1170, probably indicating that the family by that time had acquired lands in the area. His son, Adam or Alan de Singleton, born c1171, married Katherine and a tallage record, of Henry III (1219), one effectively detailing tax payable based on land tenure, associates Alan de Singleton with the *villat de Broctun*. His elder brother Richard however succeeded to the ownership of the Broughton lands and held them until he was ejected by one Theobald Walter, who was granted all the lands in Amounderness by Richard I.

In 1247-48 an inquisition was held by Adam de Hocton and others, which concluded that William le Saucer's land in Broughton formed no part of the inheritance of the now deceased Theobald Walter, and that the land had a value of two shillings and twopence a year. The dispute continued until a second inquisition in 1252, at which it was asserted that the Broughton lands had been wrongly taken from Richard, son of Uctred, and were worth 15 marks, 11 shillings and sixpence. Nine years later, in 1261, the matter was eventually settled by a Chancery inquisition when it was concluded that Theobald Walter had *by force and unjustly* ejected Richard son of Uctred, grandfather of William

15

de Singleton, who paid three marks of gold and who was now established as the legal owner of the disputed Broughton lands. In 1256 he had already acquired other lands in Broughton from Geoffrey the Cook, and in 1262 warranted a moiety of all his Broughton lands to his son Alan de Singleton.

So by 1261, the Singletons, as Lords of the Manor, had settled in Broughton, their manorial rights having been reinstated by Henry III. They had probably, as noted earlier, established a small wooden church or private chapel on the banks of Blundel Brook. William and Alan had both died sometime before 1292, when Alan's son, Thomas, was in possession of the Broughton Manor. Soon afterwards the same family estates were held by Joan, the sister and heir of Thomas and wife of Thomas Banastre of Bretherton. By 1325, Gilbert de Singleton held a messuage, a dwelling with its outbuildings and adjacent land, in Broughton, probably a structure on the site of Broughton Tower.

Broughton Tower itself was built by the Singleton family early in the sixteenth century. It was constructed in stone and surrounded by a moat, the outline of which is still evident today. Nothing however remains of the Tower: the ruins may well have provided building stone for the adjacent farmhouse on the north side of the moat.

1515 witnessed a fracas at the Tower. John Singleton of Chingle Hall, the younger son of the family, led an armed group of his henchmen, seeking to gain access to the building. At the time it was tenanted and claimed by one Arthur Standish, who had apparently provoked the attack by sending his own men to destroy hedges on Singleton land.

Singleton and his men captured the Tower and took goods, corn and cattle to the value of some £100. They broke into the kitchens, stables and barns, and felled trees to make defensive barriers. Once established, they defied the Sheriff, who appeared on the scene to proclaim that their occupation was illegal. The men inside drowned his words with bagpipe music and catcalls of derision.

A year later in 1516, Arthur Standish put in a claim for the manor against John Singleton, who was later indicted for illegally taking rents, beating and driving out tenants, several of whom were injured in the skirmish. At the hearing Sir Edward Hall, described in his testimony as *parish priest of Broughton*, gave evidence that John Singleton had eventually withdrawn his force from the scene of the battle. Both parties were bound over to keep the peace.

The show of force appears to have had a significant long-term effect: by 1567 the usurpers had gone and the Singleton family were now legally in residence. In his will dated that year, Edward Singleton states:

I, Edward Singleton of Broughton Tower, desire to be buried in my chapel within Broughton Church. To Thomas, my son and heir, I give my silver salt, which my mother-in-law gave me. Whereas James Adamson of Broughton holds of me certain lands, I will that my executors take the profits thereof to the use of my

16

four younger sons, William, Andrew, George and Richard, and I appoint Thomas Houghton, John Westby and my cousin William Singleton of Scale to be my executors.

This same Edward Singleton, who aided the escape of the Catholic priest Edward Bamber, was a devout Catholic himself. Despite sequestrations, numerous mortgages and insidious recusancy dues, the family managed to hang on to the Tower until financial persecution in the early years of James I forced them to vacate the property.

A deed of enfeoffment (a deed by which an individual was given land in exchange for service) by John Westbie of Molebeck (Mowbreck near Kirkham) dated 16th January 1575, mentions a Thomas Singleton of Broughton Tower, who had succeeded his father Edward in 1567. The will of Anne Singleton, wife of his brother William, was witnessed in 1565 by Sir Roger Sharnock, curate of Broughton.

In 1585 it was reported that Mr Singleton of the Tower harboured yet another Jesuit priest, Mr Lowe, alias Jensonne. He had been ordained in Rheims in 1579 and then set out for England. He was apprehended and, after a period in Salford gaol, was exiled.

A list of freeholders in the Amounderness Hundred created in 1600, notes a *Thomas Singleton de Teower* (Broughton Tower), which is described as *a strong, heavy structure of stone – capable of being fortified with its surrounding moat.* The family's loyalty to the Old Faith and the fines that resulted from their recusancy, left the estate somewhat impoverished.

THE LANGTON FAMILY

The Langton family, originally from Kirkham, formed an early association with the Singletons. Hugh Langton held the office of Mayor of Preston in 1431. Roger Langton was baptised in 1559 and was buried at Broughton on the 3rd April 1644. Clearly a man of some influence, power and longevity, he was Mayor of Preston on four occasions: 1605, 1616, 1632 and 1639. His son, William Langton, was elected M.P. for Preston in 1645 and continued in office, through the difficult days of the Civil War, until 1652.

In November 1589, the Langtons were allied with the Singletons in an attack on Lea Manor, the home of Richard Hoghton, and what had been the principal Hoghton home until the completion of Hoghton Tower in 1565. The site still exists today as Old Lea Hall Farmhouse on Blackpool Road, Preston, though little of the original house remains.

Thomas Langton sought to recover cattle stolen by Richard Hoghton from Mrs Singleton, recently widowed and under his protection. The cattle were impounded in the courtyard of Lea Manor. This at least was the pretext for the

17

attack: in truth however the dispute between the two families was long-standing, the origins of the feud, rather like that between Shakespeare's Montagues and Capulets, lost in the mists of time. The alleged cattle rustling incident simply appears to have been a pretext for further dispute and bloodshed.

After the theft of her cattle, Mrs Singleton rode to Broughton Tower to inform Thomas Langton, her dead husband's friend, of what had happened and he quickly rallied his retainers and supporters.

In total some eighty Langton men gathered at midnight on Preston Marsh, identifying themselves with the password: *the crow is black*. On reaching the manor house, a number of men tried to seize the cattle, while the others defended them against the thirty Hoghton retainers. The latter however had already been alerted to the possibility of attack, and armed with an array of weapons, including staves, a pike, a gun charged with *haileshot*, two pistols, one bow and arrow and numerous swords and daggers, resisted violently. The battle was bloody, and amid the blows and the darkness, Thomas Hoghton was killed while Thomas Langton was badly wounded: the cattle were not secured.

Langton was arrested as he lay wounded in his bed at Broughton Tower and was taken off to Lancaster Castle. Others, including Mrs Singleton, were also arrested and imprisoned. However so powerful and influential was Thomas Langton, that no jury could be impanelled: no-one was prepared to suffer his wrath by serving on a jury in judgement of him. After much correspondence between the authorities in London and those in Lancashire, the problem was resolved when Langton offered the wealthy manor of Walton to the Hoghton family in recompense for Richard's death – and the offer was accepted. Langton, realising that sooner or later a jury would be gathered, clearly decided that it was better to lose the Walton manor than risk the uncertainties of a trial and its verdict. So valuable a property was clearly more highly regarded by the Hoghtons than any punishment which the law might mete out.

Around the turn of the century the Broughton estates, the Tower and demesne lands passed from the Singleton to the Langton family. Roger Langton (1559 – 1644), bought the manor of Broughton, including Broughton Tower, from the Singletons in 1615.

The triple chevron of the Langton family, carved indelibly into the very stone of the church

All that remains of Broughton Tower today is the rectangular moat, stretching across the unadopted section of Tower Lane in Fulwood. It was fed by Sharoe Brook.

William's son, Richard, appears in the Preston Mayoral list of 1692 as chief magistrate. His other son, also William, was living at Broughton Tower in 1714: his grandson was the last of the Langtons to reside there. One of his grand-daughters, Jane, was married in 1735, at the ripe old age of 70, to Lawrence Rawsthorne of Preston to whom she left the Tower, which was demolished in 1800. The Arms and initials of the Langton family appear on a stone fixed in the eastern end of the church and there is a memorial plaque on the west wall above the font.

This influential family, like the Singletons, was a significant benefactor of Broughton Church.

We often speak of the Reformation almost as if it were a singular event, like a battle for example, that could be somehow pinned down to a particular date and location. It is much more useful however to think of it as a lengthy process, albeit a bloody and at times a ruthless one, spanning several decades and having a diverse and variable impact on religious life in different parts of the country over those years. For the majority of the population, the Reformation, far from being experienced as any kind of national upheaval, was almost entirely about what happened or ceased to happen in their local church.

We also tend to consider it as having its roots and inspiration in the need to reform a corrupt church, which was dominated by 'objective' ritual and ceremony at the expense of a more 'subjective' religious experience based on Bible reading in the home. Contemporary opinion however seems to suggest the Reformation, or at least its inspiration, was much more about wresting fiscal and financial control away from the Church and redirecting it to the Crown, along with the political power that obviously came with it.

Whatever it was, what it was not was a populist revolution: it had no roots in the lives of ordinary people or their demands for change. Instead it was imposed, at times savagely, from above, on people whose entire lives were shaped by the notion of obedience to those in authority, be they secular or religious.

In general terms of course it ended the Pope's control of the English Church and gave to Henry VIII not only the power to regulate the appointment of clergy but also to a large extent, to dictate ritual and the teachings of the church. Adornments, images, statues and holy relics were swept away, as well as those forms of worship considered Popish.

Edward VI, Henry's son, suppressed the chantries, such as that of the Singleton family at Broughton, and converted the endowments from them to his own use. In 1552 a national inventory was taken of all church goods, and those no longer deemed necessary for divine service according to reformed views of worship were to be sold. This would include such items as church vestments, chalices, altar cloths, and bells.

How would the people of Broughton have coped with the cataclysmic events that tore apart the rhythm of everyday life and threatened a piety that had evolved over more than a thousand years? What impact would this seismic change have had on the church and congregation at Broughton, especially during its most turbulent phase from 1547-1570? Probably, in the short term, very little. In Lancashire there existed a very strong party in favour of the old form of religion so the wholesale discarding of old institutions, artefacts and forms of worship met with near open rebellion. There is every reason to suppose that influential and devout Broughton families, such as the Singletons and Langtons, would not easily renounce their faith and abandon the church their money had benefited.

Indeed after the Reformation the Singleton family remained staunchly Catholic. Displaying a practically religious if not cognitive dissonance, they paid their recusancy fines but kept out of more serious trouble by contributing to the Church of England curate's stipend at Broughton Church: a deed of 1658 for example, records that the family paid £5 every six months towards this. In this way, superficially at least, they appeared to support the Established Church, while as we have seen earlier, privately they harboured Catholic priests seeking refuge from the authorities.

However they could not have avoided or failed to notice the changes of 1536. A revision in the observance of holy days would have had an immediate impact, especially in a rural area like Broughton: all feasts falling between July 1st and 29th September were abolished, apparently because they interfered with the gathering of the harvest and took labour from the fields. Abolished too were those high days within the Westminster law terms, as they hindered government administration. There were some exceptions, such as the feasts of the Apostles, the Virgin, Ascension Day, and perhaps most relevantly in Broughton, the nativity of John the Baptist. In practice, however, these directives were largely ignored and people continued to celebrate local saints as they always had.

In the same year the first doctrinal statement of the reformed Church appeared. The Ten Articles brought no dramatic change, though only three of the seven sacraments were maintained – baptism, penance and the Eucharist. Clergy were instructed to warn their flocks against the worshipping of images, though as yet these were not removed.

Two years later parishes were ordered to purchase a copy of Miles Coverdale's English translation of the Bible, and make it freely available to all. Saints were removed from the litany; the rosary condemned, and candles and tapers were not to be displayed before any image or picture. A further requirement, now useful to the historian but then viewed almost solely as a means of administrative control, was that:

The curate of every parish church shall keep one book or register, which book he shall, every Sunday take forth and in the presence of the churchwardens or one of them, write and record in the same all the weddings, christenings and burials made the whole week before.

The book was to be kept in a locked chest within the church: one of which can still be found in Broughton Church. Moreover, this innovation was revolutionary and a first step towards making priests and parish officers effectively agents of the state.

Mary's accession in 1553 brought any reforms to an abrupt halt and a return to the old order, which Lancashire Catholics took full advantage of. This respite for them was however brief. When Queen Mary died in November 1558, this not only put an end to the ruthless persecution of Protestants over the previous five years but also, under Elizabeth, took things back to what they had been in her father's day.

On the 23rd May 1559, a year into Elizabeth's reign, an Oath of Supremacy was ordered to be taken in Lancashire, by proclamation of the Chancellor of the Duchy. Both clergy and laity were required to attest to it. Any restored chantries were now to be used in accordance with the Reformed Church; the host was not to be elevated, and the Lord's Prayer, the Creed and the Gospel were all to be read in English. Such changes would almost certainly have been evident in the worship at Broughton church.

In 1567 the Bishop of Chester, in a letter from Queen Elizabeth herself, was reproved in no uncertain terms:

We think it is not unknown how, for the good opinion we conceived of your former service, we admitted you to be bishop of the diocese; but now, upon credible reports of disorder and contempts, especially in the county of Lancaster, we find great lack in you.

Following this reproof, the Bishop undertook a personal visitation into the more remote parts of his diocese and, as a result, felt it necessary to warn rebellious clergy and their congregations that among other things:

they use no beades and that they *abolish and utterly extirpate all manner of idolatrie and superstition out of the Church immediately.*

Curates were reprimanded for *showing and suffering candles to be burnt in the chapel on Candlemas daye, accordinge to the old superstitious custom.* These too would be changes obvious to the Broughton congregation.

However, as Fishwick asserts in his book *A History of Lancashire*:

In Lancashire the feeling in favour of the old form of religion was so strong that for some years little or no permanent change was effected, as nearly all the oldest and most powerful families were rigid Roman Catholics.

There is evidence that recusant priests conducted marriages in 1574 and said masses in Preston in 1578. In 1590 a priest was reported as celebrating Mass in the village of Broughton at the home of Widow Dilworth. William Cowell of Preston reported that he had found one Edmond Haworth *saying mass after the popish manner* in a loft at the east end of the house of Widow Dilworth in Broughton Village at about 10 o'clock in the morning. He was *attired in massing apparel*, wearing a vestment, alb and stole, and with a mass book, chalice, paten and other *furniture*. The widow was present, along with her sons and daughters and one or two others. The informant *apparently terrified with cries of, 'Strike, strike! Kill! Kill! Now or never!'* – though it is not clear from the evidence or wording whether he was the one terrified or the one who was doing the terrifying. In any event William Cowell was bribed with a gift of 7 *nobles* and promised to keep silence and return the paten and chalice he had seized. Having taken the money however, he promptly reported his discovery to the Mayor of Preston and other authorities. There is no record of the outcome of his betrayal.

Interestingly the vast majority of clergy agreed to accept the new form of religion rather than resign their livings. As a consequence, in many parishes, the vicar or rector was often a Papist in disguise. This was certainly true in the case of Evan Banester, who may have been vicar at Broughton for a brief time in the 1550s. He was identified as a *wanted* priest in 1568; by 1570 he was in Mitton; a year later he was recorded in the deanery of Amounderness; in 1580 he was still in the Fylde area. When, after 1585, it became an act of high treason to harbour Catholic priests, his fate was sealed. Whatever he had attested to, he had never actually abandoned his Catholic principles. In that same year Evan Banester was named as being illegally harboured by one William Charnock in his home on Fulwood Moor, and was accused too of saying a mass on *Lady Day in lent last*. Banester was brought before the Court Leet, found guilty and exiled

Was this same position adopted by Sir Richard Sharnocke, vicar at Broughton between 1548 and 1565? Certainly even by 1591 a report indicated that the Lancashire commission had made *small reformation* and notwithstanding the rigour of the law, churches were still empty and *there remained multitudes of bastards and drunkards*; the people *lacked instruction, for the preachers are few; most of the parsons are unlearned, many of them non-resident, and divers unlearned daily* [are] *admitted into very good benefices*. Even worse, the young were *for the most part trained up by such as profess Papistry*. The report complained too that *all parsons, vicars and churchwardens*, were not regularly examined under oath as to their obedience to the statutes governing the Church. Some *of the coroners and justices and their families do not frequent church, and many have not communicated at the Lord's Supper, since the beginning of Her Majesty's reign*. Some clergy had *refrained from preaching for lack of auditors, and people swarm in the streets and the ale-houses during the divine service time*.

Was this the case at Broughton? Had the people turned their backs on the Church? Did those who attended services do more harm than good by their *crossinge and knockinges of theire breste and sometimes with beads closely handled*.

The whole report had a strong Puritanical tone to it and, in that respect, was to prove singularly prophetic as the new century unfolded.

CHAPTER 3

THE BROUGHTON ADVOWSON AND STIPEND

Advowson is defined in English law as the right of presenting a nominee to a vacant ecclesiastical benefice.

Clearly the patronage of Broughton Church was initially in the hands of the influential families who financed it and latterly tied inextricably to that of the mother church in Preston. In 1521 the parsonage and tithes of Preston and Broughton were leased to Richard Hesketh of Howick, for a period of twenty-five years by the Dean and Chapter of Newark. After his death, his brother and executor, Thomas Hesketh of Rufford, sold the tithes for the remaining period of the twenty-five year term to Richard Hoghton of Preston. This was subject to an annual rent of £16 6s 0d, payable to his representatives.

On the 22nd November 1604, after several disputes over the preceding eighty years, the rectory of Preston along with certain glebe lands and the chapel of Broughton, were formally granted to Sir Richard Hoghton at the behest of one Roger Aston.

In 1646, at a meeting of the *Committee for Plundered Ministers*, it was decided that £20 per annum *should be paid out of the tythes of the towne of Broughton, sequestered from Sir Edward Wrightington, for and towards the maintenance of a minister in the chappell of Broughton, annexed to the Church of Preston.*

In the same year, the Committee ordered the sum of £50 to be paid out of the profits of the impropriate rectory of Poulton, sequestered from Sir Thomas Tildesley and John Greenhalgh, *delinquents*, to increase the *maintenance of the minister of the parochiall chappell of Broughton, within the parish of Preston...the said chappelrie consisting of six hundred families.*

In 1650 the stipend was set at £40 per annum, paid from monies raised through sequestrations, those incomes derived from, or the fines paid to recover properties seized from Royalists and papists. A year later the minister's *maintenance* did not actually exceed a mere 20 shillings a year and £50 was allowed from the tithes of Leyland, sequestered from one James Anderton, described as a *papist and delinquent for increase of the maintenance of James Knott, minister of Broughton and Barton*. In a confirmatory Committee order made some months later, Ralph Banister and William Osborne, *papists and delinquents* are named as contributories, out of impropriate tithe profits, to the yearly payment of £50 and *all arrears thereof incurred* since the original order had been made. Such sequestrations and the money they provided clearly ended with the Restoration in 1660

In 1658 there was probably the first significant attempt to create an endowment specifically for the Broughton living. This came through a conveyance in trust by Sir Edward Writington and several others, of part of the Langton estate, which they bought and then leased back to William Langton for a period of one thousand years at a rental rate of £10 per annum. This money was to be used for: *enlarging the means and maintenance of a preaching minister within the Church at Broughton*. It is worth noting too that the reference here is once again to the *church* at Broughton rather than a chapel.

In 1683 Sir Charles Hoghton nominated Thomas Ryley to the curacy of Broughton, and wrote to the Vicar of Preston, Thomas Birch:

Whereas of antient right (as by letters patent under the great seal of England, in the reign of our late sovereign, James, by the grace of God, of England, Scotland, France and Ireland, King) it doth appear that the nomination of a fit person to serve as curate of the chapel of Broughton doth to me unquestionably belong. I, therefore, nominate Thomas Ryley, batchelor of arts, of, Jesus College, Cambridge, as a person of his learning and piety, fit to be by the said Vicar of Preston appointed to be curate of Broughton, as soon as he shall be admitted into episcopal orders and have obtained letters of licence to serve as the said curate under the hand and seal of the Lord Bishop of Chester, witness my hand and seal this twenty fifth day of May, 1683.

In 1717 the vicar's income was recorded as £34 a year. Richard Cross had given £100 and the Vicar of Preston usually paid £4 each year.

The 1760s witnessed a lengthy dispute between the Hoghton family and the Vicar of Preston, Randal Andrews, in respect of the appointment of a successor to Broughton's curate, Joseph Cowper. The Dean and Chapter of Leicester had leased the advowson and glebe rights of Preston to the Bradshaye family, who in turn sold them to the Bold family, from whom the Hoghtons bought them. Sir Henry Hoghton produced the evidence of several indentures, dating back to 1662, to prove this purchase, which he claimed included the right to appoint the curate at Broughton. Andrews, on the other hand, claimed that the Hoghton family had on many occasions, shown no interest in patronage.

Henry Hoghton, ignoring Andrews' protestations, wrote to the Bishop of Chester:

To the Right Reverend Father in God, Edmond, Lord Bishop of Chester, Henry Hoghton of Hoghton, baronet, doth send greetings. Whereas the curacy of the chapel of Broughton in the parish of Preston, and your lordship's diocese, is now void by the death of Joseph Cowper, clerk, the last incumbent there, and doth of right belong to my gift or donation. These are therefore humbly to certify to your lordship that I do nominate John Hunter, Clerk, to be curate of the said chapel of Broughton, humbly beseeching your lordship to grant him your licence for serving the said cure.

In 1774 an augmentation to the stipend was obtained from *Queen Anne's Bounty*, which had been set up in 1704 by Queen Anne herself. Through its auspices, revenues, specifically *first fruits* and tithes of ecclesiastical benefices, which had since the Reformation been paid to the Crown, were now to be used to increase the incomes of poorer Church of England clergy. From pre-Conquest days clergy had received income from their living; the taxes due on that income were paid to the Pope until the 1530s, when they were claimed by Henry VIII.

Following the death of Queen Anne in 1714, an Act of Parliament, described as one *for making more effectual her late Majesty's previous intention for augmenting the Maintenance of Poor Clergy*, enshrined the royal benevolence in law. In 1732 the Vicar of Preston Samuel Peploe contributed ten guineas to a fund for obtaining the Bounty, and in 1774, the year an augmentation was received, Sir Henry Hoghton is listed as a donor of ten guineas. Other local people such as John Cross of Barton Hall, Thomas Boys of Barton and William Cardwell, contributed half a guinea each. It is mere coincidence perhaps that an augmentation was received from the Bounty in the same year that these donations were made,

By 1890 a total of some £176,896 was distributed nationally. Almost sixty years later, in 1947, Queen Anne's Bounty merged with the Ecclesiastical Commissioners to form the Church Commissioners.

In 1867, Sir Henry Hoghton sold the Broughton Advowson to John Bretherton of Leyland, who in 1873, transferred it to Reverend William Bretherton, his brother, who became Vicar in 1872, only a year after Broughton had become a separate ecclesiastical Parish. On his death, the Advowson was left in the hands of five trustees, three of whom: C.R. Jacson of Barton Hall, Edward Wilson of Bank Hall and John Hargreaves of Liverpool, administered its provisions and responsibilities.

The role of the Patrons, as they became known, continues today. They do not hold any lands or estate, but simply have the right to appoint the Vicar (the Advowson). Since 1885 there have never been more than five or fewer than three Patrons, who are self-appointing, so that when a vacancy occurs, they themselves appoint a successor. In one sense they act on behalf of and in conjunction with the Bishop, presenting to him their chosen candidate for Vicar at the Induction Service.

At the turn of the century the glebe inventory, tabulated and illustrated overleaf, detailed church financial and property assets as well as land, the ground rents from which supported the stipend. In addition to the usual and expected buildings and land, such as the vicarage and adjacent fields, rents were drawn from developed land in Ribbleton Lane, Brewery Street, Malt Street and Duke Street East for example.

A True Note Terrier and Inventory of all the Glebe
Lands Houses Benefaction Properties and other Rights belonging
to the Vicarage & Parish Church of St John Baptist Brighton
in the Hundred of Amounderness in the County of Lancaster and
Diocese of Manchester now in the use and possession of Samuel
Edward Collinson. Clerk. Vicar of the said Church

Imprimis   The Vicarage House with Stable Barn & other
    Outbuildings and Garden therein belonging containing

Item The Church Yard containing

Item a Field on the north side of the Church Lane &
adjoining the Vicarage Garden containing

through which there lies a foot path from the Vicarage House
to the Church but for no other purpose

Item a Field on the south side of the Church Lane bounded
on the South side thereof by Blundell Brook containing

PROPERTY / ITEM	ADDITIONAL INFO	VALUE / INCOME
Vicarage house with stable, barns and outbuildings		
Vicarage garden		
Churchyard		
Field on north side of Church Lane, adjoining vicarage and garden	Footpath passes through to give access from vicarage to church and for no other purpose	
Field on south side of Church Lane	Bordered on south side by Blundel Brook	
Hill Top Farm and farmhouse in Goosnargh	29 acres	
Aqueduct conduit passing through above property	Owned by Mayor, Aldermen and citizens of Manchester	Perpetual yearly rent of £1.5s.0d (1889)
Land forming the site of numbers 3,4,5 and 6 Milton Street, Preston	Four messuages	Perpetual Yearly Ground Rent (PYGR) of £6. 8s. 0d. (1888)
Land in Ribbleton Lane, Preston	Three messuages totalling 449 square yards	PYGR of £5.12s. 4d (1850)
Land forming the site of the mill houses adjoining Sovereign Mill in Stanley Street, Preston	1033 square yards	PYGR of £5. 5s.0d (1837)
Land forming the site of numbers 103, 107 and 107 Ribbleton Lane	Three messuages 353 square yards	PYGR of £ 4. 8s.5d (1850)

PROPERTY / ITEM	DETAILS	VALUE / INCOME
Farm and lands at Singleton Tower in Broughton		Perpetual yearly rent of £20
Land forming the site of numbers 28-32 Duke Street East; number 2 Brewery Street; number 47 Malt Street	Seven messuages	PYGR of £7 (1846)

Yearly sum in stipend	Paid by Vicar of Preston	£4
Yearly sum in stipend	Paid by Ecclesiastical Commissioners for England	£15. 6s. 0d
Capital sum of £1000	Held on behalf of the Benefice and Governors of Queen Anne's Bounty in the Augmented Livings No 1 Trust	Interest on both capital sums was payable at £3 percent per annum
Capital sum of £200	Held on behalf of the Benefice and Governors of Queen Anne's Bounty in the Harris Bequest Trust	
Capital sum of £1700	Invested in the names of the Vicar and Churchwardens	
Capital sum of £500	Invested in the name of the Vicar and Churchwardens	

In the late 1920s there was some discussion about increasing the stipend. Stocks had depreciated significantly even since 1925, and as a result income too had fallen. Gross receipts from invested capital in 1925 were in excess of £356: by 1927 it had fallen to £319. Pension deductions of some £17 reduced the sum even further, and there was a real fear that very soon the stipend from investments would fall below £300.

It was decided to add half the income from burial fees for those outside the parish to the Vicar's income, and that the Church Council would in future, pay the pension premium and the *dilapidations* charges.

By the 1950s the stipend still derived from two ancient ground rents secured upon farmland near Broughton and a small parcel of ground rents secured upon house property in Preston, the gift of a former parishioner in the 1870s. Some of the benefice income came from Government investments and some from fees received by the vicar, including burial fees. The Church Commissioners also contributed to the stipend, which from all these sources, amounted to some £470. In 1955 the Patrons of the Living agreed to augment the stipend by doubling the vicar's £50 car allowance, and by increasing the stipend itself by £100.

In April 1961 the Church Commissioners raised the basic minimum stipend for beneficed clergy to £700 per annum. To this was added the whole of the Easter offering (not the allowance of £50, as had been the custom in past calculations), the cost of rates and the dilapidation assessment. In addition, children's allowances were introduced for those clergy with children between the ages of 5 and 18. The allowance for the first child was £20 p.a., for subsequent children it was £15. Despite these improvements, the Bishop looked forward to the day when stipends, still far behind what they should be especially compared to other professionals, could be augmented substantially. He commended those P.C.C.s which already made provision for the payment of out-of-pocket expenses, such as those incurred from postage and the use of a telephone and car, hoping this would become a matter of obligation for all.

CHAPTER 4

THE SEVENTEENTH CENTURY – CIVIL WAR AND PURITAN REFORMS

God is decreeing to begin some new great period in His church, even to the reforming of the Reformation itself. (Milton – Aeropagitica – 1644)

For the Church of England, the seventeenth century was for many an age of disillusionment. For those Puritans, like Milton for example, it was, initially at least, a time for great optimism. Those generations that had lived through the events of the mid and late 1500s now witnessed a religious settlement, which was a peculiar hybrid of Protestant doctrine and Catholic practice.

At the beginning of the century Amounderness remained a *Catholic* deanery. Of the 3,322 recusants identified in 1604, some 2,661 were living in only thirteen parishes, one of which was Preston, *one of the most thoroughly recusant in Lancashire.* It was still notorious as an area in which *people were used to signing themselves with the sign of the cross on the forehead at all prayers and blessings.* Broughton Church would almost certainly share in this *vigorous resistance to official attempts to impose the new religion.*

However the growth of Puritanism in the years leading up to the Civil War, especially evident in Lancashire, so long a stronghold of Catholicism, would provide even more radical reforms to be challenged and resisted.

During the first twenty-five years of the century, there existed an antipathy but uneasy co-existence between the Puritan faction and those within the Church of England who sought to reintroduce ordered ceremonial worship. These ceremonialists, greatly influenced by Bishop Andrewes of Winchester, sought to restore the centrality of the sacraments, especially the Eucharist. For the Puritans however, this was an ordinary meal, a purely commemorative act, the Holy Table merely a table. For the followers of Andrewes, the ceremony was one in which Christ was actually present: the Holy Table was once again an altar, to be placed in a position of reverence and to be separated from the congregation by rails. It should be bowed to; steps should lead to it and it should be covered in a rich cloth. The Church view prevailed and gained authority in 1625 when Charles I acceded to the throne and in 1633 when William Laud became Archbishop of Canterbury. The latter endorsed the return to imagery and decoration in churches, seen by him as *the beauty of holiness*, a piety that celebrated and found inspiration in a powerful aesthetic element. After 1630, this reordering of churches became mandatory: for the Puritans, popery was back!

The Long Parliament, of 1640, dominated by Puritans, concluded that change in the form of religious worship was an absolute necessity. Even before then, in Puritan parishes, the communion rails were torn down and the surplices literally torn from the backs of clerics and their prayer books snatched from them and torn up. In 1641 Parliament appointed commissioners to demolish and remove from all churches and chapels:

all images, altars or tables turned altar-wise, crucifixes, superstitious pictures, and other monuments and relics of idolatry.

LITURGICAL REVOLUTION

By 1640, having gained Parliamentary power and with an army to enforce the support of their reforms, the Puritans sought to destroy any allegiance to the Book of Common Prayer and eradicate any lingering Catholic ceremony. Between 1643 and 1648 a new, Presbyterian model of Church government developed. In October 1646 Lancashire was divided into nine *Presbyteries*, Preston being linked with the parishes of Garstang, Kirkham and Poulton. These *classes*, as they were called, immediately took control of all ecclesiastical matters, and were grouped into provincial assemblies, one for each county. Representatives from each assembly came together to form a national synod at the apex of the structure. However it is certainly true that such management changes remained almost completely theoretical and only one fifth of the 40 English counties reorganised themselves along these lines – twenty-four counties did not even reply to Parliament's directive. Clearly such changes, like so many others, did not really impact on grass-roots clergy and congregations half so much as the decision by the Assembly at Westminster, over a year earlier, on January 3, 1645, to replace the Book of Common Prayer with the *Directory of Public Worship*. Its inspiration and essence can be seen in the emphasis on private and family devotion in the 1647 extract below.

The General Assembly, after mature deliberation, doth approve the following Rules and Directions for cherishing piety, and preventing division and schism; and doth appoint ministers and ruling elders in each congregation to take special care that these Directions be observed and followed; as likewise, that presbyteries and provincial synods enquire and make trial whether the said Directions be duly observed in their bounds; and to reprove or censure (according to the quality of the offence), such as shall be found to be reprovable or censurable therein. And, to the end that these directions may not be rendered ineffectual and unprofitable among some, through the usual neglect of the very substance of the duty of Family-worship, the Assembly doth further require and appoint ministers and ruling elders to make diligent search and enquiry, in the congregations committed to their charge respectively, whether there be among them any family or families which use to neglect this necessary duty; and if any such family be found, the head of the family is to be first admonished privately to amend his fault; and, in case of his continuing therein, he is to be gravely and sadly reproved by the session; after which reproof, if he be found still to neglect Family-worship, let him be, for his obstinacy in such an offence, suspended and debarred from the Lord's supper, as being justly esteemed unworthy to communicate therein, till he amend.

The *Directory*, some forty pages long, laid down no definite liturgy but was rather a guide to somewhat improvised services. It advised on appropriate themes for prayer, for example, but offered no form or words: it was not popular and eventually failed. Alongside this came the imposition of the Puritan Sabbath. Sunday was a day for meditation and prayer, a day of *holy cessation* from all sports and pastimes and from *all worldly words and thoughts*. By the end of 1645 all the feast days of the old liturgy and calendar had been abolished.

What the people of Broughton would have found difficult to ignore, even if they resisted the *Directory* and continued to embrace The Book of Common Prayer, and even if they continued to attend church and take part in *old forms* of worship, was the changed Sunday. The Sunday sports and pastimes, for so long a feature of the village green or perhaps the green areas around Broughton Church after services, were to be done away with. James the First's *Book of Sports*, published in 1618, provided opposition to the Sabbatarians of the Puritan factions. He commanded that:

...our good people be not disturbed, letted or discouraged from any lawful recreation, such as dancing, either men or women, archery for men, leaping, vaulting or any such harmless recreation, nor from having May games, Whitsun ales and Morris dances, and the setting up of Maypoles and other sports therewith used, without impediment or neglect of divine services: and that women shall have leave to carry rushes to the church for decoration of it according to the old tradition.

Despite the book's reissue in 1633, radical Puritan-dominated areas continued to proscribe such Sunday fripperies: in more reactionary parishes, like Broughton, such pastimes were viewed as the secular corollary of church attendance and as an essential element of parish cohesion and social harmony.

The Puritan faith had its base in the household not the village green: the home was the centre of devotion, prayer and fasting. The parish church was simply a place to gather to hear the word of God: hats were kept on: there was no convention of standing or bowing at the Creed. Many of the Church of England conventions, signing the cross at baptism, the churching of women, the wearing of a surplice, were regarded as mere dregs of popery and were abolished. To the Puritan, the cross and the signing of it was the *mark of the beast* and of a *harlot which stirreth up to popish lust.*

The *Directory* also hugely diminished the importance of the funeral or burial service: praying beside the corpse or at the graveside was banned as scripturally unsound. This must have been one of the most difficult changes for ordinary people to cope with, as the bereaved, with scarcely a word of comfort, saw their loved one almost thrown into the grave. The belief that the living and their prayers could do anything to help the dead had been all but erased by the Reformation: in Lancashire however there is evidence that prayers for the dead were still being said in the 1590s. Even fifty years after the publication of the Prayer Book, a strong belief in Purgatory, a state of the suffering soul only ameliorated by the prayers of the living, persisted.

Communion was seen by Puritans simply as a commemorative act to which only a chosen few should be admitted. The real presence of Christ was totally rejected and any blessing of the bread or wine was banned. Anyone wishing to receive the sacrament had first to be examined by the minister and two elders of the church, in order to assess their worthiness. This *closed communion* was however rejected by some 80 percent of parishes, Broughton among them.

Family meditation and spiritual reflection, as explained below, served to relegate communal worship and the role of the church building, its forms of worship and its ministers, to almost incidental adjuncts. Despite the word *publick* being used five times within the advice, the emphasis was undoubtedly on the family's and the individual's private engagement with God's word.

On the Lord's day, after every one of the family apart, and the whole family together, have sought the Lord (in whose hands the preparation of men's hearts are) to fit them for the publick worship, and to bless to them the publick ordinances, the master of the family ought to take care that all within his charge repair to the publick worship, that he and they may join with the rest of the congregation: and the publick worship being finished, after prayer, he should take an account what they have heard; and thereafter, to spend the rest of the time which they may spare in catechising, and in spiritual conferences upon the word of God: or else (going apart) they ought to apply themselves to reading,

meditation, and secret prayer, that they may confirm and increase their communion with God: that so the profit which they found in the publick ordinances may be cherished and promoted, and they more edified unto eternal life.

Nothing in the church building should detract from or distract the congregation from individual worship and meditation and as a result other changes followed: altars, raised communion tables, images, pictures, organs and *all superstitious inscriptions* were soon swept away. In 1646 the titles of archbishop and bishop were abolished and their possessions placed in the hands of trustees, and shortly afterwards the *title, dignity, function and office* of dean, sub-dean and dean and chapter were also done away with. The celebration of Christmas and Easter was proscribed.

In many thousands of parishes however, perhaps Broughton among them, the old services and celebrations were carried on, often behind closed doors, despite such proscriptions. The Church Survey of the Lancashire parochial districts began in June 1650 and from it we can see the state of each parish through the evidence brought before the commissioners. There were three sittings in Preston.

The Survey identified all the ministers in Lancashire and commented on their fitness for the office they held. Most were said to be *godly preaching ministers* or were *of good lyfe and conversation but kept not the fast-days appointed by Parliament.* The Survey also commented that many parishes were very large and recommended subdivision, and that some chapels were so far from the mother church, they should be made into separate parish churches. Was this the impetus Broughton church needed to become an independent parish? Certainly in 1650, according to the Survey, the minister at Broughton was allowed a substantial £40 per annum, and the inhabitants of Broughton and Haighton, some 300 families *at least*, desired to be made a discrete parish. Parish records began four years later in 1654.

The clergy and congregations, who persevered in this low-key, passive resistance and decided to *tarry for the magistrate*, were rewarded in 1660, when Charles II was restored to the throne. The Puritan dream of replacing Anglicanism with some form of Calvanist church had, during the Civil War, disintegrated into a bewildering variety of sects, such as the Quakers and the Baptists.

After 1660, the Church was restored, outwardly at least, to its ancient forms. What it lost forever however was its claim to be a comprehensive, national church. The Church's decision in 1662 not to broaden its appeal by adapting its liturgy, drove some two thousand clergy to leave and convinced tens of thousands of Dissenters to opt for separation.

In the Compton Survey of 1676, an enquiry set up by the Archbishop of Canterbury, the Broughton document gives the parish population as 636, of whom 192 people are identified as Popish recusants. In other words over one hundred years after the Reformation, almost a third of the people living within the Chapelry of Broughton were still prepared to declare their Catholic faith. Indeed this total is only of adults so attesting and does not take into account other members of the household. This has led many people, Olive Hamby among them, who has made a detailed study of the parish through wills and parish records, to conclude that a more probable figure for recusants is 323, over half the population. It is also likely that as this information was provided for the Census by churchwardens, many of them would not wish to pass on true but prejudicial or incriminating information about their neighbours or perhaps family members.

As late as 1680 John Dryden, then Poet Laureate, remained sceptical of his country's ability to settle into any form of tranquil religious stability:

> But 'tis the talent of our English nation
> Still to be plotting some new reformation.

Nine years later however, the Toleration Act of 1689 represented the formal recognition of one inescapable fact: religious pluralism in England was here to stay. It offered if not tranquillity, then at least an uneasy peace among those of different religious convictions.

CHAPTER 5

THE EIGHTEENTH CENTURY

THE SELECT VESTRY

Early in the C18th, Broughton church established its own Select Vestry of twenty-four men of the chapelry, similar in style to the *four and twenty* of the mother church in Preston.

The Preston Select Vestry had been established in January 1645 and was commonly known as the *Four and Twenty Gentlemen*. It was different from many other such groups because the twenty-four men were divided into three groups of eight, each group representing one of the three divisions of the parish. Broughton, Barton and Haighton should, geographically at least, have been included in that division termed the *Upper End*, which included Elston, Grimsargh, Ribbleton and Fishwick. Broughton was however never represented, probably because a church or chapel had existed at Broughton for a long time, and by this date it had achieved at least some measure of independence and some degree of self-government. This *separateness* almost certainly prompted the chapelry's decision to press for a Select Vestry in its own right. The decision may well also have been prompted by some opposition to the provision of funding to the parish church for its own purposes. In 1708 for example, the congregation of Broughton was asked for money to repair a specified length of wall and fences surrounding the Parish Churchyard, an obligation they were most reluctant to honour.

The Broughton Select Vestry consisted of twelve men from Broughton, eight from Barton and four from Haighton. This committee settled the local poor rate, audited and approved the Churchwardens' accounts, surveyed the roads and acted in every way as the Select Vestry of a normal parish would.

The men were chosen annually and held significant authority in almost all matters relating to the church. In 1733 for example, they informed the Churchwardens of the need for a clock and that trees should be planted in the churchyard. The Vicar of Preston agreed to these requests and the Churchwardens had to begin to raise money for the project and to apply to Mr Waddington of Chorley to make and provide a good clock.

In 1767, at a meeting held on the 21st April, the Vestry passed a resolution that in future the bell-ringers were to be paid 5s per annum and not provided with any free drink. They resolved further that on every Sacrament Day, the parson was to be paid only 2 shillings and the wardens 1 shilling each.

Three years later in July 1770, the following order was established:

Whereas it appeareth that a great part of the monies collected within the precincts of the chapelry of Broughton has been misapplied, we, whose names are hereto subscribed do declare and hereby order that the custom of dining and giving of dinners and liquor at the public charges on Sacrament days shall be discontinued and that the chapel wardens shall not expend of Guy Fawkes Day or Christmas Day more than six shillings on each of the respective days; that the established ringers shall have each of them three shillings a year; that chapel wardens shall have an allowance of one shilling when they go to buy wines, and we are determined to abide and adhere to these rules...

Although not formally constituted as a distinct Vestry until 1877, when Broughton became a separate Parish, those men involved before that date, as we have seen, exercised considerable power and authority.

In August 1828 six men were chosen for the Select Vestry: George Mayor; Charles Edmonson; John Bretherton; Richard Sharples; John Livesey and James Carter. They were appointed for six months, with the warning that: *any person chosen for Committee and not attending meeting to forfeit place.*

Three months later two members had presumably failed to heed that warning and both of them, James Carter and Richard Sharples, were replaced by Timothy Gorton and Jonas Marsden.

A meeting of the Select Vestry and local landowners was arranged on the 25th February 1882, to discuss the demolition of the old church and the building of a new one.

The last page of the extant Select Vestry record contains a comparative census of the number of papists in the township and chapelry in 1780 and in 1804. In 1780 Broughton had 215 papists; Haighton 107 and Barton 136, giving a total of 458 persons. By May 1804, as the table below shows, these numbers had increased so that within the township of Broughton at least, there were almost as many papists as Protestants.

1804	Protestant	Roman Catholic
Broughton	285	249
Haighton	52	113
Barton	224	99
Total	**561**	**461**

Between 1813 and 1821 there were 168 burials at Broughton Church. Of these, 40, almost one quarter, were of *papists* or those *of Roman Catholic persuasion,* as they were sometimes referred to in parish records. Interestingly, not only does the discriminatory nomenclature of two centuries earlier persist, but from these records we have further evidence of the religious balance of Broughton's population.

The first cemetery to provide a dedicated area for Roman Catholics, *The Rosary*, in Norwich, was not created until 1819 and municipal burial grounds in the larger cities were only just beginning to be built. Moreover, the burial of the dead of whatever religious denomination was, at the time, the responsibility of the Church of England, and the Parish Priest was obliged to read the Burial Service as prescribed in the Book of Common Prayer. Though ecumenical worship might lie two centuries in the future: death and burial were significantly inter-denominational affairs. Though it might be argued that people had little choice about where they were buried and the incumbent little choice about whether to bury them or not, the Catholic population of Broughton clearly felt sufficiently part of Broughton parish to be interred in its graveyard.

SPECIAL SERVICES

During the years that Britain was at war with the American Colonies, the Archbishop of Canterbury issued a form of Service to be used in churches throughout the period. In 1782 the Service suggested a time of fasting and penance for His Majesty's subjects. In addition, with that arrogance and self-righteousness that built an empire, a litany phrase was added: *Turn, O Lord, the hearts of his rebellious subjects in America.*

Thirteen years later in 1795 a special form of Service was used in praise and thanksgiving for the king, George the Third's, escape from several assassination attempts. In 1786 for example, when the King alighted from his carriage at the garden entrance to St James's Palace, a well-dressed woman emerged from the crowd. She held out a petition to the King but then suddenly produced a knife and tried to stab him in the chest. The blade of the dessert knife was so worn and thin however that it bent and failed to penetrate His Majesty's waistcoat. The lady, Margaret Nicholson, was disarmed quickly and so angered was the crowd that they would have killed her had not the King himself protected her. Later it was discovered that she was a barber's daughter from Stockton-on-Tees, who believed she was the rightful heir to the throne. She was declared insane and held in London's Bethlem Royal Hospital until her death forty-two years later.

CHAPTER 6

THE NINETEENTH CENTURY
A CHURCH RE-BUILT

During the C17th and C18th little appears to have been done to keep Broughton church in good repair.

In 1733, for reasons that remain rather obscure, battlements were added to the church building. Entries in the Churchwardens' accounts record:

17th August – spent at Longridge, where we went to buy battlement stones, 0s 8d (presumably the cost per stone).

Paid for battlement stones £2. 6s 8d

This ornamentation apart, no records exist of any other significant building or repair work.

By 1822, the church, which had formed a centre of worship for its community for the past three hundred years, was most definitely showing its age. Dr Whittaker is his book *Richmondshire*, published in that year, pulled no punches in his assessment of the state of repair of Broughton church. He described it as having *such an appearance of squalid neglect and decay as he had seldom seen.*

He added: *a few remnants of a more ancient fabric appear in the walls of the present fabric, which is evidently a work of the time of Henry VIII, since very little attention seems to have been paid to it, excepting to secure the handsome tower from felling by strong iron bars.*

It was beyond repair: the only solution was demolition and, the tower excepted, an almost complete re-build. In 1823 the work began, to a design by Preston architect Robert Roper (1757-1838), and lasted for the next three years. The new sandstone church was completed in what Sir Richard Glynne described with undisguised contempt, as: *the poorest quasi-early English style, with a flat, pitched roof of wide span, undivided by arcades and ugly, wide lancet windows.*

The west window and the tower were retained. The new, five-bay nave measured 69 feet by 45 feet (21m x 14m) and the floor was some 2 feet 4 inches (0.7m) higher than that of the original, old church, hence the steps needed to reach the tower floor. The interior walls were not the dressed stone still evident in the tower construction but were covered in plaster, painted to mimic stonework.

The roof of the nave was constructed as one span, covered in slates and with the interior flat, panelled ceiling still familiar today.

THE GALLERY

The church also had a gallery, which accommodated tenants, who rented the pews for a period of five years after bidding for them at auction. The rental prices of the pews reflected not only their position in the gallery but also that of the people successful in bidding for them: those nearer the front of the gallery costing twice as much as those of the rear. A Mrs Beesley paid £15 for a front pew; Mr Threlfall paid less than half of that for one in a less prominent and prestigious position.

It was more common for such wooden *west galleries*, constructed, as the name would suggest, at the west end of the church, to house the choir, as was the case at Broughton certainly in the 1870s. Many were constructed during the C18th but as a result of Victorian disapproval, most were removed during C19th restorations. They were often the home of *west gallery music*, also known as *Georgian psalmody*: sacred music made up most often of psalms, anthems and hymns. It may well be, as on the Elizabethan stage, that the choir and musicians shared Broughton's gallery with those members of the congregation wealthy enough to afford a seat next to them.

The image below of the west gallery in Preston Parish Church, illustrates what the one at Broughton may well have looked like.

In 1831, James Tuson, Broughton School's master at the time and landlord of the Church House Inn, adjacent to the church, conducted the pew auction according to the following conditions;

- ❖ Pews to be let to the highest bidder
- ❖ Biddings to be not less than five shillings in increase
- ❖ In case of dispute, the pew to be re-auctioned
- ❖ Repairs to the staircase, railings and woodwork to be carried out by the tenant
- ❖ Owners of the front pews to keep the front of the gallery in neat oak paint
- ❖ Owners of the remaining pews to keep aisles painted in oak
- ❖ Purchaser to pay one pound deposit on each pew purchased

Two documents relating to this auction are shown below. The first indicates the rules under which it was organised and the amounts paid by the successful bidders. The second illustrates where the pews were located in the gallery and gives a clear idea of the size and form of the gallery itself.

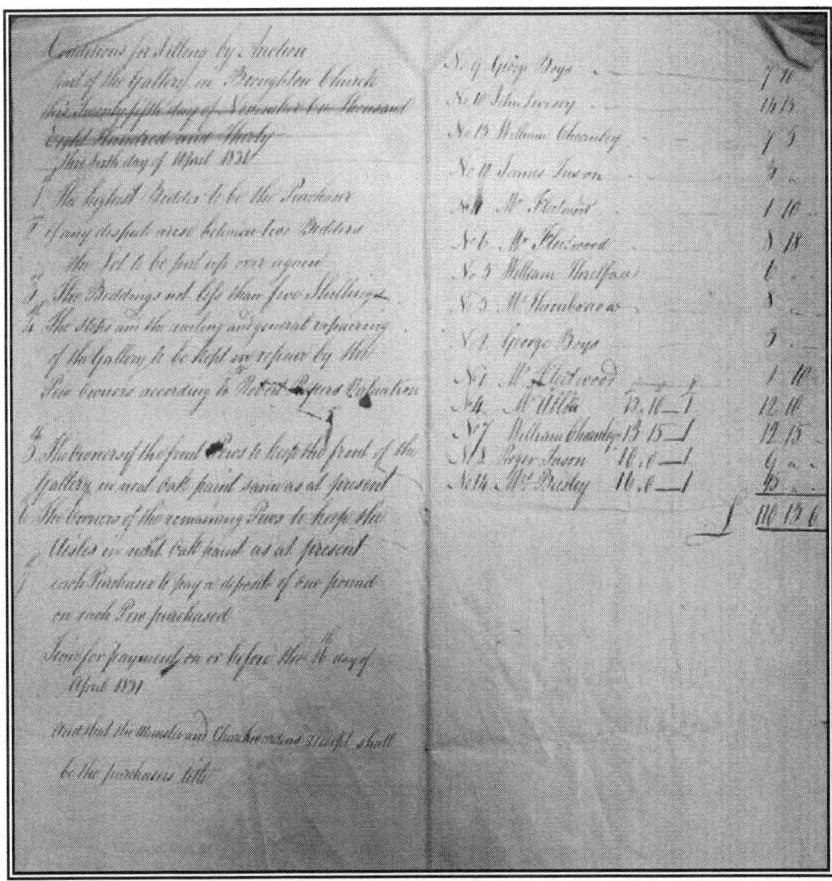

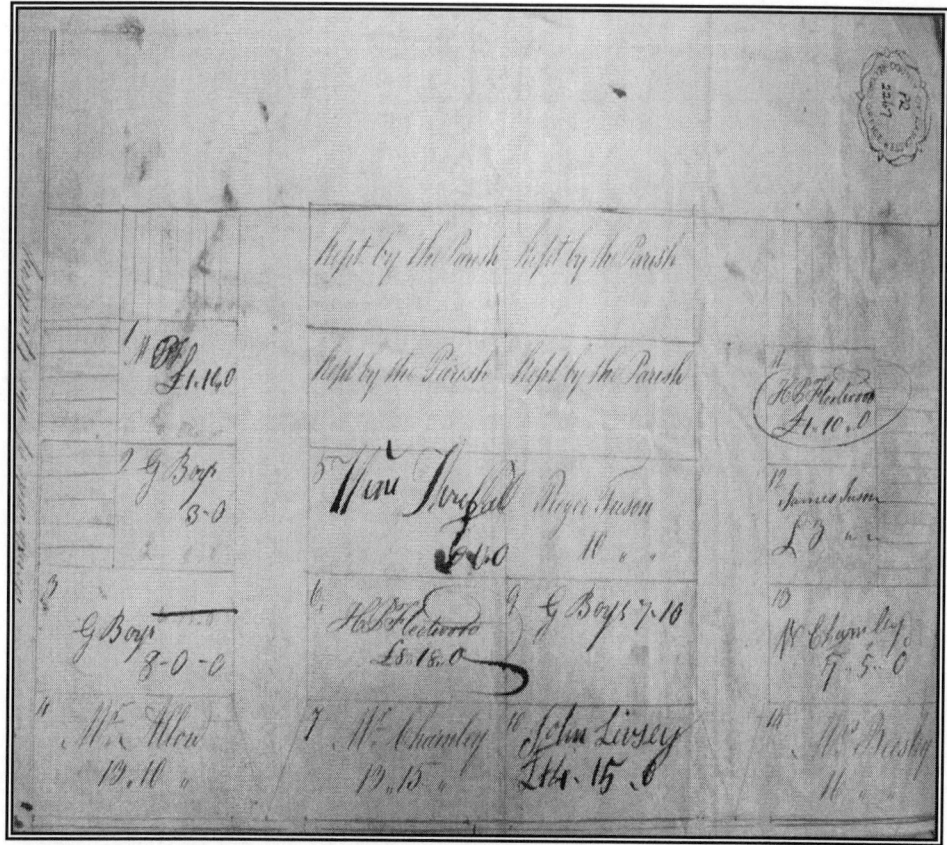

In 1872, forty-six years after its completion, *Atticus* writing in *Our Country Churches and Chapels* was a little more charitable than Whitaker in his assessment of the building, though a markedly condescending tone permeates his description.

It is a plain, heavy, slightly lopsided building – a small, quaint, coldly substantial kind of edifice – a little weather-beaten temple, good enough for all Broughtonian purposes, and quite in keeping with the requirements of the district.

He continues with somewhat restrained praise: *the general architecture of the building is strong and simple – quite devoid of ornament, homely, substantial.*

On the occasion of his visit, the morning service had a congregation of 85 adults (several of whom, he notes, were *of good position*) and 43 children. The newly built church could however accommodate about 400 people in the nave and an additional 120 persons in the gallery, which gives a good idea of the latter's considerable size. He had comments too on the congregation itself.

Matured parties as well as juveniles can get through ever so much sleep during the services at this church. In one pew we observed four healthy-looking subjects and three of them slept most peaceably during the sermon, whilst the fourth had his hands full trying to keep himself awake.

Whether somnolent or not, 128 persons at morning service from a Broughton population at the time of 590, represents a level of church attendance unparalleled today.

The vicarage was completed in 1886 at the beginning of Reverend Collinson's incumbency, at a time when it was becoming the norm for them to be built so that the clergy lived near their churches and among their people.

The photograph above, taken from Broughton Bridge sometime between 1873 and 1903, shows the completely open aspect of the church, unshaded by any of the large trees which now mask it and without its new chancel, which was not added until 1906. The large field in the foreground is now part of the church graveyard.

CHAPTER 7

CHURCHWARDENS' MISCELLANY

Churchwardens, as parish officials, began to appear shortly after the Lateran Council of 1215, which gave the laity the responsibility for the upkeep of the church nave and of vestments, ornaments and the churchyard. Congregations became organised to raise funds for these purposes and officials emerged to administer these monies.

The importance of churchwardens did not however fully develop until the fourteenth and fifteenth centuries. Generally two wardens were elected annually (women were not excluded) to be responsible for the fabric of the main body of the church, its security and the provision of all the items needed to maintain the liturgy, including cleaning, repairs and provision and replacement of vestments. They often had deputies called *lightwardens*, who as the name implies, had the job of maintaining lights in church and looking after its store of candles. The churchwardens' responsibility also extended to the churchyard, including ensuring that anyone whose animals strayed there, was prosecuted.

In the Diocese of Hereford, during the thirty years between 1661 and 1691, the following questions were put to Churchwardens by the Bishop in order to test their worthiness for office

- *Hath the steeple or tower been pulled down, or hath any of the lead or bells been embezzled or sold?*
- *Does he baptise without the required sponsors or hath he presumed to marry in private houses?*
- *Is he a frequenter of taverns or alehouses, a common gamester, profane jester, swearer, railer, scoffer or quarreller?*
- *Does he wear his hair of immoderate length?*
- *Is his apparel grave and decent, both for fashion and colour?*

The *he* referred to throughout the above, refers presumably to the incumbent.

- *Do you levy by way of distress 12d for absence from Church?*
- *Do you name late-comers, or those who depart before the service is ended, and suffer none to loiter in the church or churchyard?*
- *Do you suffer no misbehaviour?*
- *Are you careful that none lay their hats on the altar?*
- *Do you permit no minstrels, Morris dancers, dogs, hawks or hounds to be brought into the church?*
- *If you refuse to present crimes and faults, the Bishop will proceed against you in the case of wilful omission and perjury.*

Such questions not only reflected the concerns of the times but demonstrate very clearly the authority vested in the Churchwardens and the seriousness with which they were expected to carry out their supervisory responsibilities, including close monitoring of the vicar's behaviour and disposition.

The wardens had to maintain proper accounts and ensure funds were available to pay the parish clerk and the sexton. In 1822 the churchwardens, James Threlfall and Samuel Storer, issued the following statement to parishioners: *Notice is hereby given to the inhabitants of the several Townships of Broughton, Barton and Haighton that a rate of 2d per acre will be collected the ensuing week towards paying the expences (sic) of Broughton Church.* Sixty-nine people were listed as liable for these contributions.

One wonders however what the good people of Broughton thought about the churchwardens' expenditure on alcohol. They would have been content perhaps with the monthly cost of communion wine: in 1812 for example 1½ gallons of fine red port was purchased each month at a cost of £1.13s, but they may have been more grudging about the money finding its way into the tills of the Church Inn. Over a four-month period this was detailed as:

Roger Tuson	1 pint of ale	4d
Churchwardens and others	4 glasses of gin	1s 0d
Churchwardens	3 glasses of ale	
	3 glasses of gin and rum	1s 7d
Mr Charnley/ James Corless	2 quarts of ale	1s 4d
Slaters' liquor		1s 3d
Ringers' liquor		6s 8d
Churchwardens	3 glasses of gin	9d
Churchwardens et al	5 glasses of rum and tobacco	1s 9d
Singers' et al liquor		£1.18s 4d

In 1822 one receipt reads:

Dec.10 , 1822   Samuel Storer, Churchwarden, to Thos. Harding, Barton

33 Dinners...............£2. 9s. 6d
Ales and Liquors.......£7.17s 6d
                    £10. 7s.0d
The fact that three times more money was spent on drink than on food is interesting!

Eight years later, in 1830, Roger Tuson, the churchwarden, collected £18.11s. 5½d from the parish of Broughton and £9. 5s. 8¾d from Haighton. This, coupled with the *half-crown* collection from Barton, yielding £8. 5s, which when added to his predecessor's balance of £40. 5s. 5d, gave a total of £76. 7s. 7¼d.

From this, £65. 19s. 10d was disbursed to various parish projects: a new lock was purchased costing 1s; repairs to the bells and bell ropes cost 4s 2½d and coals for the vestry totalled 6s 1d. In addition, payments were made to various contractors, presumably for on-going work on the new church building. For example, George Bleasdale received 11s 3d for five days' work, while Thomas Kirkby and John Dagger received 9s each for four days' work. Interestingly additional income that year came from the sale of the old gallery pews, which raised the significant sum of £100. 13s.

The accounts for the following year give an indication of how these monies were raised based on property values. On a page headed: *An assessment made upon the several inhabitants of the Township of Broughton, after the Rate of 1½d in the pound for the necessary use of the Church*, we discover some of the principal landowners and contributors. Based on this rate:

Catherine Akers contributed 6s 9¾d
George Boys contributed 9s 10½d
Thomas Scott, with property valued at £106 5s, contributed 13s 3½d
Ellen Sharples, with property valued at £108 5s, contributed 13s 6½d

At the other end of the scale, James Corless, who owned property valued at a mere 10s, made a modest contribution of only ¾d.

The Churchwardens were also in charge of poor relief within the parish. In the case of major building projects, such as the ones at Broughton in the sixteenth and nineteenth centuries, the wardens' financial responsibilities were considerable. For all these purposes, money had to raised: this might be done through a levy on parishioners, as detailed above, through the administration of any charity bequests or endowments or, as was very common, through the sale of *church ales*.

As the copies of the Churchwardens' accounts for 1821 and 1823, reproduced on the following two pages, illustrate, there was no shortage of sales. It seems that everyone who visited the Church was entertained with liquor: the churchwardens themselves however also consumed, and no doubt enjoyed, perhaps more than their fair share of the Church Inn's alcoholic beverages. The chief purpose of the church-ale (which was originally instituted to honour the church saint) and the clerk-ale, was to facilitate the collection of parish dues and to make a profit for the church from the sale of ale by the church wardens. These profits kept the parish church in repair, or were distributed as alms to the poor.

> *The churches must owe, as we all do know,*
> *For when they be drooping and ready to fall,*
> *By a Whitsun or Church-ale up again they shall go*
> *And owe their repairing to a pot of good ale.*

"Exaltation of Ale", by Francis Beaumont

Date	Description	£	s	d
1821	Churchwardens of Broughton Church Dr to James Tuson			
July 3	Roger Tuson to 2 Glasses of Gin	"	"	6
4	Churchwardens & James Drinkward 7 Glasses Ale	"	1	2
10	Churchwardens & others when Bishop came 16 Glasses Gin	"	4	"
13	Churchwardens when Mr Roper came 4 Glasses Gin	"	1	"
20	Churchwardens and Others 4 Glasses Gin	"	1	"
Aug 5	Vestry men Meeting to liquor	1	17	8
12	Churchwardens 2 Glasses of Gin	"	"	6
21	Vestry Men and Land owners Meeting to liquor	2	16	4
23	when Church broken 2 quarts of Ale	"	1	4
24	To Glaziers 3 pints of Ale	"	1	"
26	Churchwardens 2 Glasses of Ale	"	"	10
Sept 17	Vestry Men and Land owners Meeting to liquor	1	16	6
Oct 13	Churchwardens to 1 Glass of Gin & 1 Glass of Ale	"	"	5
29	Vestry Men and Land owners Meeting to Liquor	2	6	10
Nov 3	Liquor for Ringers	"	"	5
4	To Roger Tuson 1 Glass of Gin	"	"	3
18	Churchwardens 2 Glasses of Rum	"	"	8
	To 4 Weeks Allowance removing Bones &c	"	19	10
Dec 10	To Churchwardens & Others to liquor	"	3	8
17	To Roger Tuson 2 Glasses Gin	"	"	6
25	To Ringers Liquor	"	5	"
Jany 6	To Churchwardens and Others to Liquor	"	"	6
14	To Churchwardens and Others to Liquor	"	6	"
20	To Churchwardens & Others to liquor	"	1	"
24	To Churchwardens Meeting to Liquor	"	8	4
27	To Churchwardens and Singers to Liquor	1	11	3
Feby 7	To Churchwardens and Others to liquor	"	4	7
17	To Churchwardens and Others to Liquor	"	4	8
25	To Churchwardens and Others to Liquor Meeting	2	3	6
March 16	To Churchwardens &c to Liquor	"	1	1
17	To Churchwardens &c to Liquor	"	"	8
24	To Churchwardens &c to liquor	"	"	8
31	To Churchwardens & 6 Glasses Gin and 1 Glass Rum	1	"	10
April 1	To Churchwardens &c to Liquor	"	3	1

1823   Churchwardens of Broughton Chapel Disbursements   5 9

July   To last Years Meeting liquor   "   "   "   2 10
   18   To Churchwardens &c To liquor   "   "   7 11
   14   To Plasterers 1 pint of Ale   "   "   4
   17   To Removing Seats from Barn liquor   "   3
   22   To Removing seats from Barn liquor   "   5 7
   24   To 4 Quarts and 1 Glass Ale   "   2 10
   25   To 2 Quarts ale   "   1 4
   26   To 6 Quarts ale   "   4 4
   28   To the Reverend Churchwardens liquor   3 9
Aug   To Plasterers 1 Quart Ale   "   8
   2   To Plasterers &c to liquor   "   2 2
   3   To Churchwardens & Glasses Gin   6
   4   To Churchwardens 2 Glasses Gin   6
   6   To Plasterers and Joiners 4 Quarts ale   2 8
   12   To Plasterers 1 Quart ale   8
   17   To Ringers from Stool to Meat and liquor   7
   26   To Plasterers Joiners & Masons to liquor   13 10
   29   To Plasterers Joiners 3 Glasses ale   1 2
Sep   To Plasterers 5 Glasses ale   10
   5   To Churchwardens and Others to liquor   3 6
   To Workmen 3 Quarts Ale   2 0
   To Plasterers 5 Days 1 pint &c Day   1 8
   6   To Churchwardens and Others 10 Glasses ale   8
   7   To Churchwardens 1 Glasses ale   8
   8   To Opening Ditch field Miller 1 Quart ale   4
   15   To Churchwardens & Others to liquor   1 2
   17   To a Meeting Churchwardens &c to liquor   14 8
   20   To Plasterers 1 Quart ale   8
Oct 8   To Churchwardens &c 1 Quart ale   8
   25   To Plasterers 1 pint ale   4
   25   To Churchwardens &c to liquor   2 4
   To Plasterers 3 Days 3 Quarts ale   2 0
Nov 5   To Ringers to liquor   3
   11   To Church Joiners & Plasterers 10 Glasses ale   1 10
   13   To Do Joiners & Plasterers Do   1 10
   To Plasterers 1 week 6 pints Ale   1 8
   10   To a Meeting liquor Meat & Tobacco   18 2
   25   To Plasterers 4 Days 4 pints ale   8
   To Plasterers & Joiners 2 to Quarts ale

It was almost the norm that each church had its own brew house. The churchwardens would purchase large amounts of malt, which was brewed into ale to be sold at certain festive periods, during what was euphemistically referred to, as a *church ale sale*, more accurately a parish drinking party, the proceeds of which helped maintain the church. Unfortunately, one might feel, what in all likelihood were somewhat riotous celebrations, have today been replaced by the more decorous and sedate church fete or vicar's garden party. It seems highly likely that the Church Inn, originally housed in what is now Church Cottage adjacent to Broughton Church, had its origins in such a parish brew house.

In the mid-sixteenth century churchwardens were given additional responsibilities, such as the upkeep of local roads and bridges. These financial obligations, on top of those they already had, often forced the wardens to sell church property to raise money. In other words, they were forced to choose between church goods and church fabric. During 1548 Bishop Bird during his Visitation of the Deanery of Amounderness, discovered two churches where the churchwardens had recently sold church plate to finance vital repairs, and two more where they had pawned such items for the same purpose. It would appear Broughton was not in such dire financial straits when it came to the rebuilding of the 1520s, probably because of the generosity of wealthy benefactors, such as the Singleton and Langton families. By the 1550s another Visitation revealed that half the churches and chapels in Lancashire were in urgent need of repair. However because of tithe disputes, the decline in church attendance and widespread recusancy for example, churchwardens simply did not have the funds to carry out such repairs. Once again it would seem that Broughton Church in its rebuilding, fared much better than many others.

Churchwardens, from the 1550s, were also required to record church attendance and to keep a close eye on the cleric, as noted earlier in the Hereford Inquisition, to ensure adherence to the *Book of Common Prayer*. From 1536, they had had to witness the weekly entries made by the vicar, in the church records. In these respects, in theory at least, these parish officials had become an arm of the state. In fact, as I suspect was the case at Broughton, with its conservative Catholic ethos, the churchwardens were nominated and controlled by local Catholic gentry.

If, for example, such families thought that the wardens at a Visitation would make critical or prejudicial comment about them, then they could and would replace the wardens with more compliant parishioners. There is no evidence that this was the case at Broughton Church: however, given the Catholic recusancy rife in Amounderness in general and in Preston particularly, it seems likely that its churchwardens would stand accused and found guilty of being: *infected by papistry or placed by papists or their favourites of the baddest sort*.

Not surprisingly, given their own quest for spiritual power and control, the Puritans made a petition in 1590, which was highly critical of wardens chosen, *by the singular nomination of the gentlemen and better sort of every town, without the consent of the pastor*, so that they were, *of the meanest and lewdest sort of the people, and therefore most fit to serve the humour of the gentry and multitude.*

All these duties, responsibilities and financial demands, and the often antagonistic pressures of Church, State and local gentry in Tudor times, made the office of churchwarden a singularly onerous and unpopular one. Sometimes no-one could be found who was willing to serve, an unwillingness compounded by the abusive threats made to some of them by parishioners. At Leigh in 1598 and at Ormskirk in 1640, for example, two men were *presented* for threatening the wardens with physical violence.

Whatever the shortcomings of churchwardens, other parish officers were also not above criticism. Winwick Church, from 1593 to 1596, was dominated by a perfidious parish clerk, *who conducted burials himself, had an illegitimate child by his cousin and lived with another woman, disturbed the services by piping and dancing, and made fun of the curate as he tried to perform the liturgy.*

Though the gentleman concerned might well have enlivened an especially dull Sunday service, fortunately Broughton Church seems only to have had diligent, reliable and dedicated churchwardens, who worked conscientiously to preserve both its fabric, the solemnity of its worship and its integrity as a sacred space.

The extract overleaf from the parish accounts for 1705, gives an indication of the ways in which monies were disbursed by the Select Vestry and the Churchwardens.

The Select Vestries Act

In 1818 the Act for the Regulation of Parish Vestries was passed. This set up a plural voting system in a parish vestry, depending on the rateable value of property. A landowner of property worth £50 was eligible for one vote; for every further £25 a man was given another vote up to a maximum of six votes. This scale was used later by the Poor Law Amendment Act for the election of Guardians of the Poor.

*The following year, the Act to Amend the Law for the Relief of the Poor was passed. This added a resident clergyman to the members of the vestry. Vestries were told to distinguish between the 'deserving' and 'undeserving' poor, the latter group deemed to be idle, extravagant or profligate. The Act also provided for the employment of salaried overseers, better-kept accounts and either the building or enlargement of workhouses. Under this legislation, two JPs were needed to agree to force the Vestry to give poor relief, rather than only one JP as before. This was intended to prevent "generous" JPs from helping anyone who appealed for assistance. Together these two pieces of legislation are known either as the **Select Vestries Acts** or the Sturges-Bourne Acts, after the MP who was responsible for them.*

April ye 10 / 1705 /

Thour a true and perfect acount of mony disbursed towards the use
and Repairs of the Chapell of Broughton maide to the foure and twenty
and others of the parish by James Hallton and Cristifar Clitherall
Chapelwardens for the yeare 1704 / disbursed as folowth ~ —

Inprs paide for bred and wine for three salvement days — 01 = 06 = 8
Item paide for meat and drink on three salvement days — 00 = 16 = 6
Item paide for dosing a bell — — — — — — — — — 00 = 01 = 6
Item paide for gounwork for the bell — — — — — 00 = 00 = 6
Item paide to foure briefs — — — — — — — — 00 = 07 = 6
Item spent when the bell was drosed — — — — — 00 = 00 = 6
Item spent when the foure and twenty met to Consult } 00 = 02 = 6
about the Repairs of the Church — — —
Item paide for dresing the Church on Sa: James day — 00 = 6
Item spent on sant James day — — — — — — — 00 = 02 = 6
Item paide for mending the flat — — — — — — 00 = 01 = 0
Item spent when the flat was mended — — — — — 00 = 00 = 2
Item paide for washing the Church Lining and storing 00 = 01 = 6
Item spent and paide for meat when Mr Lonam preched — 07 = 6
Item paide for meate and drink when Mr Rushton preched = 07 = 4
Item paide to the Ringars on the fift of novembar — 00 = 02 = 8
Item spent on the fift of novembar — — — — — 00 = 07 = 0
Item paide for meat and drink when Mr posley Came }
to prich besids the salvement days — — — — — } 00 = 05 = 6
Item spent on Crismas day — — — — — — — 00 = 05 = 6
Item paide for hedging wood and hedging — — — 00 = 07 = 6
Item paide to Lawout a bought for swiping the Leads 00 = 01 = 0
Item paide for foure Books making — — — — — 00 = 01 = 0
Item paide for oure acounts drving — — — — — 00 = 00 = 6

the totale is = 4 = 10

In 1770 there was some dissatisfaction with the church accounts:

Whereas it appeareth that a great part of the monies collected within the precincts of the Chapelry of Broughton has been misapplied, we, whose names are hereunto subscribed do declare and hereby order that the custom of dining and giving of dinners and liquor at the public charges on Sacrament Days, shall be discontinued, and that the Chapel wardens shall not expend on Guy Fawkes Day or Christmas Day more than six shillings on each of the respective days; that the established ringers shall have each of them an allowance of one shilling when they go to buy wines, and we are determined to abide and adhere to these rules...

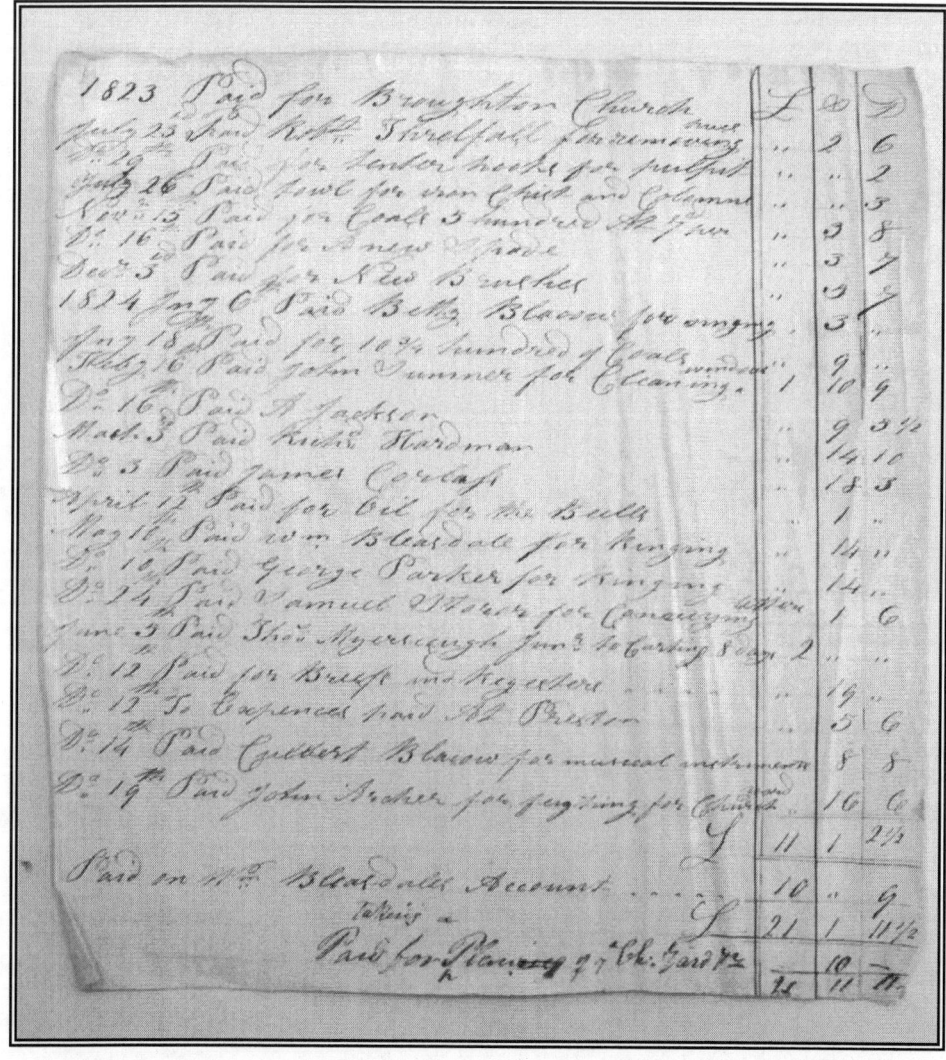

Previous extravagances having been apparently eradicated, the above extract from the 1823-24 accounts, illustrates the day-to-day concerns and expenditure of the Broughton Churchwardens. These range from the mundane - 5 hundredweight of coals purchased in November, costing 3s 8d; a new spade, presumably for the sexton, costing 3s 7d; new brushes for 5s 7d - to more interesting items: Betty Blacow was paid her annual fee of 3s for singing; George Parker and William Bleasdale were each paid 14 shillings for ringing, presumably also their annual remuneration; John Sumner received £1 10s 9d, for cleaning windows. Cuthbert Blacow was paid 8s 8d for musical instruments, and possibly the most curious item of all, twopence was paid for tenterhooks (pictured opposite) for the pulpit.

Tenterhooks were normally used to hold tightly stretched fabric on a wooden tenter frame during the drying process to prevent shrinkage. Hence the expression *to be on tenterhooks* describes someone who feels tense, who feels uneasy suspense, whose emotions are *stretched*. Why would these tenterhooks be used on the pulpit? Presumably they held taut some kind of fabric which adorned it, or perhaps a canopy.

What is interesting about all these items however, is that they were all bought or funded in the first year of the rebuilding of the new church. Clearly much had been achieved during that year and the church had continued to function as a place of worship despite the upheaval.

CHAPTER 8

THE TWENTIETH CENTURY

THE TWENTIES AND THIRTIES

Perhaps not surprisingly given the prevailing economic climate at the time, during the late 1920s and the 1930s money appeared to have been a constant source of concern at St John's. Dealing with what to us would seem paltry sums, there was a constant battle to balance the Parish books.

In 1929 for example Reverend Davies was worried that the Parish was in debt to the tune of £25. The church accounts for that year are reproduced below and give an excellent insight into income and expenditure at the time. The organ and the church gates had incurred additional expenditure and brought about this deficit. The Vicar asked that parishioners make a special contribution on the second Sunday in February in order to clear the debt.

CHURCH ACCOUNTS. TREASURER'S STATEMENT, 1928.

RECEIPTS.		£	s.	d.	PAYMENTS.	£	s.	d.
Balance from last year		1	2	5	Salaries: Organist, Sexton, Ringers	83	2	5
Collections, Special :					Organ Tuning	7	10	0
Easter Offering	71 17 8				Repairs and Renewals	54	17	1
Central Church Fund	7 14 3				Insurances	10	10	6
Sick and Poor	37 8 7				Communion Wine	3	0	0
	117 0 1				Coal and Coke	18	13	0
Extra Parochial :					Electric Power and Light	8	0	6
Miners' Distress	16 14 3				Visitation Fee	0	16	0
Infirmary (Preston)	33 9 0				Diocesan Levy (Quota)	15	0	0
Diocesan Societies	10 1 6				R. D. Conference	0	10	0
Teachers' B & O	6 17 3				Holiday Duty (Clergy)	6	6	0
Waifs and Strays	15 9 4				Central Fund (Quota)	9	0	0
Church Schools (Dioc.)	17 8 6				School Managers	1	10	0
S.P.G.	11 4 3				Choir Excursions	22	8	8
A. Ormerod Home	17 0 0				Choir Music	2	17	9
	128 4 1				Fire Insurance (Vicarage)	2	14	0
Church Expenses	214 1 9				Advertising	0	17	0
					Bank Charges	0	19	7
	460 8 4					248	12	6
Imp. War Graves Commission	0 17 6							
National War Bond—Grave Fund	0 10 0				Special Collections	109	5	10
Houghton's Charity	16 0 0				Extra Parochial Collections	128	4	1
Preston Savings Bank—Int. for								
Graves Maintenance Fund	2 5 1					486	2	5
Balance due to Wardens	24 16 6				Sexton—endowed maintenance of graves	2	15	0
					Houghton Charity	16	0	0
	£504 17 5					£504	17	5

In December 1930 a new Scout hut, partitioned for Rovers, Scouts and Cubs, was opened, furnished in what the Vicar called *a real backwoods style*. It had been built by subscription and through the efforts of parents and *friends of the movement.* A Girl Guides company had been formed some three years earlier, under the captaincy of Miss Holland. Their first Church Parade was on November 6th, 1927, and their first camping trip to Finsthwaite on Lake Windermere, was held the following year. A Wolf Cub Pack, for eight to twelve year-olds, had been formed in April 1930 under the guidance of Miss Dorothy Gregory, and the first Brownie group was started in December the same year.

WHEN *BROUGHTON* ALMOST VANISHED

In July 1931, a meeting of parishioners, or more accurately perhaps, local government electors was held at the school and was informed that Fulwood Urban District Council, wished to absorb some five-sixths of Broughton into its sphere of control. Indeed *it was only modesty on their part which prevented them from claiming the whole.*

The Broughton ratepayers unanimously voted against this incorporation, deciding there was nothing to be gained from such a merger and perhaps more importantly, ensuring that the village preserved its ancient identity.

NEW CHANCEL ... OLD TOWER...

The Reverend Davies had long considered the one hundred year-old Nave to be one unworthy of the ancient tower and splendid new chancel, which it linked. *Atticus*, never one to mince his words, had described it in somewhat mixed terms:

The interior of the Church is light, and on the whole, has a cheerful look. The ceiling is wide, square, flat and divided into panels with ornamental bosses at each angel. It looks more like the ceiling of some capacious old Hall than that of a Church. Running along each side, immediately beneath the ceiling, are various faces in plaster – queer faces containing an admixture of the tragical and comical, and looking immensely grotesque all over. Some felicity may be derived from them by the congregation, but we have not been able to ascertain the exact amount of it...

By the mid 1930s, the roof of the Nave was in need of repair and the dilemma facing the Vicar and the Church Council, was whether to spend money on repairs or to embark on a more ambitious project to restore the entire Nave. Mindful of the economic constraints of the times and acknowledging the fact that there was no endowment to cover such expenditure, the question was whether now was the right time to begin such an undertaking. The estimated cost of restoration, based on the plans drawn up and displayed near the font, was between five and six thousand pounds: the Restoration Fund had a modest £105 in hand.

By 1934 the Vicar, anxious to keep this project in the minds of parishioners but clearly with no hope that it would be begun in the near future, wrote:

In all that we do we ever keep in mind the fact that some day it will be someone's task or labour of love to take in hand the rebuilding of the nave of the church, and to restore to it some of its former beauty, which was destroyed when our forebears took down what must have been a typical English country church and erected in its place a building devoid of all architectural beauty.

His pessimism however proved more founded on reality than on mere despondency, as any realistic hope of raising money for this project effectively disappeared when an appeal was launched for each parish to contribute to the building of a cathedral church. Some £200,000 was needed over a five-year period and each parishioner was asked to take a collection box, in which to make their contribution. After a year, the Cathedral Fund stood at £37,000, donated by 4,400 people.

A year later, in 1935, following the dedication of the new central stained glass window in the south wall of the sanctuary, Reverend Davies reiterated his view that the nave needed rebuilding and reseating. Having little hope of the former, he found a crumb of hope in the latter when he asserted:

if we re-seated the nave, the improvement in appearance and comfort would be so pronounced that we would apply ourselves with redoubled energies to the larger task.

More modestly, repairs, costing £250, were carried out in 1936. The money was raised by a Parish Fund and enabled the painting of the church both inside and out, repairs to the tower roof and to the windows and doorsteps. One suspects Reverend Davies, grateful though he might have been for the money raised so quickly, saw these repairs as small consolation for his lost nave.

However at the start of 1937, his enthusiasm was renewed, following a bequest by a Mr Galloway, of £1000 for improvements to the Church. In his Parish Magazine article dated January 1st, he commented:

When the chancel was added and other restorations made…it was the intention, at the earliest possible date, to proceed with the restoration of the nave. In 1914 we made enquiries and found that the cost would be approximately £10,000. Enquiries made recently elicited the fact that the present day cost would be between six and eight thousand pounds. It is thought then that this latest gift could be placed in a sinking fund for this purpose. A second way of using the gift is to spend it on re-seating the Church, and in such a manner that when the greater work of restoration is embarked upon, the seating will form part of it.

The decision lay with the Wardens and Church Council: the Vicar's views were clear for all to see. By March, the decision was made to purchase new oak seating and Reverend Davies' disappointment is palpable:

Three members were in favour of its being put to one side to form a nucleus of a re-building fund: but finding themselves in the minority, agreed to the proposal on condition that a statement be made regarding the larger scheme.

He must have wondered whether his vision of a restored nave had disappeared forever or certainly for however long he remained Vicar.

CORONATION

The Coronation of George VI, in May 1937, was celebrated by the children of the parish, for whom Mr Roger Houghton and his Sports Committee had organised sports and games. One girl was chosen to represent 1st Broughton Guides at the Coronation itself.

THE WAR YEARS 1939 – 1945

Once again the sword has been drawn in defence of Right against might, oppression and wrong. Let our prayer be always – 'God defend the right.'
(Reverend Davies – October 1939)

As early as October 1938 many people in the parish felt what the Vicar, Reverend Davies termed: *an anxious doubt as to what the immediate future has in store for us.* So potent was this anxiety that he speculated that international tensions might have worsened significantly in the short time between the writing of his monthly letter and it being published in the parish magazine. With reassuring certainty, Reverend Davies exhorted parishioners to prayer: *If Christians will join together in praying for the right, strength and guidance will be given to them in their efforts to act aright.*

Perhaps as an antidote to *these critical and perilous times,* parishioners were also encouraged to focus on more mundane matters, the church seating for example, and on April 12th 1939, the consecration of an addition to the churchyard by the Bishop of Lancaster. This addition took up the remaining area of land between the church and the main road, the middle section having been consecrated some sixteen years earlier.

There was a plan to erect a gate between stone pillars at the north-west corner of the churchyard, leading via steps, to a footpath running east - west to the Church. This would provide traffic-free pedestrian access from the A6. The gateway itself would be a second memorial to Miss Lucy Jane Wilson. Sadly it would appear that the outbreak of war postponed this project never to be resurrected.

On September 1st 1939 the Vicar and parishioners were enjoying the newly carpeted aisles in the Church, the former making much of the double underlay that would prolong the carpet's life. A month later, war having been declared, he opened his parish magazine article with: *Conditions change with such startling suddenness.* Church carpets forgotten, it was clear *that we cannot hold our normal course.* Lighting restrictions meant that Sunday evening services were held at 3 p.m. instead of the usual 6.30. Normal service times resumed in March 1940 when Summer Time began. Scout and Guide meetings were suspended as were other evening gatherings. Sunday 1st October was set aside as a day of national intercession and prayer.

Not surprisingly Broughton Church Appeals, of necessity, became much less parochial and much more outward-looking. In November 1939 there was a request from the Church Council for the names of all those from the parish serving with the Forces and for funds so that Christmas gifts, including a slab of chocolate and a packet of cigarettes, could be sent to them. A second appeal was for comforts, magazines and books for the troops. A third request came from the Church Army, who wanted to set up centres abroad wherever troops were deployed. There was a sense too, from their letters home, that those fighting abroad would take comfort in knowing that parish life continued as normal and that they were constantly in the thoughts and prayers of those at home. Despite the somewhat sentimental tone of the Vicar's message, there is no doubting his sincerity:

May it not be that when our young men far away in a foreign land, facing an implacable foe, experiencing we know not what discomforts, know that in their old parish church at home the people there are praying for them, giving thanks for their manliness, courage and powers of endurance, their thoughts will bridge the gap and for those brief few moments, they too will no longer be on the battlefield, but back in spirit in their own home and maybe joining us in prayer.

A NEW VICAR

In the midst of these turbulent times, the Vicar announced his retirement in February 1940. After over sixteen years, he would conduct his final service on Easter Day before departing to his new home in Mevagissey in Cornwall.

What would the Trustees be looking for in his successor? Firstly a spiritual man, in the words of the Prayer Book: *discreet and learned in God's Word, who by his ghostly counsel and advice can give spiritual help to those who desire it.* Secondly they sought a good preacher and a good visitor. Thirdly, they were looking for a tactful man who was at ease in any society and who could conduct services *in a befitting manner and to the glory of God.* Finally the new incumbent should have a sound knowledge of church music. Fortunately perhaps, the Trustees realised, *no-one will expect to find a man who displays all these qualities to perfection* – they would ultimately appoint a man not an angel!

The man they appointed in May 1940, was the Reverend C.M.S. Clarke. His induction by Archdeacon Newman, was held on Tuesday, 6th July at Broughton Church. One of his first tasks was to write to all the parishioners serving in the Armed Forces: from his own World War I experiences he had a profound empathy for what they were feeling and suffering.

DIGGING IN THE GRAVEYARD

In October 1940 the Vicar watched as a *Ruston Bucyrus* chewed up the churchyard. This was not some rampaging dinosaur, nor some invasive, parasitic plant virus, but a huge mechanical digger creating mounds of earth along Blundel Brook. This work formed part of a scheme of defence: the small, sluggish brook which for centuries had babbled by Broughton Church had its course changed and its pace quickened, never to be the same again. Reverend Clarke saw in this transformation an allegory for the times. The work was symbolic of the huge changes taking place in every aspect of life.

England is changing or being changed, familiar places are being destroyed by bombs, and habits are being rooted up as men and women rally to defend the England which they have known and loved.

His powerful address to the Parish concluded with an affirmation of the power of faith. There was nothing more imperative:

than the development of that strong faith in the living God, which steels the hearts of men and stiffens their courage to face any danger, in the firm confidence that God can save by many or by few. It is essential that we spare no effort for equipping ourselves materially against the assaults of the enemy but it is still more important that we do not neglect the greater need of equipping ourselves spiritually for the utmost limits of endurance in withstanding the strain that Hitler's fury may impose upon all of us.

Towards the end of 1940, parishioners were encouraged to invite servicemen stationed locally into their homes *for a friendly chat and a smoke*. In addition, Reverend Clarke was appointed officiating Chaplain to the R.A.F. unit stationed at Barton Hall.

NEW RULES FOR THE GRAVEYARD

For some time there had been concerns about the appearance of the new portion of the churchyard; that it should be in keeping with the stonework of the Church and Tower. With this in mind, three regulations were drawn up:

- Headstones shall not exceed 2 feet 6 inches in height
- Curbs shall not exceed 6 feet 6 inches in length
- Only local stone of the Longridge or Grit stone type shall be used – this would exclude white marble or coloured granite

60

FESTIVAL

In June 1941 the inaugural *Day and Sunday School Festival* was held. As the Vicar said: *In these days of war, when so much is being smashed, it is good to build up a new tradition which, with the help of God, shall bring strength and joy to the community.*

On a beautiful day, a children's choir sang a special hymn and the collection, which amounted to some £31, was ear-marked for the maintenance of both schools. It was hoped that in future the Festival would be celebrated annually, bringing not only *much inspiration and blessing upon the Parish* but also reminding parents of the *vital necessity of helping children not merely to learn but also to practice the principles of the Christian Faith* – a mission statement as relevant today as it was seventy years ago

FIRE AND INSURANCE

Perhaps not surprisingly, War Damage Insurance greatly occupied the collective minds of the P.C.C., especially in the early years of the war. It was unanimously decided that the Church should be insured to the maximum affordable amount. The Government had given assurances that the actual building would be replaced if it were damaged or destroyed but it was up to the P.C.C. to insure the *furniture* within the building. It was decided to insure for £8,000, which over the next six-month period, would cost £45. The position would be reviewed quarterly.

At the same time, the Vicar appealed for additional fire-watchers to work alongside existing volunteers: the Vicar; Mr Smithies, Headteacher at Broughton School; Mr Hargreaves, Churchwarden; Mr Jolleys and Mr Simpson.

AIR-RAID PRECAUTIONS

Broughton School was designated as a Rest Centre for any families whose houses might be damaged in an air-raid. With the hope, of course, that the scheme would never need be operated, the Rural Dean organised the local clergy into four teams to cover Preston and the surrounding area. In the event of an air-raid the clergy would be on hand to comfort and advise distressed people: special clergy were also assigned to the mortuary; the Casualty Bureaux, where names of the wounded would be posted; the Assistance Board and the hospitals.

THE 1950s AND POST-WAR OPTIMISM

THE WAR MEMORIAL EXTENSION

On Sunday November 12th, 1950, the extension to the Broughton War Memorial was dedicated at a service held in Broughton Church. Later that afternoon, the Anglican and Methodist choirs, along with Brownies, Cubs, Guides and Scouts, the immediate relatives of those commemorated and ex-servicemen, processed along the A6 to the Memorial. Air Marshal Sir Hugh Walmsley officially unveiled the new extension. The work was completed by Messrs Croft and Sons, at a cost of something in excess of a thousand pounds.

The memorial and its extension, commemorate the nine Broughton men who gave their lives during World War I and the twenty-five people of the Parish who made the same sacrifice during the Second World War. They are:

1914 – 1918 War

Eric Osmond Collinson
Robert Evans
Charles Edward Hoyle
Tom Jackson
Thomas Astin Page

Frank Roberts
William Sykes
James Thornton
Joseph Benjamin Watson

1939 – 1945 War

Denis Anthony Bentley
Ronald John Buckley
Thomas Leonard Cain
Arthur Carr
Clifford Carr
Bryan Inglis Cannell
John Edwin Chadwick
Geoffrey Thomas Chapman
Thomas Crossfield Derham
Anthony Chambre Dickson
Joseph Ignatius Holden
Eleanor Leigh
Norman Henry Leigh

Terence Anthony Lendrum
James Mason
Samuel Myerscough
Charles Naylor
Norman Parkinson
Donald Robertson
George Telford Stevenson
George Nevil Sutton
William Wallbank
John Walmsley
John Nelson Wilkinson
Henry Wrennall

During the 1950s the focus at St John's was on two other major building projects and raising the monies to fund them.

Broughton School Appeal Fund.

Your QUESTIONS to Me

Q.—How much do you want?
A.—£4375, by June 30th THIS YEAR!

Q.—Do you honestly think you can get it?
A.—Honestly—and with faith and hard work—YES!

Q.—How do you expect to get it?
A.—(1) By Direct Giving.

If 600 people each sent £5 our goal would be reached. Of course, some can send MORE (perhaps much more), others must send LESS (perhaps much less). Our Treasurer will be grateful for five shillings as well as five guineas. An *average* of £5 from 600 people would save our School from State control. MY JOB IS TO PERSUADE YOU AND 599 OTHER PEOPLE TO SEND IT NOW!

(2) By Social Efforts.

The way in which our workers are getting busy is splendid and heartening. They will work all the better if they know that the donations are coming in. Already they have gathered in 15% of our receipts and they are ready to keep at it until the end of June or until they drop!

(3) By Special Efforts.

Look out for announcements about a Mile of Pennies (April); a House-to-House Envelope Collection (May); and a Grand Vicarage Garden Party (June).

Q.—Will £4375 guarantee your School?
A.—Nothing can be guaranteed in this world. But all parties support the Education Acts which require us to raise this money and our School is in the Development Plan of the Lancashire Education Authority AND DON'T FORGET, THIS MONEY IS FOR A NEW SCHOOL, not to patch up the old. It will compare with any other School in the country.

My QUESTIONS to You

Q. Do you believe that the State is getting too much power and undermining our character and initiative? If so, the School Appeal provides you with a chance to ward off the danger. If you say, "Why should I bother? Let the State run education," you give away your right to criticise its increasing control, you have handed more power to the State by your answer.

Q. Is your only answer to those who say that Churchmen are to blame because they neglected their schools in the past that *you* will neglect them *now*? Two blacks don't make a white!

Q. Are you content to let the burden fall on a few churchgoers who have not only sent donations themselves but are working hard to raise shillings when by a stroke of the pen you could send pounds? IF YOU HAVE HAD ANY BENEFIT FROM BROUGHTON SCHOOL, show your gratitude by sending whatever you can.

Q. If I made no effort to save this School, BUILT BY BROUGHTON PEOPLE AND WITH BROUGHTON MONEY, would you not deplore such a lack of spirit? But if the effort fails because you failed to respond, who will you blame then? And think of the pride and satisfaction you will feel when you see a splendid new School from the money you helped to raise.

Q. Are you content to let it be said that Broughton could not find £4000 for its School.

On Thursday, January 13th a public meeting was held in the school dining hut. A leaflet issued to the local community prior to the meeting and reproduced above, explained the problem and what needed to be done by the parish.

In brief, under the 1944 Education Act, it was deemed that Broughton School could *not be adapted or extended to conform with Building Regulations, due to cramped nature of site and difficult levels...* . The plan was to rebuild the school at some time between 1952 and 1963 at a total cost of £35,000. Half of this sum would come from the Ministry: the other half had to be borne by the School Managers if the school was to be maintained on a voluntary or 'aided' basis and so remain inspired by the Church of England faith. This meant that the parish had to raise £17,500 by 1963 at the latest. More pressing was the need to raise £4,375, a quarter of that total, as a sign of the parish's willingness and ability to save the school, by the end of June 1949 – in other words in six months!

Though the original meeting had been poorly attended by only some thirty people, parishioners responded rapidly to the Appeal itself. By the end of January the Appeal had raised £851. Through gifts, donations and money-raising events such as coffee mornings, whist drives and dances, the total had grown to over two thousand pounds by the end of March. Despite this encouraging start however, by the beginning of June there were still doubts that the target would be met. There was an air of desperation in the Reverend Oatridge's exhortation: *we can get there if everyone is determined to do it.*

Despite the Vicar's concerns however, on the 10th July a Sunday Thanksgiving Service celebrated the Appeal's success and marked a wonderful achievement. The August edition of the parish magazine carried the good news and an interim statement of account. The Appeal, under the trusteeship of A.E. Dickson, F. Eden Wilson, R.D.Houghton and O. Taylor, was to remain open for further donations: ultimately a further £10,000 had to be raised.

SCHOOL APPEAL INTERIM STATEMENT.

	£	s.	d.
1945 Gift Day	100	0	0
1948 Vicarage Garden Party ..	167	19	1
Receipts from Donations and Efforts	3234	13	3
	3502	12	4
Less Expenses	31	6	2
	3471	6	2
Later Donation	10	0	0
	3481	6	2
Garden Party (June 30th) £407 14 1			
Less Expenses .. 30 16 1			
	376	18	0
Sports Gala (July 2nd) 244 18 11			
Less Expenses .. 62 10 4			
	182	8	7
Mile of Pennies (July 9th) 220 0 0			
Less Expenses .. 1 10 0			
	218	10	0
Thanksgiving Sunday (July 10th)	96	6	9
Miscellaneous	20	1	4
	£4375	10	10

SCHOOL APPEAL.

Day-to-day financial problems were also of concern in the early 1950s. While parish income remained fairly stable, running costs were rising steadily. Reverend Oatridge noted especially that the dilapidation charge on the vicarage had risen from £21 in 1946 to £62 in 1951. Similarly the annual contribution to the diocese had more than doubled, from £70 to £147, over the same period. Monies from such sources as the Vicarage Garden Party were needed therefore just to balance the books rather than being donated to charitable causes.

Another source of income was the churchyard. From burial fees it brought in revenue of £373 in 1951. The vicar's concern was how that sum would be replaced when the churchyard was full, which he anticipated at the time, would be some eight to ten years in the future. Church collections over the four years from 1947 to 1950 had remained very stable at an average of £1,098 per annum

One solution to the Parish's financial plight was the *Duplex Scheme.* This scheme was described as *a simple and effective method of church finance in use in every diocese in England.* The Parochial Church Council had a duty to frame the annual budget needed to maintain the work of the Church and to take the necessary steps to raise the funds required. The Duplex system, similar in many respects to the envelope scheme still in place today, involved people being sent 52 numbered envelopes dated for each Sunday of the year. It was different however as each envelope was divided into two sections. One was for money donated for *Maintenance* (Church expenses and charities at home); the other, labelled *Extension*, was for money intended for the work of missions abroad. These two elements gave the scheme its *duplex* name.

STIPEND CONCERNS

In the early 1950s there was another growing financial concern - the declining value of the vicar's stipend. The Parochial Church Council decided to launch a Benefice Endowment Fund, using the church collections from December 21st 1952 as *seed money.* At the time the Benefice derived from several different sources, ranging from agricultural rents to a *Christmas Box* of £4 from the Vicar of Preston.

All of these sources, augmented by income from what had been called *Queen Anne's Bounty*, provided an income of some £470 per year.   The Parochial Church Council felt that the absolute minimum stipend should be £600 and consequently the additional £130 would have to come from the General Church Expenses Account. It was in order to avoid this, and the pressure it would place on other necessary church expenses, that the Endowment Fund was created. This was not to be a continuous or sustained appeal but one which was to be occasionally highlighted in parish notices and publications. Money was raised through events such as the Vicarage Garden Party and through individual donations, such as the £500 left as a bequest by the late Mr John Sumner. In addition, legacies left to the Vicar and the Church would be invested and the interest paid into a stipend account.

Consideration was also given to extending the graveyard in order to sustain the income from that source. A list of fees from 1953 is reproduced overleaf.

MARRIAGE AND BURIAL FEES

It is, perhaps, worth repeating from time to time the nature and scale of fees in connection with weddings and funerals, which are now regulated by the Church Commissioners.

Marriage

(1) After Banns

(a) Without music :

	£	s.	d.
Church	1	2	0
Certificate	0	3	9
	£1	5	9

(b) With music :

	£	s.	d.
Church	2	13	0
Certificate	0	3	9
Organist	1	1	0
	£3	17	9

(2) By Licence

(a) Without music :

	£	s.	d.
Church	1	10	0
Certificate	0	3	9
	£1	13	9

(b) With music :

	£	s.	d.
Church	3	1	0
Certificate	0	3	9
Organist	1	1	0
	£4	5	9

Burials

	Parish'n'rs			Non-Parish'n'rs		
	£	s.	d.	£	s.	d.
First Interment (Single breadth)	1	0	0	*100	0	0
Burial of Cremated Remains	1	0	0	*100	0	0
Burial of Stillborn Infant	0	5	0			
Re-opening Grave	1	0	0	1	1	0
Surplice Fee	0	10	0	1	1	0
Morning Funeral (before 1 p.m.)	1	1	0	2	2	0
Sexton's Grave - Digging Fee	1	1	0	1	1	0
Tolling Passing Bell	0	5	0	0	5	0
Headstones	0	15	0	2	2	0
Inscription on Headstones	0	10	0	0	10	0

* The Vicar may exercise his discretion in regard to Non-Parishioners who are regular worshippers in Broughton Church or who have lived mostly in Broughton and only recently left the district as Parishioners.

If music is required at a funeral, the following additional fees are charged : Church, £1/11/-; Organist, £1/1/-. At both marriages and burials, the services of choirboys are also charged as an extra. If the Bells are desired, Mr. J. Jolleys, of Church Cottage, Church Lane, the captain of the Bellringers, should be approached direct.

Graves

Headstones and kerbs are permitted, but the former should not exceed 2ft. 6ins. in height. Only local stone of Longridge or Grit stone type should be used ; this excludes white marble or coloured granite. Relatives who wish for graves to be maintained should see Mr. Catterall, of Besford House, Durton Lane, the Sexton, with whom they may make their own arrangements, or send 15/- a year to the Vicar for weeding, washing and planting. It is worth adding that it is illegal for a Vicar to reserve a grave space, as this would prejudice the rights of future Vicars, who are, for their term of office, master of the Churchyard with the sole right of saying where any body may be interred. The most that a Vicar can do in this matter is to promise a person that, if that person should die while he is still Vicar of the parish, he will be prepared to bury him in a certain portion of the Churchyard ; but no promise is binding on any succeeding Vicar.

17

To mark the Coronation of Queen Elizabeth II, a programme of events was arranged for Saturday, 5th June 1953. The page from the parish magazine reproduced below illustrates the delights on offer.

Parishes of Broughton and Haighton

....

CORONATION OF
QUEEN ELIZABETH II

....

1.—To mark this occasion the following programme of events is being arranged by a joint committee representing both Parishes to take place on **Saturday, June 6th, 1953.**

(a) Sports Gala and Field Day on King George V Playing Field, Broughton Village, from 2 p.m. to 5 p.m. for all children resident in the above Civil Parishes or attending Broughton or Haighton Schools.

(b) Free Tea Party in Broughton Institute from 4-30 p.m. to 6-30 p.m. for such of the above children who will be 15 or under on June 6th next. These children will also each receive a Coronation Souvenir Mug and a tin of chocolates.

(c) Free Tea Party in Broughton Institute at approximately 5-30 p.m. for old people resident in the above Civil Parishes who are 65 or over on June 6th next. These people will each receive a Souvenir Canister of Tea.

(d) Coronation Dance in the Broughton Institute commencing 7-30 p.m.— admission 2s. 6d. Tickets from Scouts, Guides and members of Coronation Committee.

2.—Although the Education and Local Authorities are contributing towards the celebrations, a large part of the cost will have to be raised by voluntary effort, and you are therefore invited to send a donation to Mr. Broadbent and so assist in making the day a really happy and memorable one for young and old alike.

3.—A committee of ladies from both Parishes is arranging the catering both on the Sports Field and at the Tea Party and will welcome all gifts of tea, sugar, butter, margarine and other food-stuffs.

Lady helpers will also be required to assist with the catering and serving. Telephone Mrs. Robinson, 27, Yewlands Drive (Tel. 79001).

▬▬▬▬▬▬▬▬▬▬▬▬▬▬▬▬▬▬

BROUGHTON & HAIGHTON PARISHES

CHILDREN'S

CORONATION SPORTS GALA

on

KING GEORGE V PLAYING FIELD,
BROUGHTON VILLAGE

on

SATURDAY, JUNE 6th, 1953

commencing 2 p.m. sharp

———

ADMISSION FREE   ALL WELCOME

———

Sports for all ages (children); Bicycle, Sack, Flat and Relay Races; Tug-o'-War (Broughton v. Haighton); Obstacle Race; Children's Roundabout and Swings; Prizes for all events; Marquée; Teas and Refreshments; Ices; Minerals.

———

PLEASE BOOK THE DATE

———

Donations towards expenses gratefully accepted by
The Hon. Treasurer (Mr. C. Broadbent)
District Bank Ltd., Broughton, nr. Preston

7

The second major building project considered during the 1950s was that of a Parish Hall. This idea had first been mooted a decade earlier, originating in a remark by the Bishop of Blackburn in 1946 to Mr Eric Dickson, one of the Patrons of the Broughton Living. He suggested that a new church ought to be built at the southern end of the Parish to cater for the rapidly growing number of parishioners living in the new Fulwood housing estates. The idea was initially put on hold until the future of the school was decided. If a new school was to be built, then it was thought that one of the empty old school buildings could be bought from the Ministry and used as such a centre. The Parochial Council had the option of a site in Lightfoot Lane but was reluctant to take on the additional financial burden of building a new hall plus on-costs, such as employing a caretaker for the building.

Almost every meeting of the PCC during the early 1950s devoted discussion time to the provision of a parish hall, without being able to come to any real decision. One entry in the PCC Minutes for April 1950 sums up why the Committee struggled to reach a firm conclusion. It was acutely aware of *the need for a church hall or centre in the Fulwood part of the parish, the population of which was rapidly increasing* but *there was divided opinion as to whether this hall or centre should be strictly a parochial church hall or community centre.* There was divided opinion too about the site for such a building – for several years the one on Lightfoot Lane was the favoured option. Just about the only thing that could be agreed upon seemed to be that a parish hall was needed.

At the beginning of 1953 there was still no decision. Three sites were still *being considered*: Lightfoot Lane; *some site near the Church*; *the site of the present old cottage near the school*. Superficially at least, three years' discussion had produced very little but further conjecture.

By 1955 however the provision of a parish hall was becoming more urgent and necessary as the parish extended to the south west and it was felt that social facilities should be provided for this rapidly increasing population. The school had been saved: now the Parochial Church Council devoted their energy towards building a Parish and Mission hall. The mission element was key to the new proposal and was the main reason for abandoning any thought of using school buildings when and if they became vacant. Such a hall would not be near the majority of people it served and it was felt that the Church ought to go to the people. If it was to do so, then a hall in the Black Bull area, west of the A6, would be of immense value, both as a social centre and, indirectly perhaps, as a vehicle for encouraging new worshippers at the mother church. Because of the number of new houses built in the parish and the resultant growth in population since 1936, it was thought that the parish would be eligible for a substantial Diocesan grant towards the building of a hall and also for a £250 annual grant towards a curate's stipend.

It was decided, at last, to purchase a building plot of some 6,800 square yards, between Janice Drive, Broadway and Northway as the site for the Parish Mission Hall, at a cost of approximately £1700 plus road charges. The eventual sale price rose to some £2100 plus1600 road charges. An appeal was launched seeking to raise £16,000 in four years and £4,000 by the end of the year. By November 1955, almost £1500 had been raised through a whole variety of events. In the same month a Gift Day, was held at which every family in the parish was encouraged to contribute £5 towards the Appeal. This raised a further £750, though the vicar had reservations that the Appeal had not reached those people at whom it was directed – those who did not regularly come to church but who felt strongly that there was a need for a Parish Hall and that the Church should provide one. Perhaps in order to exert a subtle pressure on these people, a list of donors was published on a regular basis, without showing the sums donated.

By June 1956, money was coming into the Appeal at the rate of £100 per week, raised largely through many small-scale social events. Even this however was not sufficient and a number of men, drawn from the Men's Meeting on May 15th, carried out a house-to-house canvass of the parish. The letter they distributed, which brought in an additional £406, is shown overleaf.

NEW VICARAGE OR NEW HALL?

By the early 1950s it was becoming clear that the vicarage was beginning to show its age and in need of significant repair and modernisation. It was decided at the PCC meeting of March 1953, that because of the costs involved, it should be sold and a new vicarage built. A sub-committee was created to explore and develop this project.

Indeed this appears to have been the golden age of the sub-committee: a different one was created to consider almost every aspect of church life, no matter how small. In 1954 for example a sub-committee was set up to provide *about two dozen small tables for church functions*. A year later another sub-committee was formed to look into the provision of a chancel carpet. By 1956 however, the number had been reduced to a more manageable nine: Finance; Altar Linen; Church Yard; Electoral rolls; Fabric; Magazine; Social; Youth Fellowship and Parish Hall Appeal, the titles of many of which would be recognisable today.

This title of this last named sub-committee offers a clue as to why the one tasked with the building of a new vicarage, was short-lived. The building of a Parish Hall became almost the sole focus of Parish finance and fund-raising : the PCC had no choice but to finance, with the help of the Diocesan Dilapidations Fund, the renovation of the old vicarage rather than seek to build a new one.

A NEW PARISH HALL FOR BROUGHTON

Dear Friend,

In this letter we aim to challenge your conscience as a member of a growing community.

At Broughton, in our lovely old Parish Church of St. John Baptist, the Church is very much alive to its responsibilities. Are you?

The bright Services, excellently attended, are led by a splendid Choir. There are grand bodies of Scouts, Rovers, Guides, Cubs, and Brownies, a well-supported Women's Service, a lively Youth Fellowship, a successful Day School, an active Sunday School, and a fine spirit of devotion to an ideal.

This ideal is to take the Church to the people. The rapid development of the district south of Lightfoot Lane emphasises the need for a Parish Hall designed for spiritual and social purposes, and plans have gone ahead as follows:—

(1) A site has been acquired bounded by Northway, Broadway, and Janice Drive. A start will be made on the building in the spring of 1957, and it is hoped to complete it in twelve months.

(2) The total cost is estimated at £25,000.

(3) Over £3,000 has been raised by donations and congregational efforts.

(4) £4,000 has been given by the Diocese.

(5) Thus we still need about £18,000.

(6) There are approximately 1,500 houses in the Parish, many of whose occupants may well wish to help, once they know what is going on. Hence this letter to you.

If you are among the many who have responded to our previous appeals, we thank you for your support. If not, will you think again as to what you can do to help on this project.

The Church is not simply a place where people are baptised, married, and buried. It is—or ought to be—a brotherhood of Christian folks going out to help their neighbours. We do this in a small way at Broughton Church through our services, youth organisations, and other activities. It will be done in a bigger way when the Parish Hall is built. It is vital to our expanding needs.

Do you accept this challenge? Would you be ready to contribute a weekly or monthly amount, however modest, to our Parish Hall Fund? If you are, Church workers are ready to arrange a regular collection time at your convenience. Alternative ways of giving are listed below, and you are invited to fill in or delete as required. Our messenger will be glad to call for your answer in a few days' time. Please let the other members of your family read this letter.

Thanking you in anticipation,

Yours sincerely,

N. C. OATRIDGE, Vicar.

W. J. REYNOLDS, Warden.

J. B. HARGREAVES, Warden.

— — — — — — — — — —

Broughton Parish Hall Appeal Fund

(1) I am ready to subscribe at monthly/weekly intervals.

(2) The most convenient time for your Collector to call is ....

(3) Alternatively, I will make a:

(a) Standing Order to my Banker.

(b) Form of Covenant (Forms are available at Church or can be sent).

(c) Single Donation.

(d) Interest-free Loan for .... years.

(e) Loan at ......% interest for ...... years'

Signed ....

Address ....

The letter distributed throughout the Parish to encourage donations to the Parish Hall Appeal

70

By March 1957 tenders had been sent out to a number of firms. The lowest tender of £19,819 by the company of W.J. Turner of Preston, was accepted and the architect, Mr Mellor of Lytham, was appointed. The aim was to keep the total costs, including road charges, down to a ceiling figure of £25,000. Work began in August and approximate costs became clear:

Cost of land: £2,200
Building: £19,000
Architect's fees: £1,500
Cost of roads: £1,500
Cost of furnishing: £1,500

This gave a total cost of approximately £26,000, of which some £6,250 had been raised during the three years of the Appeal. The balance would be made up by a gift of £5,000 from the Diocese of Blackburn, a loan of £4,000 and an interest-free loan from a parishioner of £2,000. The remaining balance required, of £8,750, would have to be raised either through a building society loan or through further money raised by *every professing Church person* in the parish.

A large thermometer, created by Mr Smithies and displayed in Church, indicated the overall progress of the fund as the total reached £21,500. This meant that a balance of around £6000 would have to be raised by a bank loan. Annual Gift Days throughout the 1960s, went some way to paying off this additional sum.

On Sunday, December 7th 1958, the new dual purpose Parish Hall and Chapel was opened and dedicated by Bishop Baddley of Blackburn: the first Communion Service took place the following Friday.

On the 6th February 1966 Bishop Claxton of Blackburn named and rededicated the Chapel section within the building, as St Martin's Chapel. The Bishop himself had suggested the name because of his connection with St Martin's-in-the-Fields in London. From 1962, when St John's Church had its first assistant curate, it was possible to celebrate Family Communion at St Martin's every Sunday.

YOUTH FELLOWSHIP

Parish concerns however did not revolve entirely around financial matters. At the end of 1956, Broughton Church Youth Fellowship, founded by Mr A.J. Barker, celebrated its third year. It was open to young people between the ages of 14 and 20, who had been confirmed in the Anglican Church. Meetings were held in the Woodwork or Cookery Room in the school on Monday evenings from 7.00 to 9.30 p.m. The principles of the Fellowship were to promote a true spirit of Christianity among the youth of the parish, encouraging fellowship, co-operation and selflessness, and seeking to help members develop their particular talents and gifts and to use them in the service of others.

71

By the end of 1956 however, the members had spent almost a year renovating the left hand Cottage, pictured below, in order to convert it into a recreational centre to be used, for quiet activities such as chess, draughts and similar games. This building, having almost collapsed, was demolished ten years later in 1966.

The cottage was opened as a youth centre, on January 7th 1957 by Mr Barker and the Fellowship's February programme gives an idea of its activities:

Feb 4 (Monday)	General Meeting
Feb 6 (Wednesday)	Members' Committee Meeting
Feb 11 (Monday)	Brains Trust
Feb 18 (Monday)	General meeting
Feb 24 (Sunday)	Tenderfoot hike
Feb 25 (Monday)	Ballroom Dancing Instruction

In January 1959, the Fellowship left the cottage and held their meetings in the newly opened Parish Hall, which, under the guidance of Mr and Mrs Breakall, the Youth Club Leaders, offered the opportunity for many more recreational activities, most notably drama productions.

THE 1960s AND 70s

During these two decades of enormous national and international cultural and social change, parochial life at St John's was characterised by stability and consolidation. Established clubs and organisations - the Mothers' Union, the Church Youth Fellowship, the Cubs, Scouts, Brownies and Guides, the Choir – all continued to flourish and develop. The new Parish Hall offered opportunities for new groups such as the Young Wives Group, to be established.

In March 1961 for example, The Hall Players drama group, funded by a loan from the P.C.C., was formed. Its first production, in November that year, was the comedy *Quiet Weekend* by Esther McCracken. In 1964 a Coffee Club, supervised by adult volunteers, was started in the Parish Hall, where young people could meet after Evensong for coffee and conversation.

An Assistant Curate, the Reverend Michael Taylor, was appointed in January 1962. A bachelor, he came to the parish from St James in Chorley and found rooms initially at 26, Edenway. He left in September 1964 to take up the post of Chaplain at St Boniface's College in Warminster. He was succeeded in October by Reverend William Fielding, from St Michael's Church in Ashton. The parish purchased a house for him and his family at 16, Chestnut Drive in Fulwood.

GARDEN OF REMEMBRANCE

At the end of 1963 it was suggested that a Garden of Remembrance be created on the northerly part of the new graveyard, for the interment of cremated remains. It took some six years for this idea to become reality but in 1969, laurel bushes were removed and the ground levelled near the gate entrance to the churchyard on Church Lane. A Book of Remembrance, in which the names of those cremated were recorded, was purchased and kept in a glass case in Church. The Garden was finally opened, with a service of Dedication on September 28th, 1969. Following a generous donation in 1970, a low wall was built on the Church Lane side of the Garden. At the same time the P.C.C., helped by the efforts of the Verger, were able to remove the kerbstones from some graves in an attempt to create a more open churchyard with the long stretches of turf between the rows of headstones which can be seen today.

IN THE MIDST OF LIFE WE ARE IN DEBT!

Further financial concerns arose in the mid-1960s, a £1500 deficit in the 1966 budget for example. Leaflets commended seven year covenants and that parishioners join the Simplex envelope scheme, which had replaced the Duplex Scheme of the past, and as the name suggests, now involved a single donation to Parish finances only. Such efforts were supplemented by the annual Gift Day on Sunday, 6th November, which sought to raise £500 both to cover that year's financial deficit and to help pay off the £3000 debt still owing on the Parish Hall.

In June 1967, Reverend Fielding left the Parish to take up the benefice of St Oswald's in Knuzden near Blackburn. A new curate, Reverend Ronald Hollinghurst, joined the Parish in August and lived at 22 Brookside Road, a house purchased for him by the P.C.C. at a cost of £3,400, and for which a 10% deposit of £340 had to be found. The house bought previously at 16 Chestnut Drive had proved too small, offering no room in which the curate could meet people privately. The original plan was to sell this property but it was later decided to keep the house and offer it as part of a job package to a couple willing to combine the duties of Verger and Parish Hall caretaker. The previous Verger and Sexton, John Rowcroft, had died suddenly on Sunday, 21st May, after collapsing in the north gateway of the church.

The final instalment of £1000 was due to be paid on the Parish Hall but it was hoped to defer this and the money used in the purchase of the Brookside Road property. Even if this were possible, there still remained something in excess of £2000 to be found. With this in mind, the P.C.C. looked for some kind

73

parishioners to make £100 interest-free loans in order to reduce the amount needing to be borrowed from the Bank.

A new Verger, Mr Midgeley, was appointed in November 1967. The title verger comes from the fact that he was the attendant who carried the verge or staff of office, usually carried before a bishop or other ecclesiastical dignitary. In some parishes the verger preceded the choir to and from the vestry – in the olden days he literally cleared a path through the congregation for the procession as people were not seated but simply crowded into the nave. In more recent times the verger is also the cleaner and caretaker of the church and may well also have some responsibility for the churchyard, generally helping the Vicar and Churchwardens to carry out their duties.

Financial concerns loomed large again in 1968. Church collection income and that raised through the envelope scheme was falling and there was a rise in liabilities. The houses provided for the curate and verger; the cost of renovating the organ and of installing oil central-heating in the Church; the parish's responsibility to the Deanery in relation to William Temple C of E School; the remaining debt owing on the Parish Hall – all of these plus the rising cost of insurance on the Church and Parish Hall, put a severe strain on parish finances. Though there were mutterings among the congregation that it should be abolished, the solution was yet another Gift Day in November.

As if all these money worries were not enough, 1969 brought additional concerns when the Church Commissioners, following their survey of the vicarage, concluded that not only did it require total redecoration and necessary fabric and central heating repairs, but advised that structural alterations and a revised layout of rooms were needed. The estimated cost of this work was £6000. Some grants were available: £400 from the Dilapidations Fund; a grant from the Dilapidations Board of £2000; a Church Commissioners' grant of £1800, but this still left some £1800 to be found by the Parish. Indeed the Commissioners' grant was dependent upon the sum being matched by the Parish. The initial costings did however prove somewhat optimistic and the final sum to be found eventually totalled £2,500. By April 1969 just over a thousand pounds had been raised or promised.

Once again there was an appeal for interest-free loans in units of £25. It was hoped alterations could be completed before the new Vicar, Revd. Canon John Adam, took up his post. His Institution and Induction took place on Saturday, 1st March, 1969: the former was carried out by the Bishop of Blackburn; the latter, whereby he was given possession of the church building and of the temporal rights of the benefice, was carried out by the Archdeacon of Lancaster. In the event, the building work could not be completed by the beginning of March and so temporary accommodation was needed – the P.C.C. with tongue firmly in cheek I'm sure, - explained that they hadn't entirely dismissed the possibility of caravan dwelling in the Vicarage grounds! Fortunately Mr and Mrs Loveless, proving to be the very antithesis of their name, put their home in Barton at the disposal of the Vicar and his family for some five months. Building delays meant that the Adam family could not take up residence in the refurbished vicarage until October 1969. In December 1970 an *At Home Sherry Evening* was held at the vicarage, both to allow parishioners to see the improvements and to raise money to pay for them.

After two years Reverend Hollinghurst left the Parish in March 1970 to take up an appointment as Vicar of St James' Leyland. He was replaced by Reverend Maurice Sunter in November. A year later, in November 1971, Reverend Sunter departed for the treacle mines of the parish of St Nicholas in Sabden. He was replaced by the Reverend Kingsley Charles Jones, originally from Wiltshire but who was, prior to his appointment, curate at Penwortham. He worked in the Parish until March 1974 when he was appointed to the parish of Woolaston in the Hereford diocese. At the time of his departure the Church of England was facing significant problems in the shortage of clergy: in simple terms twice as many clergy were retiring as were being presented for ordination. As a result no immediate replacement was likely, though the Reverend George Jackson, Vicar of Woodplumpton, would spend the final year before his retirement working at Broughton Church, from October 1974 to October 1975. His work as Deputy – Vicar would also cover the inter-regnum between Canon Adam's retirement in December 1974 and his successor being appointed. In addition Mr Birket, one of the first clergy to be ordained for auxiliary work in the diocese, would work at church on Sundays and some evenings while continuing his day-job at County Hall

THEATRE WORKSHOP

In November 1970 a group of about forty young people, between the ages of 12 and 16, gathered at the Parish Hall to form a junior theatre workshop, the Saint Martin's Youth Theatre Workshop. The children formed their own committee under the guidance of Miss Lesley Vaughan, Miss Megan Tudor-Thomas, Mrs Doreen Roberts, Mrs Barbara Hill and Mrs Marjorie Tudor-Thomas, and explored all aspects of theatre and drama production.

STEWARDSHIP IN BROUGHTON

At the start of 1971 the P.C.C., through its newly formed Forward Planning Committee, launched a campaign to develop the notion of stewardship within the Parish. Perhaps for the first time, this was an attempt to be proactive rather than reactive in organising parish affairs and finance.

Initially the scheme was concerned with people who already had a connection with the Church and how, through them, it could increase its regular income. A longer-term plan was aimed at people outside the Church and would have a more pastoral objective. The initial strategy was to compile a list of families

75

attached to the two churches and then produce an informative brochure presenting the activities, aims, financial needs, priorities and targets of Broughton Church, which would be personally distributed by a team of visitors. A third strand would take the form of a Church Week from May 16th to the 23rd, to include normal services, a pageant of Church life and a grand Parish Social Gathering. Finally each family in the Parish would be visited and the visitor would explain personally how best the Parish could be helped through regular financial donations.

In the past money-raising campaigns had been organised along the lines of a commercial company in response to some urgent need and not as part of any planned strategy. Now the P.C.C. felt that Broughton Church was entering a memorable period in the history of the Parish, in which people would be become more committed to give not only financially but also of their time and talents in support of the Church's work.

The visitors would encourage people to take part in the new Envelope Scheme, giving the Church a steady, predictable weekly income, which would clearly greatly aid future planning. It was hoped too that more people would agree to a Covenant, an undertaking to give a certain sum over a period of years, which enabled the Parish to gain a considerable sum over and above the amount given by individuals.

The second phase, to be carried out during the Autumn of 1971, was concerned with a much-needed reorganisation of the pastoral system within the Parish. Through Street and Road-Wardens, taking responsibility for their immediate locality, and being willing to visit their neighbours and the sick for example, it was hoped to create a pastoral support network. It was hoped too to increase the amount of publicity going to homes in the Parish, perhaps in the form of a quarterly Parish newspaper to run alongside the magazine and with a less Church-centred bias.

PATTERNS OF WORSHIP

In the early 1970s the P.C.C. decided to experiment with Holy Communion at 6.30 p.m. on Sunday, in place of the usual Evensong. It was felt that the changing patterns of the traditional Sunday made it difficult for many people to attend a morning Communion Service. The first Service was held on February 22nd 1970, its format an interweaving of the usual Communion liturgy with the musical features of Evensong – a psalm, *Magnificat* and *Nunc Dimittis*. Two other different formats were tried over the next two months.

The experiment proved popular and it was decided to hold an evening Communion Service at 6.30 p.m. on the third Sunday of the month, from September to December. In addition, it was also decided to try out a version of the Family Service already in place at St Martin's but involving the uniformed organisations on the second or fourth Sundays during the same period.

At the end of 1971 two new building projects were being considered. The first was an additional wing to the Parish Hall containing games and meeting rooms, a small kitchen and a lounge with bar. The architect was Mr K. Pinder. The approximate cost would be some £15,000 but it was hoped to raise a large part of this, if not all, by making more fruitful use of part of the field adjoining the Parish Hall. This would include building a new curate's house, selling the one on Brookside Road, and the construction of a hut for Guides and Brownies, the latter at a cost of some £9,000. In addition two plots of land would be auctioned in April 1973. Building was underway by August that year and completed by April 1974.

By March 1975 the house built near the Parish Hall for assistant clergy, was ready - sadly there was no assistant or curate to move in. It was therefore offered to a suitable tenant who could look after the property and who would agree to move out as soon as a curate was appointed.

The second project was much more ambitious – a new church-aided, 280 pupil school and Worship Centre to be built in the Broadwood Drive area of Fulwood, the expanding eastern part of the parish. On June 29th, 1973 the last service was held at St Peter's Church in Preston. The parishioners were however keen to preserve and keep alive the church's name in the Preston area. With this in mind, the Broughton P.C.C. unanimously agreed to adopt the name for the new school and worship centre. As a thank you, the old church gave an altar cross, communion silver, hymn books and a lectern Bible to the new St Peter's.

The architect appointed to design the new building was Mr David Bennett and work was underway by December 1974. Initially it was hoped that the building would be completed in time for the Autumn term 1975. In fact the official opening and dedication by the Bishop of Blackburn, did not take place until the 6th July, 1976.

The Church's contribution to the building costs was in excess of £40,000, yet another fund-raising headache. One of the more original money-raising ideas to fund the new building was a Mediaeval Market, in preparation for which parishioners could buy 5p savings stamps to be collected on a card and spent at the market held on November 16th 1974. In addition, in May 1976, parishioners were invited to become a Friend of St Peter's and to join the annual subscription scheme in order to pay off the remaining £9000 debt on the building.

As if all this new building was not enough, in January 1975 plans were afoot for a new Choir Vestry, the existing one, built in 1906 when the choir consisted of about 12 boys and a few adults, being totally inadequate. There were now some thirty boys and over twenty adults and teenagers in the choir. Moreover the adjoining Clergy Vestry, also built in 1906, was far too small for the Vicar and Churchwardens. The Tyson Trust, founded by the late John James Tyson, a bank official who lived at *Kranholm* on Garstang Road, offered to donate

£15,000 to fund the project. The old Choir Vestry would be released for the use of the Vicar, while the Vicar's present vestry would be used by the Churchwardens.

Mr Kevin Fletcher was the appointed architect for the new building, to be dressed in matching stone and sited on the south side of the Church, with external access and a door into the nave. Some forty-five graves would be affected by the new build and its adjoining terrace. Though most of these were dated in the last century, statutory notices were placed in the Press and posted in the Church and Parish Hall. Attempts were also made to contact near relatives of the interred persons. Those gravestones which were removed would, as far as possible, be used to pave the new terrace.

A NEW VICAR

A new vicar, the forty-four year-old Reverend William Gerald Armstrong, the successor to Canon Adam, was instituted and inducted on Thursday 24th April, 1975. In September 1976, Cyril Birket, who had been a part-time assistant curate for some months, gave up his job at Lancashire County Council to take up the post on a full-time basis. Later, in February 1979, he was appointed Vicar of Wesham near Kirkham and left Broughton at Easter.

In July 1977, a second curate joined the ministry team, Reverend Gerald Field, who had been ordained Deacon at the beginning of the month. Some two years later he appears to have left the Parish under something of cloud. In August 1979 the Vicar wrote somewhat enigmatically in the Parish magazine:

It was with very deep regret that we had to announce the departure of Gerald Field from the staff of Broughton Parish. It is perhaps true of clergy more than any other professions that people are not usually very interested in what you have done right, but they are immediately interested in where you have gone wrong. I pray that Liz and Gerald will be remembered for the many good things they have done for this parish and particularly for young people.

LET THERE BE LIGHT

In March 1978 plans were underway for the rewiring of the church and the provision of new lighting. The latter, designed to be more in keeping with the old candelabrum in the centre of the nave consisted of eight clusters of five lights and two of eight lights, costing £40 and £76 respectively. Parishioners were invited to fund a light cluster as a memorial or a thanksgiving. The lighting was installed by August 1978 and dedicated on the 8th October.

CHAPTER 9

TOWARDS THE NEW MILLENNIUM

The last two decades of the Twentieth Century appear to have been, for the most part, a period of certainty and consolidation at Broughton Church. After the major building projects and many funding appeals of previous years, life at St John's, though far from stagnant or complacent, settled into a vibrant routine involving many different social groups within the growing Parish. There were of course moments of crisis and sadness such as the departure of a Vicar and later a headteacher, both in unhappy circumstances; there were moments of unease and debate, such as those surrounding the sharing of the *Peace*, which appeared as part of the Communion Service in the early 1990s.

Despite, and completely overshadowing, such controversies however, a variety of organisations flourished - The Hall Players; Mothers' Union; Women's Fellowship; Scouts; Guides; Cubs; Brownies; Bible Study Group; Friends of St Peter's; Young Wives; the Bell Ringers and of course the Church Choir - all these organisations and many others, created a true sense of community, within what had become something of a sprawling parish.

During the spring and summer of 1983 however, the people of the Parish had to deal with a particularly difficult situation. For several months there had been some concerns among members of the PCC about possible financial irregularities in wedding and funeral fees paid to the Vicar.

The matter had initially been raised in comments made in the PCC Treasurer's report of the 13th December 1982. He commented: *I have formed the opinion that I am unable to satisfy myself that all parochial fees have been properly accounted for.*

More specifically he continues: *Firstly, I am not able to confirm that all fees properly due to the PCC under the Ecclesiastical Fees Measure (1962) have been received by the PCC. Secondly I am not able to confirm that all amounts paid in respect of other parochial charges have been properly accounted for.*

In March of the following year, the Vicar offered his apologies to the PCC for what had happened and the problems it had caused. At the same time he expressed a wish to leave the Parish and asked the PCC to approach the Bishop with a view to his taking up an alternative living after a period of sabbatical leave. This proposal was agreed *in accordance with the Christian principles of compassion and forgiveness.* Immediately after this meeting the Archdeacon had contacted the Churchwardens to inform them that the vicar would be taking indefinite leave of absence.

At their April meeting the PCC unanimously agreed to the proposal that Reverend Armstrong be asked to resign the Broughton living no later than the 30th June. In addition monies paid by the Parish as part of the Vicar's stipend would cease to be paid after the 15th June: instead they would be deposited in a new, separate account until a new incumbent was inducted.

At an Extra-ordinary Meeting, held on the 18th April, it was proposed that the police be authorised to investigate financial discrepancies regarding wedding and funeral fees, as well as a payment of £530 made with regard to the installation of a burglar alarm at the Vicarage, some of which may have been used fraudulently to fund a similar installation at the vicar's private house in Bentham.

In June, the Vicar's seventeen year-old son, Nicholas Armstrong, was convicted of stealing £220 from the Church safe. He claimed in court that he had taken the money to get back at the Church authorities, who had accused his father of malpractice and as a response to what he described as a smear campaign in the local press.

In July, after Reverend Armstrong had quit his post, the Diocesan Pastoral Committee, acting on behalf of the Bishop, suspended the Living, in theory for five years. This was the maximum term before a new order was required: in practice the living could be restored at any point once problems were resolved. The Diocese also ordered a review of the whole parish, especially with regard to its size. There was certainly a feeling among some officials that it ought to be divided into two or three smaller parishes.

After an inter-regnum of almost a year, during which Reverends Edgar Ambrose and Arthur Rhodes, along with Churchwardens Betty Crane and Don Dow, managed the business and religious life of the Parish, a new Vicar, Reverend Stanley Finch, was instituted on 31st July 1984. He was joined in October by deacon and second assistant curate, the Reverend Peter Pike, who following his ordination as Priest, remained in the parish until August 1988, when he moved to the church in Woodplumpton.

ECUMENICAL UNITY

In August 1986 Reverend Finch was at the forefront of the move towards Church unity, which he had first championed a year earlier. Many of the local Churches, at least those which were already members of the Fulwood and Broughton Council of Churches were considering entering into a local ecumenical covenant. They were agreed on two things: unity did not mean uniformity and that such unity would only develop out of a growing together rather than through any imposed, bureaucratic scheme.

In these early days, the covenant would only involve a commitment to continuing along the road to unity. Indeed the Vicar was keen to point out that such a process would not bring any loss of independence. What this small step did mean was that Churches would share more activities and explore their faith together. In years to come such unity might mean that Churches shared together in Holy Communion: for now the first stage was simply a full acceptance of each other, despite differences in the detail of Christian belief and action and significant differences in organisation. The draft Covenant was published in the parish magazine in April 1987 and is reproduced overleaf.

Despite what today would appear to be the unexceptionable, inchoate nature of the document, there were some misgivings among parishioners at the annual Church meeting in June 1987. However the overwhelming response among parishioners was generally extremely positive: indeed such was the strength of feeling among some of those who fully supported these embryonic moves towards unity, that dissenting voices were labelled bigots and trouble makers, a response which prompted a plea for tolerance from the Churchwardens.

The Covenant was signed by representatives of local Churches on January 24th 1988 in Fulwood Methodist Church. Seventy people from each congregation were allocated places to witness this historical agreement to *foster a growing unity in prayer, worship and fellowship*, an agreement unthinkable to those Broughton parishioners who, hundreds of years earlier, lived through the turbulent years of sixteenth and seventeenth century reforms, persecution and bigotry.

ROGER DONALD HOUGHTON

The whole parish was greatly saddened by the death of Roger Houghton on the 8th May 1988, just a few days short of his eightieth birthday. For much of that time he had been at the very centre of Parish life at Broughton. Born on the 24th May, 1908, he was educated at Cheltenham and Wadham College, Oxford, where he obtained an Honours Degree in Law. He was then articled to his father's firm of solicitors, *Houghton, Revely, Craven and Wilkins*, in Preston. He became a partner in 1935 and, apart from the War years, practised there until his retirement in 1978.

During World War II, he was commissioned in the Royal Army Service Corps, and after service in France, was evacuated from St Nazaire in 1940. He spent a further three years in India and saw action against the Japanese in the critical battles of Kohima and Imphal.

TRIBUTES

ON Friday, 13th May, Broughton Choristers said farewell to a very dear colleague and friend.

For over 50 years Roger Houghton sang week by week in the stalls at the Parish Church. It goes without saying that he was a very competent musician - few choral blemishes at practices or services went unnoticed by him, and it was little use choirmen glancing at their watches at 9 o'clock on a Wednesday night if that anthem wasn't quite right!

Roger was tireless in his work for the Church and its music. During the past 25 years there have been two organ rebuildings; the choir has been re-robed twice; the music library has been extended considerably; the present Choir Vestry has been built; (the envy of every visiting choir) and at the centre of all the planning, preparations and fund-raising was Roger.

Who will ever forget the magnificent Jubilee Dinner. Twelve months prior to the event Roger was contacting ex-choristers the length and breadth of the British Isles to bring about that splendid reunion.

But it was Roger's ability to relate to the young choristers which was so delightful. Their interests were his interests - be it music, sport, fishing, bird watching (the list was endless) - he could share their enthusiasms. And how he and they together enjoyed the Choir Sports and the Choir Trips, with memorable moments such as the annual Treasure Hunt or the Sausage Sizzle on Great Orme!

Roger's enthusiasm for Church Music however was not purely parochial. As a member of the Council of the Royal School of Church Music, and as a member of the Diocesan Music Committee, he worked tirelessly for the cause of Church music throughout the area, and many parishes have benefitted from his guidance.

We shall miss Roger enormously and one wonders how we will cope with all the tasks he so willingly undertook. However, of one thing I am certain:- Broughton Choir will go from strength to strength in the years ahead - the dedication and tremendous work of Roger Houghton has ensured that this will be so.

JOHN CATTERALL

From 1946, he worked as a member of Broughton Parish Council, serving as Chairman from 1951 to 1955. He rejoined the Council in 1972 and remained in office until his death.

Though a man of many interests, his greatest love was undoubtedly the Church and Church Music, especially Broughton Church and Choir, of which he was a member for over fifty years. He became a member of the Council of the Royal School of Church Music in 1962 and served until his death. He was largely instrumental in the building of the new Choir Vestry and spear-headed many other fund-raising appeals: the organ appeal of the late 1970s and early 1980s was one in which he, almost single-handedly, battled doggedly to raise some £20,000. Roger Houghton's indefatigable energy, determination and tireless commitment to Broughton Church and its Choir was amply expressed in the Choir Master's tribute to him in the parish magazine of June 1988, which is reproduced on page 81.

CURATES COME...AND CURATES GO

Following the departure of Reverend Peter Pike, a new curate, Robin Davill, was ordained Deacon in October 1988, before joining the Parish. Originally from Nottinghamshire and yet a member of Yorkshire Cricket Club, Reverend Davill worked for eleven years as a teacher before entering the Ministry, and completing his training at Westcott House, Cambridge. He remained in the Parish until April 1991, when he left to work at Howden Minster in the York Diocese.

His successor was Dr Stephen Hunt, who, after an academic career as a lecturer in Biochemistry, which culminated in his becoming Reader in the Biology Department at Lancaster University, was ordained and took up his post in September 1991. He remained in post until February 1995 and was replaced in July that year by Rev. Jim Percival. He worked in the Parish until 1999, when he moved to the Parish of St Stephens in Little Harwood near Blackburn.

Reverend Robin Pettit arrived in the Parish in January 2000 as Senior Curate responsible for St Peter's Chapel. A second curate, Reverend Satoru Kato, originally a Buddhist priest, who had converted to Christianity and worked for several years as an ordained minister of the Church in Japan in Tokyo, was appointed a few months later. Unfortunately Rev. Pettit left his post suddenly, on grounds of ill-health, in March 2001. The following month, he was replaced by Reverend Terry Scholz, a former lecturer in Management Studies and Industrial Law.

BYPASS PROPOSED... AND REJECTED

After public consultation in September 1991, alternative routes emerged as for a proposed bypass around the centre of Broughton. Those in favour of such a scheme were asked to express a preference between:

Scheme A – widening the existing stretch of the A6 from Broughton roundabout to a new roundabout near Broughton Park Hotel (The Marriott), and then east of the village, cutting through Whittingham Lane, between the Village Club and Old Hall.

83

Scheme B – from a new exit off Broughton roundabout, cutting across D'Urton Lane and part of the Church car park, to a new roundabout between the Church and *Brooklands*, along the south side of Blundel Brook and east of the school playing fields to merge with the line proposed in Scheme A.

Not surprisingly the P.C.C., Broughton Parish Council and the Annual Parents' Meeting at Broughton School, all expressed a preference for the much less intrusive and damaging Scheme A. However Lancashire County Council and the majority of people responding to the public consultation, preferred Scheme B.

The debate re-emerged in 1994 - 95 but this time the Opposition campaign, spear-headed by Chris Couper, Secretary of the *Land and Buildings Committee,* and the Broughton Bypass Review Group, was more vociferous and organised. Despite a number of parishioners, who lived in Broughton Village, being in favour of the scheme, in April 1997 Preston Borough Council decided to exclude the controversial Route B from its Local Plan. This was not the end of the matter however, as Lancashire County Council continued to favour the plan.

In 2001 a new, enlarged and even more intrusive scheme was proposed and again faced significant opposition from the PCC, Broughton School Governors and the Broughton Bypass Review Group. Again the weight of opposition as well as financial constraints, appeared to silence the proposals, only for them to reappear a decade later.

Twenty years on …the debate and controversy continue.

CHANCEL CHANGES

During the latter part of 1991 and the early months of 1992, there was some discussion about the reshaping of the Church chancel. More radical proposals included removing the oak reredos and the altar rail, moving the altar itself forward to a position between the current choir stalls, and extending the latter and moving them back to where the altar presently stands. It was thought that such dramatic alterations would allow more of the congregation to see and hear what was happening at the altar, as well as making room for an ever-growing choir.

Unsurprisingly not everyone agreed with such significant alterations and thankfully no changes were made.

CHURCH COTTAGE

There were no such qualms about what needed to be done to save Church Cottage. In 1989 the building, once the local inn and schoolhouse, for a time simultaneously, and latterly the home of the Jolleys family, was virtually derelict. One half had already been demolished in the mid-1960s, and the remaining half had been condemned as unfit for human habitation but gained a reprieve while

Mrs Jolleys, who had lived there all her married life, remained resident. Ironically by the time of her death in the mid-1980s, the opinion had changed dramatically and Church Cottage was now considered a Listed Building.

Given its new status, it was no longer possible therefore to demolish the building. Offers were made to buy it as a house; there were thoughts of it being acquired by the Church to develop and use as offices; it could be developed by the School to use as a study base. However the most original suggestion, that it be restored in keeping with a particular historical period and furnished with suitable artefacts as a living museum, was the one which found most favour.

In 1993 the School Governors initiated a scheme to restore and convert the building into a living museum of Tudor life, at a cost of some £50,000. An Appeal was launched, to which British Aerospace contributed a magnificent £24,000. Work began in 1994, the main contractor being Bill Wolstenholme of Longridge, and the thatching being restored by John Burke of Nantwich. In October that year, with most of the substantial work completed, an Open Day show-cased this unique building. The following year, on the 11th July 1995, Church Cottage Museum was officially opened by Princess Alexandra.

A NEW MAN AT THE HELM

In July 1998, after some fourteen years at Broughton Church, the Vicar, Reverend Finch, moved to what he described as a *retirement post* in the Cotswolds, at St Mary's, Great Washbourne.

After an inter-regnum of some six months, his successor, Reverend David Jenkins was appointed by the Patrons.

FINANCIAL CRISIS

Money, or rather the lack of it, ever the dull backdrop to parochial life, once again, in the mid-1990s, dominated the Broughton stage. In 1996 the PCC Treasurer, Norman Gore, highlighted what he saw as a *severe financial challenge*.

For seven of the previous nine years Parish expenditure had exceeded income. In 1995 there had been a deficit of some £1,524 despite a significant rise in Direct Giving. It came as no surprise therefore to reveal that cash reserves, over the same period, had fallen from £68,000 in 1986 to £32,000 at the end of 1995. At that rate the Parish would in essence be bankrupt by the end of 2005.

Mr Gore highlighted some of the Church's financial commitments – it cost £250 every day just for it to pay its way. Insurance costs amounted to £3,600; heating and lighting just in the Parish Church ate up a further £1,334; £450 was spent on wine and wafers for Communion Services. Far and away the greatest expenditure however was in fulfilling commitments to the Diocesan Quota and

Clergy Stipends. Broughton was called upon to make a higher contribution to these funds to compensate for poorer parishes struggling to maintain a ministry at all. In 1990 St John's total payments into these two funds was £26,389: in 1996 the commitment would be almost double, at £51,681. The formula used to assess parishes depended on two factors, its level of annual income and the number of people on its electoral role.

How was this potentially disastrous situation to be resolved? Annual income from Parish events such as the Garden Party and Christmas Fair was normally about £2000. The Parish Hall was paying its way. Interest on reserves brought in some £5,000, less than in previous year due to falling interest rates. The key was to increase both the number of people taking part in Direct Giving through freewill envelopes and Covenanting, and also to persuade people to give more, the average contribution per envelope being a modest £2 each week.

To some extent people responded positively to this clarion call; revenue from Direct Giving in 1996 increased by over three thousand pounds and that from Covenants by over £500. The deficit however remained, indeed it had grown to almost £8,000.

The situation in 1997 appeared to worsening rapidly. Despite further increases in the revenue from plate collections and Direct Giving, and a Gift Day, which raised £938, the deficit for the following was forecast to exceed £9,000.

By June 1998 the crisis appeared to have been averted. Parishioners had responded so positively that the actual deficit was only £1996, a quarter of that forecast. Direct Giving had increased by almost 15%, and an Advent campaign persuaded more people to give through standing orders.

MILLENNIUM FESTIVAL

Amid popular rumours of global cyber meltdown and urban myths of imminent Armageddon, Broughton Church took a more optimistic view of the coming of the new Millennium, organising a Festival from the 28th April to the 8th May 2000. It began with a Parish Ball and the week-long celebration included a teenage disco, a Family Day It's a Knockout, a Quilters' Fair, Choir Concert, Barn Dance, Silent Auction and Pet Show.

LITURGICAL CHANGES

With effect from the First Sunday of Advent in 2000, the Church of England adopted a new form of Common Worship. After the 31st December, the Alternative Service Book would no longer be licensed for use in parishes. The new Lectionary had been introduced over a year earlier and to this would now be added a new Eucharistic Rite, Funeral Service, Baptism, Confirmation and Wedding Services.

Unsurprisingly not everyone welcomed these changes, and the Vicar felt obliged to reassure parishioners that these were exciting developments and the opportunity for a fresh look at and an evaluation of forms of worship. The changes were permanent and mandatory – there was no opting out – they needed to be embraced positively. Cranmer, the author of the Book of Common Prayer, had sought to render the liturgy into everyday English and so make it accessible to the common man. Reverend Jenkins sought to persuade his congregation that the Church in the new Millennium also needed to look at what was appropriate language.

For the traditionalists there was the comfort that the 1662 Prayer Book Services, the 8 o'clock Communion, Mattins and Evensong, would remain unchanged, and be said according to the Prayer Book.

PARISH HALL REFURBISHMENT

In August 2000 the Parish Hall complex was closed for three weeks for a major overhaul, its first since being built forty years earlier. The work included replacing external doors and windows, exterior painting, kitchen refurbishment, installation of a loop-sound system and general internal redecoration. It was hoped to raise the £26,000 needed through an Appeal launched the following month. Gift Aid envelopes were made available and the 600 parishioners on the electoral roll, were encouraged to donate £5 per week during October and November.

By November the internal work was completed and a Thanksgiving Service was held in St Martin's Chapel.

CHAPTER 10
BROUGHTON INCUMBENTS 1353-2012

1353 **NICHOLAS DE BROUGHTON**

He was titled *chaplain* and his name appears in the essoins, a submission of excuses for not attending court, taken before the Justices in Preston in 1353.

1358 **JOHN LE CLERC**

His name appears in the Assize Roll of 32 Edward III (1358)

1377 **GEOFFREY**

He was nominated chaplain of the hermitage of Broughton and is named in a deed of 1377.

1368-1396 **WILLIAM DE ERLESGATE**

He was named in 1371, as chaplain in a feoffment of land in Goosnargh upon which services and rents were due to Richard of Caterhole (Catterall).

Though there is no absolute or definitive proof, it is highly likely that the three individuals above were priests at a chapel in Broughton. They are certainly listed as such in Farrar and Brownbill's *A History of the County of Lancaster* published in 1912 (Vol 7 pages 117-124)

1441 **HENRY DE BROUGHTON**

He was the priest at Broughton, mentioned in a lease dated the 19th year of the reign of Henry VI (1441). In addition he is named in a quit claim (September 1441) of all messuages and lands held by one John Migehalgh by feoffment of Robert Migehalgh his father.

1515 **SIR EDWARD (EVAN) WALL**

Fishwick notes that in a deposition taken in 1515, Sir Edward Wall was described as the *parish priest* of Broughton.

1530 **SIR HENRY HELME**

He was chaplain at Broughton and received a stipend of £2 a year. He is named in a subsidy roll c1530, the family originating in Middleton and later making its home at Church House, Goosnargh.

1554   **DOMINUS VANUS (EVAN) BANESTER**

Dominus was the academic title of Bachelor of Arts and usually translated as *Sir* in English universities. Most priests and curates were graduates hence the epithet *Sir* became their customary title.

The Guild Roll of 1562 identifies a Nicholas Banester and his two sons, George and Evanus. The latter was one of the clergy at Preston but is described as an *extra*, which may well suggest that he was 'loaned' as curate at Broughton.

In 1586 he was reported to the Privy Council as a Marian priest of Preston, being harboured by Mistress Jane Eyves at Fishwick Hall.

1548-1565   **SIR ROGER SHARNOCKE (CHARNOCK)**

He was named in the Chester Visitations Lists for 1548 and 1562 and three years later was nominated in the will of Anne Singleton, wife of William Singleton of Broughton, dated 13th December 1565, as *Roger Sharnocke curet at Broughton.*

1597   **JOHN or ROGER MARTIN (MARTON)**

Fishwick gives his Christian name as *John*, while Jackson offers the name *Roger*. He was described as *clark and curate of Broghton* and in his will dated 10th June 1597, expressed the wish to be buried in the Church at Broughton. He bequeathed his nag and four sheep to his grandson, Henry Martin: to his nephew, another Henry Martin, he left two sheep. He also made a bequest to the children of Richard Taylor, leaving to each of them one sheep. John Simpson also received one sheep and the curate's *best breeches*, while the remainder of his estate, with a total value of £19 18s 6d, was left to the children of Richard Martin and Thomas Kirkby.

1604-1610   **JOHN WITTON**

He was described as *stipendary minister* but as *noe preacher*, which suggests either that he was singularly ineffective or more likely that despite his position, he was not permitted or was unlicensed to preach.

1622   **JOHN LOMAX**

Little is known of the life and career of John Lomax but he is mentioned in the Chester Visitations list for 1622.

1626   **PETER ADDISON B.A.**

1628   **ROGER FARRAND**

Born around 1587, he was commonly known as Sir Roger Fishwick. He was curate of Preston from 1613 to 1616 before moving to Woodplumpton, where he remained for the next twelve years. While there, In 1621 – 22, his name appears among those financial contributors to the King for the recovery of the Palatinate. James 1, in the early stages of the Thirty Years'

War, was anxious to furnish his son-in-law, Frederick V, Elector Palatine, with men and money to recover the Palatinate lands. The conflict was however as much about religious differences as territory, and Farrand's contributions were a clear statement of his staunch Protestant loyalties.

On the 4th October 1625, the high regard in which Farrand was held and the confidence which he inspired in others, were clearly demonstrated by the fact that he was admitted free of the *incorporation* in *consideration of his pains heretofore employed and hereafter expected.*

Following his resignation from the curacy of Woodplumpton in 1628, he took up his post at Broughton, though he continued to live at Eaves. He married and fathered four children: the curiously if aptly named Eaves Farrand of Fishwick, whose burial was recorded in Preston on the 19th July, 1667; Alice, baptised in Preston on the 19th June, 1612; John, baptised on the 31st December 1616, who died in infancy and Elizabeth, baptised on the 7th June, 1620.

His singularly Protestant credentials were again demonstrated in 1641. His name heads the list of those who signed the *Protestation* in an effort to maintain the Protestant religion against all *Popish innovations* and in response to the growing threat, as they saw it, of Cromwellian Puritanism. Signed by those over the age of eighteen, it was in effect an oath of allegiance to King Charles I and the Church of England. No one could hold a Church or state office without signing.

He died in 1660 and his burial is recorded in the Preston registers.

1650   **JAMES KNOTT**
He was identified in the Church Survey of 1650-51 as the minister at Broughton. Initially, in 1650, his allowance was £40 per annum but a year later the *Committee for Plundered Minsters* reported that he had only received twenty shillings the previous year and ordered an increase in his yearly allowance to £50. During 1651-52 he was minister at Barton and Broughton and was still in post in January 1653 when £39 8s 6d was paid to him as part of his salary arrears.

1661   **JOHN WINKLEY**
John Winkley was identified as curate in charge at Garstang during the six years from 1637 - 43. Thirteen years later, in October and November 1661, his signature as minister can be found in the Broughton parish registers. He was the son of Edward Winkley, a Preston salter, identified in the Guild Rolls of 1662. He married Margaret, the daughter of Thomas Butler of Kirkland, and they had two sons, Thomas and William.

1674 – 1714   **WILLIAM WOOD**
He was certainly curate at Broughton in 1676, when he was signatory to the Broughton document compiled in response to the Compton Census. His initials could also be found on the tower bells cast in 1681. In

90

1678, he was deprived of the living because of a secret marriage and it is possible that one **Thomas Rylie**, a graduate of Jesus College, Cambridge, stood in for Woods during his enforced absence.

Nothing is known of Woods' time in the ecclesiastical wilderness or of the fate of this first wife but in 1682, Woods was reinstated, perhaps because he had entered into a more orthodox marriage in February that year, when he married Dorothy Billington at Broughton. However the Vicar of Preston, despite retracting his previous decision, still refused to pay him the normal £4 per annum. With the support of some of his parishioners, Woods challenged this ruling and entered a suit against the Vicar. Whatever the outcome of this legal action, Woods was identified as *curate and schoolmaster* at Broughton in the Bishop of Chester's Visitation List for 1691 and named in the will of Roger Langton in 1714.

He and Dorothy had five children, all baptised at Broughton: Ann and Dorothy (1685); Elizabeth (1687), who died in the same year; John (1690) and a second Elizabeth (1693). Woods died in 1720 and was buried at Broughton.

1683   **THOMAS RYLIE**
            He was nominated in 1683 by Sir Richard Hoghton and may have served the parish for a year at least while William Woods was temporarily deprived of the living.

1721   **WILLIAM CHARNLEY B.A.**
            Charnley was born in Balderstone on the 24th January, 1697 and baptised at the church of St Mary the Virgin in Blackburn. He was the son of Henry Charnley, a Lancaster grocer, and was educated at Threshfield Grammar School near Grassington in the Yorkshire Dales. At the age of seventeen, he entered Trinity College, Dublin but four years later, on the 17th of May 1718, he completed his undergraduate studies at St John's College, Cambridge, taking his B.A. degree in November of the following year. His first curacy was at Tarleton before moving to Broughton on the 9th February 1721, where he remained for the next decade. He and his two immediate successors were nominated by the Vicar of Preston.

He later became Vicar of Brayton and Selby in North Yorkshire.

1727   **JOHN STARKIE**
            The son of Nicholas Starkie of Preston, Starkie was born about 1702. He entered Christ's College, Oxford, aged nineteen, on the 21st March 1719 and graduated with a B. A. degree four years later in 1723. On the 20th November 1727, at the age of twenty-five, he was nominated by the Vicar of Preston to *officiate* at Broughton. As this nomination was made while William Charnley was still in post, the word *officiate* may well have indicated that rather than an actual appointment being made, Starkie was simply acting for Charnley on a temporary basis. It is not clear whether he was ever sole curate.

91

After leaving Broughton he became Rector of Hanaker near Chichester and died in 1748 without issue.

1731-1761   JOSEPH COWPER M.A.
Having been instituted in January 1731, Cowper first preached at Broughton a year later. Twenty-three years into his Broughton tenure, he wrote to the Bishop of Chester to complain that in all that time he had served without a fit residence. He further commented that *as I advance in years I have infirmaties upon me such as hoarse colds, which render the execution of my office more precarious*. With these two complaints in mind, he put forward a plan whereby the current schoolmaster at Broughton, Robert Cragg, already paid £25 per annum, could be ordained and paid an additional £10 a year to assist with services. This plan was put into action when Cragg became curate in 1756.

Cowper died in 1761 and was buried at Walton-le-Dale on the 10th March.

1761-1774   JOHN HUNTER
Following the death of Joseph Cowper, John Hunter, on the 21st April 1761, became the first Broughton Vicar to be nominated for the post by the Hoghton family. Initially he had been headmaster of Churchtown Free School near Garstang and also curate at the chapel there before his resignation in 1741. On 1st October, 1774 he left Broughton to become curate at Pilling, a post he held until his death in 1781.

1774-1780   RANDAL ANDREWS
Andrews was the son of, and shared the same name as, the then Vicar of Preston. He was born on the 6th June 1751 and baptised at Preston Parish Church. Having matriculated at Oxford in 1769, he gained his B.A. degree in 1773 and his M.A. three years later, in 1776.

Two years earlier, on the 16th October 1774, he had been appointed to Broughton and described then as a Fellow of Worcester College. His curacy was augmented by the governors of *Queen Anne's Bounty*. Without resigning from his post at Broughton, Andrews was also instituted as Vicar of Ormskirk in February 1780 and appointed George Charnley as his curate at £26 a year *with dues*. He held both livings until his death and was buried at Ormskirk.

1780-1809   GEORGE CHARNLEY
Charnley was re-appointed in 1793 at £26 per annum. He was the last curate to simultaneously hold the post of schoolmaster at Broughton, a position he had held since 1773. He died on the 15th December 1809 and is buried in Broughton churchyard.

1810-1817   HUGH HODGSON
He was probably working as assistant master at Whitechapel School in Goosnargh from 1798 to 1801 but was certainly appointed curate

there in 1804. His nomination by Sir H.P. Hoghton, described him as being *of Goosnargh, clerk*. He died at Broughton on 4th May, 1817, aged 76 and his memorial in the churchyard noted that he was *much respected*. This memorial was recorded on the pedestal of the sundial adjacent to the choir vestry but sadly has long since disappeared,

1817-1872   WILLIAM DIXON

William Dixon, the son of Reverend Robert Dixon of Rampside, was born on the 10th February, 1790 at Dalton-in-Furness near Lancaster. He was educated at St Bees College, Cumberland and his first curacy was at Kirkby-on-the-Moor in Yorkshire.

At the time of the 1841 Census Reverend Dixon was identified as living at Parsonage House, Broughton, along with his wife Jane, born in Topcliffe, Yorkshire, and their six children: Charlotte Agnes (1821), Lucy (1824), Jane Isabella (1824), Damaris (1827), William Wetherill, given his mother's maiden name as a middle name (1828), and John George (1829).

William and Jane had married on the 26th May, 1819 at St Peter's Church, Brafferton, in Yorkshire: their first-born daughter, Jane Isabella, was born the following year but sadly died aged only 3.

Aged 61, at the time of the 1851 Census, he was still incumbent at Broughton with his 55 year-old wife and five of his children, all now in their twenties.

A decade later he was described as *permanent incumbent* at Broughton. Four of his six children, aged between thirty and thirty-seven, remained in the family home. Three of them, in their forties, were still there in 1871, living with their 81 year-old father and their mother aged 75.

William Dixon died a year later on the 23rd March, 1872, aged 82. He was buried on the south side of the churchyard, where his gravestone (illustrated overleaf) commemorates not only his own life as *clerk in Holy Orders* and *Minister of Christ in this chapelry* but also the deaths of his wife Jane, who was born 1795 and died in 1876, and those of his children. Charlotte died in 1863; William, who followed in father's footsteps as a minister, died in 1865, aged only 37; Jane Isabella, named after her youngest sister who died in infancy, herself died in 1881; Lucy died in 1895 and Damaris in 1896.

The memorial plaque displayed inside the church and illustrated on page 141, demonstrates the affection felt by parishioners for the genial, devout and devoted Reverend Dixon, who had served the parish for so many years.

The reverse side of the grave memorial commemorates William's father Robert, who was born in 1767 and died in 1831, his wife Agnes and their son, John, who like his father and his brother, was also an ordained minister. It commemorates too William's other brother, Thomas, who died in 1870, and their grandmother, Elizabeth Dixon, who had died half a century earlier. An adjacent stone was erected as a tribute to Jane's sister, Isabella Wetherill, and to William and Jane's son John George, yet another clerk in Holy Orders, who rather intriguingly died in Australia in 1871.

1872 -1885   WILLIAM BRETHERTON

William Bretherton was born on the 15th December, 1826, the son of Jennet and Henry Bretherton, a farmer of 72 acres in Clayton, near Preston. One of eight children, he began his education at Leyland Grammar School and completed his studies at St Aidan's College, Birkenhead. In the 1861 Census he was described as a thirty-four year-old student but was still living in the family home.

On the 5th October, 1865 he married Frances Ogden Ashton, the daughter of Charles Ashton of Dukinfield. Six years later he was in his final year as curate at Christ Church in Harpurhey near Manchester. Prior to this he had held curacies at St Mary's, Newton Moor and St John's, Duckinfield.

His brother, John Bretherton of Leyland, had purchased the advowson (the right of patronage) of Broughton Church in April 1867 from Sir Henry Houghton for £1000 and five years later was able to ensure William was instituted there on the 9th April. Less than a year later, in an act of great generosity, John transferred the advowson to his brother William.

Under the Scheme of 1877, Reverend Bretherton became one of the first co-opted governors of Broughton School.

He died without issue, on the 21st August, 1885, at the relatively young age of fifty-nine. In his will, dated 9th March 1882, he offered the following testament:

I give and devise all that Advowson Donation, right of Patronage and presentation of, in and to the parochial chapelry or vicarage of Broughton, with all and singular Houses, lands, farms, tithe, rent, charges, payments, rights and appurtenances thereto belonging unto and to the use of Charles Roger Jacson Esq. of Barton Hall and Edward Wilson Esq. of Broughton House, Joseph Clayton of Broughton Bank, Marquis de Rothwell of Sharples Hall near Bolton, John Hargreaves of Rock Ferry, their heirs and assigns.

To clarify the legalese, the five named people were appointed William Bretherton's trustees, or Patrons as they became known, who upon his death, were given the authority to present a *fit person to be instituted and inducted as incumbent Curate*, a process which still continues today. The residue of his estate, after funeral expenses, was left to his *dear wife,* Frances Ogden Bretherton, the executrix of his will, and her heirs. Frances, who died in 1909, survived him by some twenty-four years.

William Bretherton's and his wife's striking monument in Broughton churchyard.

Samuel Collinson was born in 1853 in Alnwick, Northumberland, the eldest child of Thomas Collinson, a schoolmaster from Derby and his wife Hanna Sophia. His mother died, possibly in childbirth, in June 1858 in Alnwick, leaving his thirty-seven year-old father to bring up three young boys, all under the age of six.

His father married his second wife, Catherine Ann Sharpe, in September 1863 in Derby. By the time of the 1871 Census, the family was living in Alnwick, where Samuel was employed as an 18 year-old apprentice ironmonger. At some time during the following decade, he clearly rejected this somewhat mundane career and decided to make greater use of his intellectual ability. By 1881 he was a twenty-eight year-old student of Theology at Durham University. Interestingly on the day of the Census, he was actually a visitor at Coates House in Edinburgh, the home of his younger brother Thomas Collinson, a precocious talent, who at the tender age of twenty-two, was already a Professor of Music.

He graduated in 1882 with a Licentiate in Theology and four years later, after time as a curate at St Alban the Martyr in Leeds (1883 –1884), and two years in Preston, he was appointed vicar of Broughton, aged only thirty-three. The current vicarage was built in 1886, when Rev. Collinson began his Broughton ministry. By the time of the 1891 Census, he and his wife Sarah Eliza, along with their three children: Constance Mary, aged 5; Irene Beatrice, aged 3, who was deaf and dumb from birth, and Eric Osmond, aged 2, were established there.

A decade later, at the turn of the century, his 13 year-old daughter was being taught at home by Ellen Pyper, a specialist teacher of the deaf and dumb, while his other daughter, Constance Mary, aged 15, was a boarder at the Clergy Daughters' Institution in Warrington. The family had one general servant, thirty-one year-old Agnes Miller.

In 1911 both unmarried daughters remained in the family home: his son, Eric Osmond, enlisted as a private in the 50th Gordon Highlanders, Vancouver, the first Canadian contingent in the Great War. A plaque in the clergy vestry commemorates his death in action at Festubert in 1915, at a time when his father was himself a temporary chaplain to the Forces.

During his time at Broughton, a parish at the time of 1015 souls, Reverend Collinson received a stipend of some £250 from a gross income of £280 per annum. This, according to Crockford's Clerical Directory for 1909, was primarily made up of:

- Rent Charge..........................£77 with Glebe
- Vicar of Preston.....................£ 4
- Queen Anne's Bounty.............£33

- Ecclesiastical Commissioners…£15
- Other sources………………..£80

NOTICE.

I, the undersigned, on behalf of the Commissioners to whom and by virtue of the provisions, of "The Incumbents' Resignation Act, 1871," a Commission has been issued by The Right Reverend William, Lord Bishop of Manchester, for the purpose of making enquiry into the truth of the ground alleged in a certain representation made by the

Reverend *Samuel Edward Collinson L.Th.*

Incumbent of *St. John the Baptist Broughton*

in the County of Lancaster, within the Diocese of Manchester, as his reason for desiring to resign his said Benefice, and upon the expediency of such resignation, and otherwise to proceed as therein mentioned, Do hereby give Notice that the First Meeting under the said Commission will be holden on

Wednesday the *16th* day of *May* 19*23* at *11-0*

o'clock in the *fore* – noon, in *The vestry of the Parish Church Preston*

then and there to proceed on the said enquiry.

Given under my hand this *27th* day of *April* 19*23*.

Edward A. Cheney

Registrar of the Diocese.

I, the undersigned, do hereby certify that on Sunday, the *29* day of *April* 19*23* I published a Notice, of which the above is a true copy, by affixing the same in the usual place for Public Notices, at the Church of *St. John the Baptist Broughton* previous to Divine Service on the morning of the said Sunday, and that I left the notice so affixed as aforesaid.

Dated this *20th* day of *May* 19*23*.

Richard Hardman } *Warden*

Reproduced above is a copy of the Commissioners' notice of enquiry into the resignation of Reverend Collinson in 1923.

During his incumbency Samuel Collinson oversaw enormous changes to the fabric of the church, especially the building of the chancel, vestry and organ chamber. He died, aged 72, on the 18th December 1923 at Port St Mary on the Isle of Man, and his huge contribution to the parish is commemorated in the East Window installed by parishioners in his memory.

1923 -1940   DAVID RICHARD DAVIES

As his name might suggest, David Davies had strong Welsh roots, being born in Tonypandy, Glamorgan in 1882. After gaining a B.A. in 1903 (and an M.A. in 1907) at St John's College, Cambridge and completing his theological training at St Michael's and All Angels College, Aberdare, he served as a curate at St James' Church in Latchford, then a small township just south of Warrington, from 1904 to 1906.

In September 1908, he married Anita Mary Todhunter in Bucklow, on the Lancashire – Cheshire border, the couple having met while Reverend Davis was curate at St Peter's Church in Lymm during 1906 and 1907.

Three years later, at the time of the 1911 Census, the couple, married for just over two years, were living at Lyndale on Furness Road in Heysham, along with their one year-old son, David Phillip, born in Windermere while his father was a curate in Kendal from 1907 to 1909, Anita's sister, Minnie Elizabeth Todhunter, and Ann Soulby, a domestic servant. Reverend Davies remained at St John's Church, Heysham until 1913, when he took up a new post as Vicar of St Peter's Church in Finsthwaite in Cumbria, with a stipend of some £390 per annum. During the war years he served overseas as an army chaplain before returning to Finsthwaite in 1919.

While there, he presented the church with a set of brass altar vessels, which had been made by men of his Company for the celebration of Holy Communion on Christmas Day 1919 in Treviso, Italy. The chalice and two patens were fashioned from shell cases, while the cross and box for bread and wafers were made from an oak plank taken from a pontoon bridge that spanned the river. These unique items can still be seen in a display case on the north side of the chancel in Finsthwaite church.

David Davies came to Broughton in 1923. During his time a new sitting room was added to the vicarage and, reflecting his sporting interests, a tennis court was created in front of it. He was also responsible for the inauguration of the Nine Lessons and Carols service, not only a celebration of Christmas but also of the high standards achieved by the Choir itself.

In 1940, he moved some 350 miles south to Cornwall, to St Peter's Church in Mevagissey. His final parish however was rather ironically a second dedicated to St John the Baptist but this time in Oakwood Hill in Surrey. He died there of a heart attack in 1946, after which his wife, Anita, returned to live in Broughton. His son Philip was also a curate in a long-established parish near Woking.

1940 – 1946   **CHARLES MAURICE STRETTELL CLARKE**

Charles Clarke was a pupil of Rossall School and a graduate of Queens' College, Cambridge, as were, among others, T.H. White the author and Stephen Fry. His education was interrupted by the Great War, when he joined the R.A.M.C. in 1915. He was awarded the Military Medal in 1918. After the war he completed his education, gaining a B.A. degree in 1921, before moving to Wescott House Theological College, Cambridge.

The son of Canon Clarke, Vicar of Christ Church, Preston (1894 – 1913), he was ordained in 1922 and worked as curate at St George's Church, Bolton. In 1928 he was appointed Vicar of St Simon and St Jude's Church in Great Lever, Bolton, and seven years later, Vicar of St Mary's, Crumpsall.

He served as Vicar of Broughton during the difficult years of the Second World War before moving to St Mary's Church, Melton Mowbray, where he was also Rural Dean. He also became an Honorary Canon of Leicester Cathedral in 1952 and remained in office until 1965.

1946 – 1968   **NORMAN CHARLES OATRIDGE**

He was born in Deal, Kent on St Patrick's Day, 1903, the son of William Oatridge, a baker and pastry cook, and Kate Lambert Oatridge, some thirteen years his junior. At the time of the 1911 Census, the family was living at 45 Beach Street in Deal. His eldest sister, nineteen year-old Ethel, worked at home while Norman, aged 8, his brother Ronald, aged 12 and his sister, Kathleen, aged 10 were all described as scholars. The youngest child was one year-old Betty Margaret Lambert Oatridge.

Norman was educated at King's School, Canterbury, whose notable alumni include Elizabethan playwright Christopher Marlowe, Field Marshal Montgomery, the authors Somerset Maugham and Michael Morpurgo, and England cricketer David Gower. After graduating from St Catherine's College, Cambridge, where he took part in Union debates and, along with the 1960s' television celebrity Gilbert Harding, was a member of the university debating team that visited America, he worked briefly for the Bank of England.

He was ordained in 1931 and became curate at St James' Church in Preston, where, two years later, he married Evelyn Joyce Halliwell. After a spell working for Dr Barnado's Homes, he became vicar of All Souls Church in Southport. His time at Broughton was marked by two significant challenges: saving the church school for the parish and building the Parish Hall and St Martin's Chapel in Broadway. In 1967 he published his book *Bernard Shaw's God*, the profits from which went to the Parish Hall Building Fund. Essentially a shy man with a quiet sense of humour, the later years of his ministry were dogged by ill-health but he struggled bravely to continue his work, ably assisted by three successive curates.

He and his wife and their unmarried children retired to Rose Cottage in Broughton village on the 31st October, 1968, after several years of ill-health. He died some two years later, in 1970.

1969 – 1974   JOHN MARSHALL WILLIAM ADAM

John Adam left Oxford in 1933, having gained an M.A. at Oriel College. He began his ministry in a Sheffield parish and then at the Cathedral. As a member of the Cambridge Mission to Delhi, he travelled to India to serve both as a chaplain and a lecturer at St Stephen's Christian College, a constituent college of the university there. He later rejoined the Sheffield Cathedral staff before becoming Vicar of Paddock in Huddersfield.

In 1946 he took office as Home Secretary of the Missionary Council of the Church Assembly in Westminster. Nine years later he moved to the Rectorship of Friern Barnet in north London. In 1963 he was appointed Vicar of Preston and also Rural Dean.

On the 1st March 1969 Revd. Canon Adam was instituted at Broughton and during his time there undertook several key construction projects, notably at the vicarage and the Parish Hall but, most significantly, he was the prime mover in the building of St Peter's School.

He retired on the 1st December 1974 after a ministry of some forty-one years. He and his wife Marietta went to live at *Windhover Cottage* in Caton near Lancaster. Canon Adam died in 2007, aged 98.

1975 – 1983   WILLIAM GERALD ARMSTRONG

Gerald Armstrong was educated at Durham School and the Universities of Nottingham and Oxford, where he gained a B.A. degree. He was ordained by the Archbishop of Canterbury, Michael Ramsay, in York Minster. His first curacy was at Beverley Minster and then at Sutton in Holderness, before becoming Vicar of Charlesworth and later Rector of Ashbourne in Derbyshire.

He was instituted at Broughton on the 24th April, 1975 and, in controversial circumstances, resigned the living in 1983.

1984 - 1998   STANLEY JAMES FINCH

Having been brought up in Longridge and attending Preston Grammar School, Stanley Finch gained an M.A. from Merton College, Oxford. He trained for the ministry at Wells before becoming curate at Lancaster Priory. Later he was appointed Precentor at Leeds Parish Church, before becoming Vicar of Habergham near Burnley and subsequently Vicar of Holy Trinity Church in South Shore, Blackpool.

Following his appointment to Broughton, he also worked as Rural Dean of Preston from 1986 to 1992 and as a member of the Diocesan Audit Commission in 1994. His time as Vicar coincided with the growing ecumenical movement within Christian churches, and Stanley Finch was at the forefront of the Ecumenical Covenant being Chairman of the Ecumenical Council for two years. He was appointed Honorary Canon of Blackburn in 1991.

1999 – 2004   DAVID HAROLD JENKINS

As a thirty-seven year-old, Reverend David Jenkins and his wife Sarah, moved to Broughton, his Institution and Induction ceremony being held on the 28th April 1999.

A native of Belfast, he was educated at the city's Royal Academy, a Protestant public school. At the age of eighteen he moved to England to read History at Sidney Sussex College, Cambridge, and while a student was confirmed as an Anglican, having previously worshipped as a Presbyterian. Like two of his predecessors, Canon Adam and Rev Pike, he was a Companion of the Order of St Francis.

After graduation he worked briefly in the personnel department of IBM before resuming his studies at Ripon Theological College near Oxford. His first post as curate was in Cambridge, not amidst the gleaming spires but on the Arbury estate – a tough introduction to the ministry.

Two years later he moved to St Peter's Church in Reading, where he worked until 1993 when he took up his first incumbency at St Michael's and All Angels with St Luke's in Staining near Blackpool.

2005 – to date   SIDNEY FOX

Sidney, a native of South Yorkshire, was educated at Rotherham Grammar School and the town's College of Technology. Until 1971, he worked as an assistant engineer at *Dean's Electrical and Engineering Company.* As a boy, he was Head Chorister at St Stephen's Church, where he met his future wife, and later became a Scout Leader. He left his home town in 1971 to take up a post with Cleveland County Council as an engineer. Four years later, aged twenty-eight and married with two children, he took the life-changing decision to abandon this career path and to begin training for the Anglican priesthood at Lincoln Theological College.

Four years later, in 1979, having graduated as a Bachelor of Theology at Nottingham University, he was ordained Deacon at Petertide in York Minster. Sidney's first post was as curate at St Oswald's Church, Middlesborough. His ordination as priest came a year later, again at York Minster. In 1981, at the age of thirty-four, he became parish priest at St Oswald's, his licensing taking place on the 8th December.

101

He spent some seven or eight happy years in the parish before moving to St Mark's Church in Newby near Scarborough, a place of many happy memories as eighteen years earlier he had spent his honeymoon there. He was instituted and inducted on the 16th November 1987 by the Bishop of Hull.

What characterised his work in both these parishes and has been the hallmark of his work ever since then, both in Scotland and at St John's, Broughton, has been his energetic involvement in so many different aspects of parish life. Never content to simply conduct services and open the occasional bazaar, he took part in drama productions, organised the fund-raising for urgent church repairs and the building of a new meeting room, before, in 1992, taking the huge decision to resign from the Church of England and move to Scotland to become Rector of St Andrew's Episcopal Church in Brechin.

1995 was for Sidney, a year of great joy and deep sadness. In March he published his first book: *What's in it for us? Christian Mysticism for Ordinary People*, a study of three Anglican precursors of the revival in spirituality, William Inge, Evelyn Underhill and F. P. Harton. In May, following a prolonged illness, his wife Margaret died. Despite his private and personal loss and profound grief, the public smile never faded as Sidney continued to lead his church community and to take a leading role in all aspects of parish life, including the intriguing *Great Nappy Run*, celebrated on Palm Sunday 1996. Parishioners collected a mountain of nappies as part of an emergency aid programme for Romania.

The new millennium brought new beginnings for Sidney when, sporting a rather dashing beard, he and his second wife, Susan, were married in May 2001. He continued to work tirelessly both for his parishioners and, as Brechin Rotary Club President, for many other projects and charities. He was also Chairman of the local Christian Aid Committee and vice-convenor of Angus Independent Advocacy, an organisation providing a voice for people with learning and mental difficulties.

After thirteen years, Sidney, without the beard, moved south to St John's in May 2005, where he continues to display the same dedication and innovative approach to both the spiritual and practical needs of his parish, the latter being tested by the need for massive restoration work on the church and his role as Computer Technology guru.

CHAPTER 11

CHARITABLE TRUSTS

There were originally four charities connected with the Church, funds from which were distributed either by the vicar and churchwardens or by private trustees.

- Thomas Houghton's Charity
- William Daniel's Charity
- Miss Damaris Dixon's Sick and Poor Charity
- Royal Air Force Bequest

Thomas Houghton, through an indenture dated 16th July 1649, conveyed land in Broughton and Woodplumpton, now known as Houghton House Farm, to trustees. Miller House Farm near Nog Tow, on the boundary of Broughton and Woodplumpton, also belonged to the Trust and its rent provided an additional part of the income.

The trustees were required to divide the income from these lands among the *poor, needy and impotent* people living in the township of Broughton, the monies being traditionally disbursed annually on St Thomas's Day, the 21st December.

1854 however saw a significant change in the way the funds were administered. Firstly the Churchwardens took over the running of the charity from its long-standing trustees and secondly they instigated a much more rigorous process for deciding who was eligible to benefit from it. There was a concern that previously the rules concerning the distribution of monies had not been strictly adhered to.

The present Wardens have enquired into the nature of the Trust and so far as they are able to judge, they think that for a length of time the funds payable to this township have not been strictly applied. Indeed they think that his (the Founders) intentions have been much lost sight of ...

In the same letter to the Charity Commission, the Churchwardens issued a warning that those who *usually in years past received assistance from that dole* should not expect that they would continue to be granted funds in the future. They were determined to ensure that money was paid only to those who were legitimately the *poor, aged, needy and impotent* of Broughton. In particular they were anxious to define *aged* as applying to persons over the age of fifty! Following consultation, the Commissioners agreed with their judgement.

The Charity's income in 1854 was £14 2s 6d: following deductions for the purchase of a new Minute Book and the cost of printing application forms, £13 12s 10d was available for distribution among some thirty-eight people.

Memo.

Posted on the Church doors, for three Sundays.

"Thomas Houghton's Charity"

Notice, — is hereby given that the portion of the Income of the above Charity, which is payable to the Township of Broughton, for this Year, will be distributed by the Church Wardens on St Thomas' day the 21st instant. —

The distribution will take place in the Girls School Room at 4 o'clock in the afternoon and papers of application for relief may be had, free of charge, from W.S. Bleasdale, the Sexton. —

These papers must be filled up and sent to the Wardens on, or before, the 14th Instant. —

No parties are eligible to receive relief from this Charity except such as are "poor Aged, Needy or Impotent" and who "dwell in the Township of Broughton"

(Moore: Wilton)
(Wm price Hoole) Wardens

N.B. No application will be entertained which is not filled up in all particulars. —

Reproduced above is a copy of the Churchwardens' notice for
1854, which was posted on the church doors for three weeks prior
to St Thomas's Day.

Under the new regulations not all applicants were successful in securing financial help as the page from the Wardens' Minute Book, illustrated below, indicates. The extract also gives a good idea of the amounts given to those who were successful: in 1854 these ranged from 11s 10d to 2s. It will also be noted that the Wardens had allowed a year's grace before applying the new age limit of fifty.

Name	Age	State	No. of children under 12	Amt. granted	Remarks
			Brot forward	8 9 ..	
Cuthbert Catterall	48	Married	Three ✓	8 .	very poor
Johanna Sharples	47	Widow	Two	2 0 +	a weaver
Ed. Wilson	45	Married	Four ✓	6 ..	Work uncertain
Wd. Poulton	45	as a Mother	Six ✓ 1	.. ..	very poor
Jas. Corless	40	Married	Four ✓	2 0	bad health – parents well off
Joseph Abbott	39	do	Two	Refused in good work. Wife strong. dog not help
Wm. Harpeeny	39	do	Three	6 ..	Poor – uncertain Work
Rich. Hosker	38	do	Four ✓	5 ..	Fair Wages but not strong
Jno Carter	38	Widower	One ✓	10 ..	Wife died the day before distribution
Richd Smith	37	Married	Five ✓	6 ..	Industrious well behaved
Richd. Rossall	37	do	One	Refused	In constant Work
Wm. Crompton	36	do	Two ✓	3 ..	Work uncertain, but keeps cows
Wm. Abbott	35	do	Four ✓	5 ..	Wife very delicate
Jas Bleasdale	33	do	Three	Refused	Constant employment – good wages
Ed Sharples	32	Single	None ✓	10 ..	Unable to work from Rheumatism
Jas Harrison	30	Married	Four ✓	5 ..	very poor
Thos Higginson	29	do	One ✓	2 6	Work uncertain
Jas Redgreaves	39	do	Two	2 6	+ Wife delicate
Robt. Tallabone	56	do	Three ✓	5 ..	very poor
Rich Sharples	53	do	None ✓	Refused	Well to do
Jas Appleby	57	do	One ✓	2 0	Tailor – Work uncertain
Robt Holloway	43	do	Two	2 0	very poor
				£13 13 ..	

The comments appended to each applicant in 1854 are, for the most part, objective and related to the newly clarified application criteria. By 1886 however the Churchwardens' observations on some unsuccessful applicants had taken on, perhaps inevitably, a much more subjective, judgmental and moral tone.

Warden, Richard Hardman, noted:

A woman named Singleton as stated on the list and living in a cottage near the Black Bull Inn Broughton, sent her boy for relief, said not to have been married and known to be of very low character, was refused.

Another unsuccessful applicant, who called herself Mrs Howarth, was: *living with a man named Thomas Howarth in the village of Broughton, a saddler by trade and can earn good wages but of very intemperate habits himself, having told that she was not his lawful wife. On this account refused.*

Moneys from the Charity continued to be paid until St Thomas's Day 1972, when the income was £20 and there were eleven recipients: eight received £2 each, three received £1 and £1 was paid to the Governors of Broughton School.

Between 1854 and 1972, the Charity's annual income varied little and was generally somewhere between £14 and £20. During the years of World War II, the income settled at some £22, while between 1913 and 1918, it reached only five or six pounds. However, while the funds available remained fairly stable, the number of applicants reflected changes in the demographic of Broughton township and the economic circumstances of the people living there. In short it became a more significantly middle-class suburb and much less a rural village. In 1857 there were 36 applicants for the relief offered by Houghton's Charity. By the 1890s this had fallen to an average of 16 applicants a year, and thirty years later, the annual numbers had fallen even more substantially to perhaps only five or six.

This economic change and the decreasing demands made on charity relief, especially after the inception of the Welfare State in the late 1940s, had a marked impact on another of Broughton's charities and on the way that all of them would ultimately be structured and administered.

William Daniel, by an indenture dated 3rd November 1656, conveyed land in Broughton, including Highest Fields and Little Meadow, to trustees, who were required to pay *a yearly sum of twenty shillings lawful money of England* to the churchwardens for the *maintenance of a grammar school at Broughton or for want thereof for the maintenance of the church and church bridges*. The money was to be paid in two equal instalments at Whitsuntide and Martinmas. These several 'closes' were to be held for one thousand years after the death of William Daniel and his wife.

106

William Daniel died without issue and his widow Margaret, by an indenture dated 29th July 1690, granted a further £20 to be paid to the trustees after her death for the benefit of the poor of Broughton.

From 1734, after the payment of 20 shillings as directed, the remaining funds were used for the purchase of white kersey to make coats for indigent people living in Broughton. Monies were only to be given to those who:

should be found to have the greatest necessity having a more particular respect to such as were most sober, honest and industrious in their callings and conversations and were the greatest frequenters of the Protestant Churches.

Financial help was also given:

for the relief and benefit of such poor people and their children, inhabitants in the said township towards finding them apprentices to honest callings, buying of Bibles and other orthodox books towards their instruction in the Reformed Protestant religion, and that more special regard and preference should be had to widows and householders and such that have no allowance from the township and were no common beggars and also to such of the poor which lived in Broughton Row.

The charity became known as the *Petty Coat Charity* and a field in Broughton of some five and a half acres, originally divided into three, Brook Paddock, Lower Petticoat and Higher Petticoat, retained the name *Petticoat Field*.

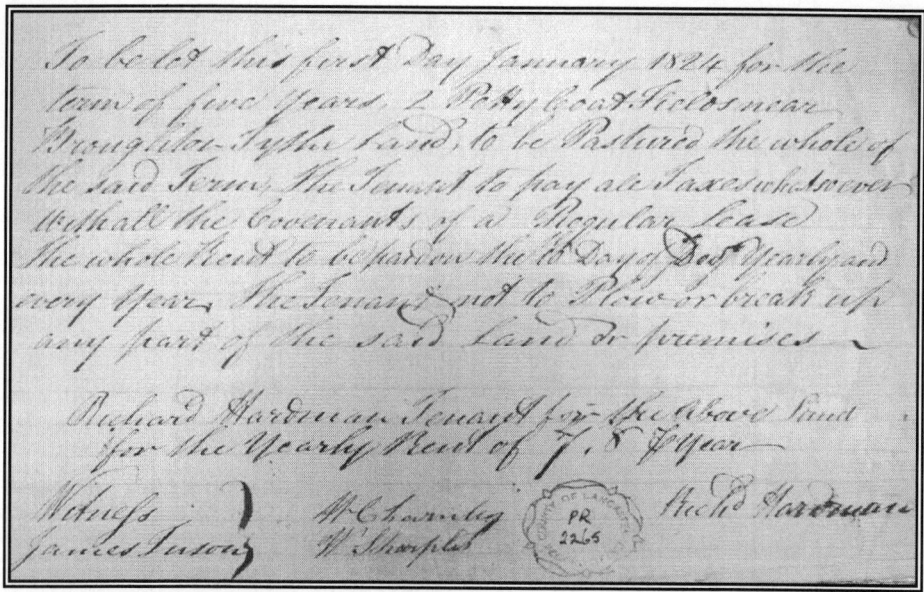

Reproduced above is a copy of the tenancy agreement for Petticoat Fields for 1824.

For many years it was farmed by the Kirkham family, their last annual rent being some £45. Following the building of old people's bungalows off Woodplumpton Lane in Broughton, it became the custom for the moneys deriving from the charity to be paid to those living there at Christmas time, each receiving five pounds.

In June 1981 the Central Lancashire New Town Development Corporation made a compulsory purchase of the land known as Petticoat Field so that a new distributor road, Eastway, could be constructed through it. £8,250 was paid in compensation to the trustees, substantially increasing the Charity's annual income. A stone tablet, which used to be displayed on the west wall of the church, commemorated the original gift.

Miss Damaris Dixon, the daughter of the Rev. William Dixon, Vicar of Broughton, bequeathed in her will dated 12th September 1895 and proved in Lancaster on the 11th December 1896:

to the Minister and Churchwardens of Broughton the sum of £1000, in augmentation of the endowment of the benefice, for the endowment of a Charity for the sick and poor of the Parish, the said sum to be invested in the name of the Vicar and Churchwardens, and the income to be applied in their discretion for the relief or nursing or otherwise for the benefit or support of the sick and poor of the Parish.

From 1908 until 1946 the income from this fund was paid to Broughton and District Nursing Association, an organisation which shared similar aims and objectives, but which, with the advent of the Welfare State, in particular the National Health Service Act of 1946, had become defunct. Between 1947 and the mid 1980s the monies had therefore been paid into the Vicar's *Sick and Poor Fund.*

In 1952 the Charity Commission had suggested an amalgamation of the Damaris Dixon and B.D.N.A. but there were long delays in effecting this consolidation, pending government legislation, which culminated in the Charities Act of 1960, and under which all charities had to register. Accordingly, after a lengthy procedure both Charities were registered in the early 1960s. About this time too, it was proposed by Mr F.E. Wilson that an approach might be made to the Charity Commission for the amalgamation of two other Charities – *Daniel's Charity* and *Thomas Houghton's Charity*. The Commission eventually agreed two schemes, one for the amalgamation of the Dixon and B.D.N.A. Charities and one for that proposed by Mr Wilson.

In 1976 the first of these amalgamations was agreed and two years later, in 1978, the Charity Commission approved the Scheme and a final order was sealed, whereby the accumulated funds, some £6000, of *The Broughton and District Nursing Association*, were incorporated into the Dixon Charity.

In 1983 the scheme was revised to create a body of trustees, other than the Vicar and Churchwardens, to administer the funds. In January 1985 the new proposed trustees met for the first time, under the chairmanship of the then Vicar, Rev. Stanley Finch

Money once distributed by the vicar as part of the discretionary fund, is now allocated on the more general basis of *relief of need* and its disbursement restricted to those living within the ecclesiastical parish of Broughton-in-Amounderness. Recent accounts are detailed below:

Accounts date Income Spending

Accounts date	Income	Spending
31 Dec 2009	£1,153	£925
31 Dec 2008	£1,485	£1,670
31 Dec 2007	£1,382	£890
31 Dec 2006	£1,251	£1,660
31 Dec 2005	£1,330	£1,095

The **Royal Air Force Bequest** of £100 was made by the Commanding Officer and other officers of R.A.F Barton Hall when it closed at the end of the Second World War. It had been the base of Number 9 Fighter Group from August 1940 to September 1944. The income is added to the vicar's discretionary fund and is now merged with the Damaris Dixon Charity.

CHAPTER 12

THE CHURCH INTERIOR

The north porch, the usual entrance and exit used by the congregation, was dedicated by the Bishop of Lancaster in 1987 and was financed by a bequest made by Lilian Wood the previous year.

This porch was dedicated
in memory of
LILIAN WOOD
by The Rt. Rev. Ian Harland
Bishop of Lancaster
on the 5th day of April 1987

The interior of the church, before the chancel restoration, was described by *Atticus* in his usual somewhat mocking tone:

The interior of the Church is light, and on the whole, has a cheerful look. The ceiling is wide, square, flat and divided into panels with ornamental bosses at each angle. It looks more like the ceiling of some capacious old Hall than that of a Church. Running along each side, immediately beneath the ceiling, are various faces in plaster – queer faces containing an admixture of the tragical and comical, and looking immensely grotesque all over. Some felicity may be derived from them by the congregation, but we have not been able to ascertain the exact amount of it, and on that account shall not speculate.

Sadly those gargoyle faces, which may have entertained the congregation during especially dull or lengthy sermons, vanished during the 1906 restoration but the panels remain.

Immediately left, along the north wall of the church, are displayed three memorials. The first, a tablet from the old, pre-1826 church, reads:

NEAR THIS PLACE LIE INTERRED THE REMAINS OF JAMES CARDWELL OF BARTON, YEOMAN, WHO DEPARTED THIS LIFE, APRIL 16TH AD 1803 IN THE 72ND YEAR OF HIS AGE. ALSO WILLIAM HIS SON, DEPARTED THIS LIFE APRIL 3RD 1806, IN THE 28TH YEAR OF HIS AGE

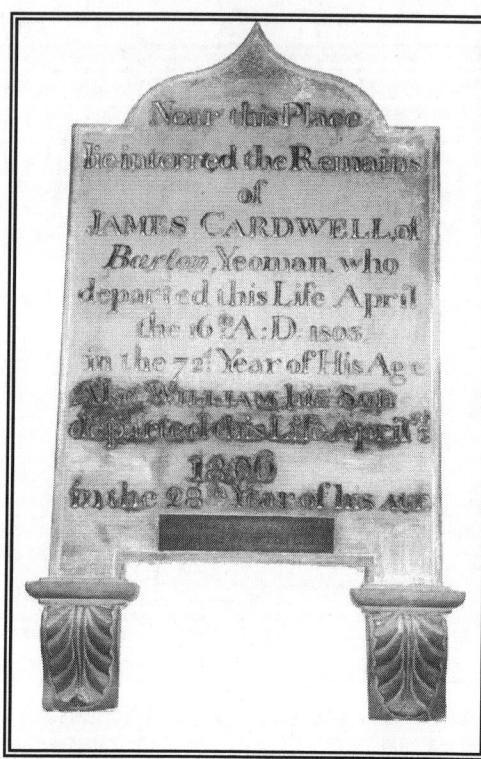

On a brass plate, which was inserted after the tablet was replaced in the newly-built church, is further recorded:

ALSO ANN, RELICT OF THE ABOVE WM. CARDWELL WHO DIED ON MAY 6TH 1832 AGED 53 YEARS

James Cardwell was christened on the 9th June 1731 at Barton, the son of William and Ann Cardwell. On the 8th March 1757, aged twenty-six, he married Margaret Lewtas and the couple had six children: Elizabeth (1725); James (1731); Robert and Thomas, both christened in 1733; William (1736) and Richard (1739). James, as the eldest son, inherited Tunsteads Farm on Brass Pan Lane in Barton when his father died and as a yeoman, a free man holding a small landed estate, he farmed there until his death in 1803. Thereafter, as his will indicates, the farm passed to his son William, who unfortunately was only able to run it for some three years before his own untimely death in 1806. As the tablet indicates, he was survived by his wife Ann Cardwell (nee Bois).

Further along the north wall can be found a second plaque dedicated to members of the Jacson family. It reads:

TO RECORD THE MORTAL EXISTENCE OF THREE DAUGHTERS AND TWO SONS
THE HOPE NOT OF THIS LIFE ONLY
OF GEORGE JACSON OF BARTON, ESQUIRE, AND CHARLOTTE HIS WIFE
CHARLOTTE ANNE:
BORN DEC.20 1813; DIED MARCH 21 1839:BURIED AT BEBINGTON

111

FRANCES, WIFE OF JOHN RICHARDSON
OF POPLAR VALE, MONAGHAN, ESQ: BORN MAR 17, 1815:DIED JAN 7
1851
BURIED TY HOLLAND IN THE SAME COUNTY
MARY ISABELLA, BORN FEB 28 1825: DIED MAY 15, 1841
BURIED AT WORTHING, SUSSEX
GEORGE, BORN Aug 26, 1816: DIED DEC 12 1831: BURIED AT
WINCHESTER
ROGER, BORN NOV 18, 1821:DIED SEPT 25, 1853
BURIED AT BEBINGTON

Charlotte Anne, the first child commemorated in the tablet and the ninth child of George and Charlotte, died aged only twenty-six. She was buried at Bebington, where her grandfather was vicar.

Her sister Frances married John Richardson on the 23rd September, 1840 at Broughton Church. The couple moved to Poplar Vale in County Monaghan, Ireland. Charlotte died there in 1851 and was buried in Tyholland, the smallest parish in Monaghan.

The third daughter named on the memorial, May Isabella, was the eleventh child of George and Charlotte, and died aged only sixteen.

George, his first-born child, died aged only 15 and was buried in Winchester, presumably as he was a student at Winchester College at the time of his death.

The final child named in the memorial tablet is Roger Jacson, the fifth child of George and Charlotte, who, after lengthy illness, died in 1853, aged only 32. He too was buried at his grandfather's parish church in Bebington on the Wirral.

His life may have been relatively brief but he did leave a diary, which described experiences somewhat more adventurous than most. In 1847 he travelled by sailing ship with a cargo of cotton to Canton in China to work for a shipping firm. In many respects he could not have chosen a more dangerous time to arrive, in the midst of the First Opium War and the wake of the Second Battle of Canton only six years earlier. The fighting, the civilian rebellion against the British and the uneasy peace that followed the battle, all served to create a profound distrust of foreigners in general and the British in particular. He was involved in a dangerous argument with local Chinese, who took exception to foreigners occupying land on the Honan side of the river. A new boathouse was set on fire and a mob of over one thousand irate Chinese demolished it. The British Consul requested the local police disperse the mob but was ignored. Finally two boatloads of British Marines, from a ship moored in the Pearl River, landed and cleared the crowd. As if to underline the very real peril Roger was in, shortly afterwards six Englishmen were murdered.

In his spare time Roger sailed a small cutter in the river estuary. The humid climate, high temperatures and strong winds did little to improve his health however, and business suffered along with it. He travelled to Manila in the Philippines in search of additional commercial opportunities but with little success: the enterprise ultimately wound up and he returned home.

A second memorial tablet, pictured below and again relating to the Jacson family, can be found a little further along the north wall.

It records the burial of Charlotte, George Jacson's wife, in the vault beneath and that of their son Henry, who died in 1839, aged only sixteen.

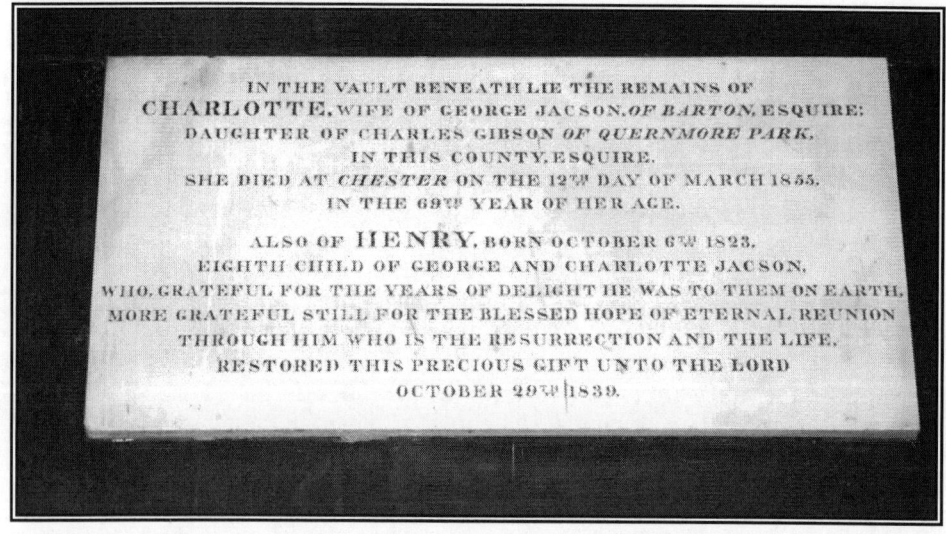

IN THE VAULT BENEATH LIE THE REMAINS OF
CHARLOTTE, WIFE OF GEORGE JACSON, OF BARTON, ESQUIRE:
DAUGHTER OF CHARLES GIBSON OF QUERNMORE PARK,
IN THIS COUNTY, ESQUIRE.
SHE DIED AT CHESTER ON THE 12TH DAY OF MARCH 1855,
IN THE 69TH YEAR OF HER AGE.

ALSO OF HENRY, BORN OCTOBER 6TH 1823,
EIGHTH CHILD OF GEORGE AND CHARLOTTE JACSON,
WHO, GRATEFUL FOR THE YEARS OF DELIGHT HE WAS TO THEM ON EARTH,
MORE GRATEFUL STILL FOR THE BLESSED HOPE OF ETERNAL REUNION
THROUGH HIM WHO IS THE RESURRECTION AND THE LIFE,
RESTORED THIS PRECIOUS GIFT UNTO THE LORD
OCTOBER 29TH 1839.

A third tablet, in the north-east corner of the chancel, above the archway leading to the vestry, commemorates the burial of George Jacson himself.

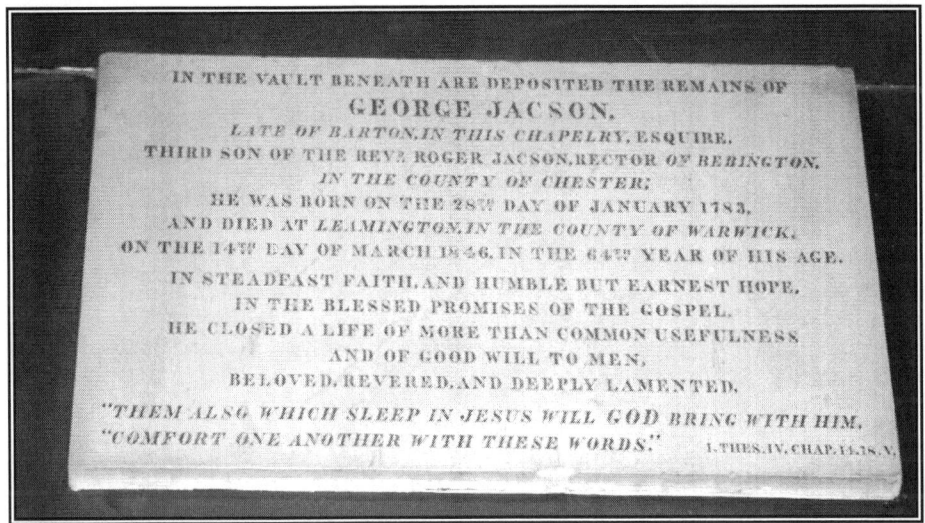

IN THE VAULT BENEATH ARE DEPOSITED THE REMAINS OF
GEORGE JACSON,
LATE OF BARTON,IN THIS CHAPELRY, ESQUIRE.
THIRD SON OF THE REV? ROGER JACSON,RECTOR OF BEBINGTON,
IN THE COUNTY OF CHESTER;
HE WAS BORN ON THE 28? DAY OF JANUARY 1783,
AND DIED AT LEAMINGTON,IN THE COUNTY OF WARWICK,
ON THE 14? DAY OF MARCH 1846,IN THE 64? YEAR OF HIS AGE.
IN STEADFAST FAITH,AND HUMBLE BUT EARNEST HOPE,
IN THE BLESSED PROMISES OF THE GOSPEL,
HE CLOSED A LIFE OF MORE THAN COMMON USEFULNESS
AND OF GOOD WILL TO MEN,
BELOVED,REVERED,AND DEEPLY LAMENTED.
"THEM ALSO WHICH SLEEP IN JESUS WILL GOD BRING WITH HIM,
"COMFORT ONE ANOTHER WITH THESE WORDS." 1.THES.IV,CHAP.14.18.V.

George Jacson, the third son of Roger Jacson, the Vicar of Bebington, and his wife Francis, was born on 28th January 1783 and came to Lancashire aged sixteen to join the Horrocks textile firm in Preston. He rose from apprentice to partner in the company, which then became known as *Horrocks, Jacson & Co.* He was actively involved in the political and social life of Preston, and represented St John's Ward as a councillor (1836). During his time of office he became involved in the navigation of the River Ribble and made several innovative suggestions about how to ensure Preston developed as a key port. He became an alderman two years later and in 1840 was both a chief magistrate and the borough's Mayor.

He married Charlotte, the eldest daughter of Charles Gibson of Quernmore Park, on the 23rd January, 1813 at St Mary's Church, Lancaster, and the couple had twelve children.

In 1825 he rented Barton Hall and eight years later bought the estate and manorial rights of Barton from Mr James Shuttleworth, lord of the manor. The manor was in a dilapidated state and Jacson, as the new squire, repaired the buildings and improved the land. He sold fifteen acres of land to the Lancashire and Preston Junction Railway Company for the construction of the railway through Broughton and Barton for £1,437, on condition that the line be built straight and that trees be planted along the main road to shield the residents of Broughton Lodge from the visual affront it caused. As he said:

I never like to see a crooked line when it can be made straight.

Even though he raised several further objections to the railway, the Parliamentary tribunal agreed to its construction but did grant George Jacson one interesting concession. He was allowed to build a cottage near the railway station at Barton, on what was then called School Lane and is now Station Lane. This cottage was to provide him and his friends with a private railway stopping place: they could stop any second class train if necessary either to board or alight. The Company even agreed to pay some £30 towards the cost of building the cottage.

Barton Hall is pictured here in about 1950 but largely unchanged from the impressive house owned by the Jacson family until 1893.

After his purchase of the property, George Jacson moved into Barton Lodge. The old hall was converted into a farmhouse and the Lodge renamed Barton Hall. The imposing building can still be seen on the hill to the right of the A6 as the road climbs to Barton village. The animal welfare centre, run by the Veterinary Laboratory Agency, now occupies the site.

George Jacson died on the 14th March 1826 in Leamington, Warwickshire, aged sixty-four, having lived a life *of more than common usefulness and of good will to men.*

THE CRUCIFIX

On the wall, just below this memorial plaque, is a crucifix picked up by **Major Arthur Theodore Ransome Houghton**, Company Commander of the 4th Loyal North Lancashire Regiment. He found it in 1916, when he and his men were billeted among the ruins of a monastery near Ypres. The figure appears, at first glance, to be made of stone but is in fact a wooden carving and, as can be seen below, suffered some shell damage during the fighting.

Arthur Houghton was born in Preston in 1880, the son of Cedric Houghton, a solicitor, and his wife Gertrude. His father incidentally was a discerning collector of pottery and porcelain, and after his death in 1910, bequeathed over 400 items to the Harris Museum. Many of these can still be seen exhibited on the second floor.

Having graduated from Oxford, he followed his father into the legal profession and in 1904 joined the Preston firm of *Houghton, Craven and Company.* In 1906 he married Ruth Ponting and six years later, the couple moved into The Stone House in Whittingham Lane, Broughton, which had been built for him.

During the Great War, he was commissioned and in 1917, as Captain Houghton, was awarded the Military Cross for gallantry during the battle of Menin Road in the Ypres salient.

Between 1932 and 1950 Major Houghton was clerk to the Ribble Fisheries Board, and in 1952 published a book, *The Ribble Salmon Fisheries.* He was a member of Lancashire County Council for some 20 years and also served as a County Alderman.

Arthur completed fifty years as a chorister, forty of them as a member of Broughton Church Choir. His musical interests and talents did not end there: in his private workshop, he made several cellos and a viola. He was also an active supporter and sponsor of many religious and secular causes, and as Chairman of the County Records Committee, was a key mover in the creation of the Lancashire Record Office. This *Renaissance man* was also President of the Preston Scientific Society, a former president of Preston Law Society and Preston Symphony Orchestra and a frequent member of Agricultural Land Tribunals formed by the Agricultural Act of 1947 to settle land disputes. He was vice-President of Preston Grasshoppers Rugby club, where, in his younger years, he had been a playing member.

As Vicar's Warden in the 1950s, Major Houghton also produced several papers and articles relating to the history of Broughton church, relating particularly to old deeds discovered at the time in an old safe in the church vestry and to the church's stained glass. Arthur Houghton died suddenly aged 72, on the 13th November 1952, and is buried in Broughton churchyard, along with his wife Ruth.

Displayed at the end of the north wall, opposite the crucifix, is a fragment of a painted capital from the old pre-1826 church

This window, donated by members of the Houghton family, was dedicated on the 3rd September 1961 by the Bishop of Blackburn, Charles Claxton, in memory of Major Houghton and his wife Ruth (see previous page). Seen at its best in the light of the setting sun, it was designed by A.S. Erridge, with a central feature illustrating the calling of the fishermen, Simon Peter and Andrew, to be Apostles. At the base the Holy Family in Nazareth are depicted in the carpenter's shop, symbolising the sanctity of family life, and at the top are three cherubim, angelic symbols of church music, one of the great passions of Major Houghton. The other two images also reflect his other passions of fishing and carpentry. The general theme is that of service and harmony within family life.

THE JACOBEAN TABLE

Beneath the crucifix, in the north-east corner of the nave, is a Jacobean table, which was formerly used, in the old church, as the High Altar. At the back of the table is a re-table, consisting of a piece of a carved oak beam held between two pieces of modern oak, which was possibly a part of a rood, chancel or tower screen, again from the old church

117

In the corner between the pulpit base and the chancel wall can be found a rough-hewn, octagonal holy water stoup.

In 1893 it was found at the bottom of a ditch near the church and it seems likely that originally it belonged to the pre-Reformation church. It measures 19cm high with a top diameter of 20cm and a base diameter of 11.5 cm.

THE PULPIT

The oak pulpit, incorporated into the new chancel design, was gifted to the church by the Wilson family, in memory of Eliza Maria Wilson, a member of the Pedder family, who died in 1904. Prior to 1906, the previous pulpit had stood on the opposite side of the church, where the lectern is now located.

This gift is recorded in a carved inscription of the stone base of the pulpit: *This pulpit is dedicated to the Glory of God and in memory of Eliza Maria Wilson by her sons and daughters.*

118

This detail from the carved panelling of the pulpit, repeated on all three of its facets, represents perhaps the twin doors of an altar tabernacle, the dwelling place of the divine presence. The suggestion is that it is through the words of the priest, spoken from the pulpit, that the divine presence is revealed.

THE CHANCEL

In 1904 the decision was made by the vicar, Reverend Collinson, and members of the congregation, to improve the church by removing the east wall and adding a new chancel *of splendid proportions* measuring some 38 feet long and 22 feet wide. Reverend Oatridge described the east end of the building prior to this major renovation.

There was a modest triptych reredos behind which a latticed window in plain glass was framed on each side by wooden panels inscribed with the Ten Commandments. The slightly curving altar rail terminated at each end in box pews facing north and south and there was a small pulpit on the side on which the bible lectern now stands. Lighting was provided by oil lamps mounted on stands. One of the oak chairs, which now occupy a place in the sanctuary, could be seen.

The new chancel, designed by the firm of Austen and Paley of Lancaster, was completed in 1906 and incorporated an organ chamber on the south side and choir and clergy vestries, with under-floor heating, on the north side: the former occupying the site of the pre-1826 chapel dedicated to the Singleton family and the latter on the site of the Lady Chapel of the Barton family. Six broad steps led to the Sanctuary. In addition some fifteen feet of the original flat panel ceiling was removed, in order to accommodate the height of the chancel arch, and became the pitched section nearest the chancel we see today. Original plans for the new chancel are illustrated on the following pages.

119

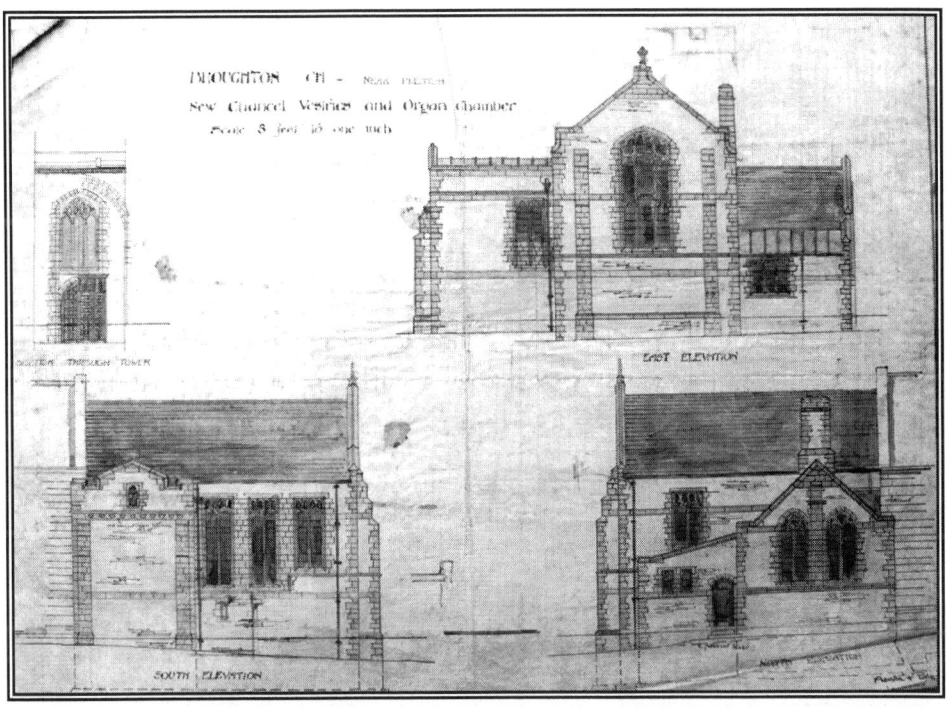

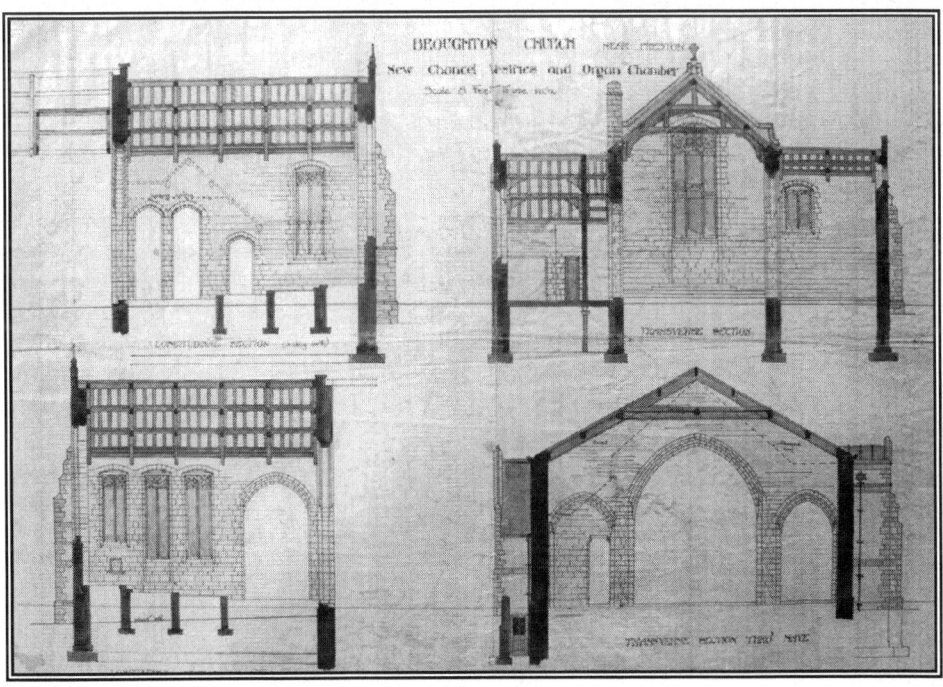

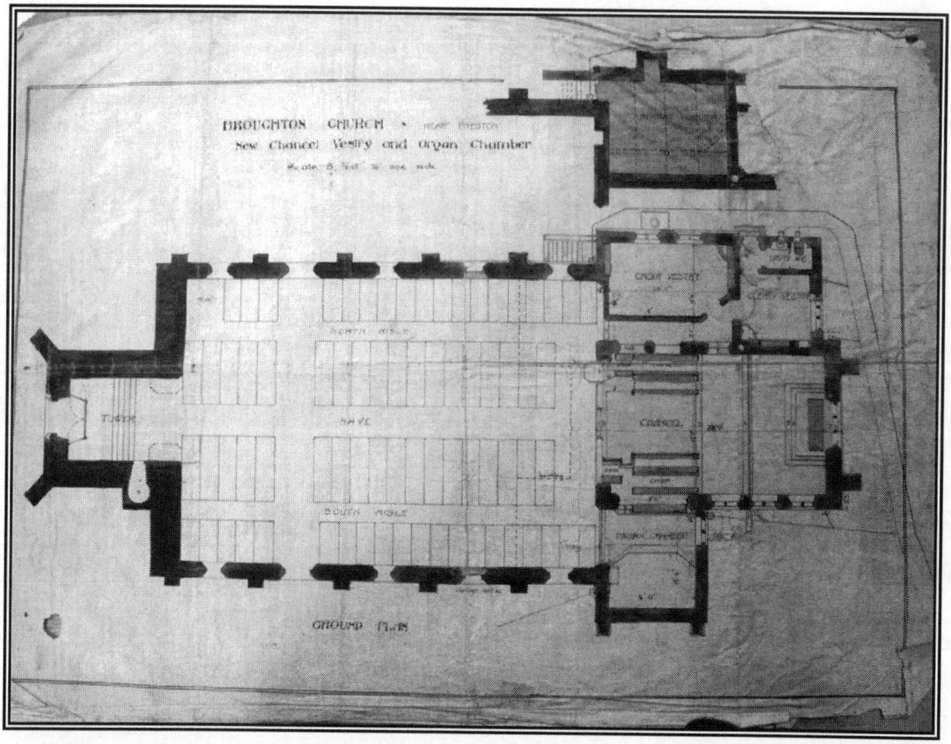

During these alterations, the gallery, which ran north to south along the opposite, west wall, was removed along with the box pews housed there. The timber from them was used by Mr Richard Hardman, the village joiner, Churchwarden and chorister, to improve the seating in the nave. Despite his efforts, this *temporary* seating was allegedly very uncomfortable and continued to mortify the flesh of the congregation for the next thirty-two years, when a bequest of £1000 from William Wilding Galloway of Bilsborough Hall along with donations from the Herling family and other parish members, paid for the oak pews still used today. The legacy is recorded on a pew at the rear of the church (illustrated opposite)

The vicar at the time, Reverend Davies, wrote a short booklet on the history of the church, which was sold to augment the monies already donated for these new pews. They were dedicated, along with the memorial window dedicated to Lucy Jane Wilson, by the Bishop of Blackburn at the Harvest Festival service on October 2nd 1938.

In addition, the old principal west doorway in the tower, previously part blocked and part used as a window, was opened up and masonry covering the old arch was removed, opening up the tower to the nave. As, since the re-building of 1826, the floor of the latter was significantly higher, a flight of four steps was constructed to lead down to the base of the bell tower.

The sanctuary floor was covered with a carpet of unique design, based on lines from Psalm 91: *Thou shalt tread upon the lion and adder: the young lion and the dragon shalt thou tread under thy feet.* The carpet was later removed and replaced by the tiles seen today.

The total cost of the entire 1906 restoration was some £3,500.

THE NORTH WALL OF THE CHANCEL

On the north wall of the chancel are two plaques commemorating members of the Wilson family.

The arrival in the area of professional and upper middle class families like the Wilsons during the early part of the C19th, marked a distinct change in the population of Broughton and the congregation of its church. For centuries the area had been populated by farmers, labourers, trades people, gardeners, dressmakers, washerwomen and a number of handloom weavers. In one sense the professional and manufacturing gentlemen who saw Broughton as a pleasant place to build their new residences, replaced those Tudor and Stuart families like the Singletons and the Langtons for example, who in the past had been lords of the manor. Like such families too, these nouveau riche incomers also became enormously generous benefactors of Broughton Church and were responsible for many improvements and additions.

Certainly by the middle of the C19th the church's congregation had become a more balanced mixture of wealthy middle and upper middle class worthies and their families, and the labouring, trade and farming classes. Interestingly from the 1930s onwards, the congregation again began to change as the suburbs to the south grew and introduced a much more urban element into what had been an almost exclusively rural parish.

The Wilson family, who typified the wealthy incomers and church benefactors of the time, came to the Preston area in 1833, when John William Richard Wilson, a Preston solicitor, built Broughton House, now the Lancashire County Council Ambulance Headquarters, on the western side of the A6 just opposite the church. Eleven years earlier he had married Lucy Shuttleworth and the couple had three children, all destined to die in childhood, when they took up residence in Broughton.

122

The lower tablet records the burial of John William Wilson and other members of his family:

IN THE CENTRE OF THE PORTION OF THE CHURCH-YARD
ENCLOSED BY THIS CHANCEL, BUILT IN 1905, WERE BURIED
JOHN WILLIAM RICHARD WILSON OF BROUGHTON HOUSE
WHO DIED 10TH OCTOBER 1875, AGED 80
LUCY HIS WIFE, DIED 2ND OCTOBER 18939, AGED 37
JOANNA MARY, THEIR ELDEST DAUGHTER, DIED 4TH JANUARY 1841,
AGED 8
LUCY ELIZABETH, THEIR YOUNGEST DAUGHTER, DIED 8TH
JANUARY 1841, AGED 3
SARAH ELLEN THEIR SECOND DAUGHTER, DIED 12TH JANUARY
1841, AGED 6
ROBERT WILLIAM THEIR FOURTH SON,
DIED 1ST FEBRUARY 1841, AGED 11
JAMES, THEIR FIFTH SON,
DIED 17TH FEBRUARY 1841, AGED 10
CHARLES ANOTHER SON
DIED 21ST AUGUST 1861, AGED 25
ALSO ELIZABETH MARY HIS SECOND WIFE,
WHO DIED 29TH DECEMBER 1882, AGED 72
AND THEIR SON FREDERICK
WHO DIED 8TH MARCH 1872, AGED 20

Did ever words fail so utterly to describe the tragedy that struck the Wilson family during January and February 1841? During six horrific weeks, five of John William's children, aged between three and eight years old, died after drinking infected water from the well in the grounds of Broughton House. Only one of his children from his first marriage, Edward, survived into adulthood.

John William's marriage to his second wife, Elizabeth Mary Clayton, in 1842, produced a further seven children born during the 1840s and 50s: Frederick, William, Sarah, Frances Mary, Margaret and Arthur, several of whom contributed much to the life and fabric of Broughton Church.

The upper tablet on the north chancel wall, commemorates John William's son Edward Wilson, who inherited the Broughton House estate.:

NEAR THE WESTERN ENTRANCE OF THIS CHURCH LIE THE
REMAINS OF
EDWARD WILSON OF BROUGHTON HOUSE
WHO DIED ON THE 5TH DAY OF DECEMBER 1908, AGED 82 YEARS,
ALSO
ELIZABETH HIS WIFE, WHO DIED ON THE 4TH DAY OF AUGUST 1901
AGED 73 YEARS

IN APPRECIATION OF THEIR DEEDS OF BENEVOLENCE TO THIS
CHURCH AND PARISH, THE PARISHIONERS AS A MARK OF ESTEEM
ERECTED THIS TABLET TO THEIR MEMORY.

Edward, having become a partner in the family law firm in 1843, married Eliza Maria Pedder nine years later in 1852. By the time of the 1861 Census, he and his family were living at Broughton House. Six children had been born during the first nine years of their marriage: Lucy Jane (1854), Henry (1855), Edward Thomas (1857), Charles (1858), Ada (1860) and Sarah Julia (1861). His father had retired some three years earlier and Edward's brother, Charles, also a partner in the firm.

Rather curiously, a decade later the entire family appeared to be boarding with a Mary Ellen Lewis at number 10 Beach Street in Lytham. A further three children had been born: Albert William (1862), Johanna Mary Helena (1863) and Elizabeth Ann (1870). By the time of the 1881 Census however, the family had returned to Broughton House. Two of Edward's sons, Edward Thomas and Henry Francis, were articled as solicitor's clerks, about to follow their father and grandfather into the family firm.

Henry Francis was educated at Rossall School and Trinity College, and after a spell working in London, returned to Preston to work as a solicitor in his father's office until his retirement at the age of 80, in 1935. For many years he walked from Broughton House to his office in town, refusing offers of lifts. Later he would walk as far as Withy Trees and then take the tram. This daily exercise clearly served him well: he lived to the age of 96. In summer he always wore a brown or grey bowler hat and in winter donned a black one. So punctual was he that locals could set their watch by him. In church on Sundays, he always wore a top hat and full morning dress. For fifty years he served as Churchwarden at St John's and was presented with a silver salver on his retirement. After he was widowed, he moved to Cornwall to a house overlooking the Falmouth Estuary. He is buried in the churchyard in St Just's in Roseland.

His brother, Albert William Wilson, died aged 89, within four days of his brother. He had also been a Rossall School pupil but his career took a totally different course after he attended the Royal Agricultural College in Cirencester. He worked as a land agent in Preston, and like his brother devoted much of his time to Broughton Church, where he taught at the Sunday School and was Treasurer of Broughton School before moving to Dolphinholme. He was survived by a widow and five sons.

His sister, Lucy Jane, also never married but also worked as a Sunday School teacher at Broughton Church for some 50 years until her death in 1937.

Edward Thomas succeeded his father, Edward senior, as Under Sheriff of Lancashire and in 1887, married Mary Wharton. They had two sons – Cecil Edward and Robert Meredith. Sadness and loss however seemed to haunt the Wilson family. Cecil died in 1907, aged 17, while a pupil at Charterhouse School following an infection picked up after a nail in his football boot pierced his foot. His brother Robert, commemorated in a tablet on the south chancel wall, died during the First World War.

The new chancel, costing some three and half thousand pounds, was largely funded by the Wilson family. The oak reredos was given by Miss Lucy Wilson, then living at The Cottage, Broughton, in memory of her nephew and godson, Cecil Edward. The pulpit was funded in memory of Eliza Mary Wilson.

THE LITANY DESK

The desk is inscribed:

DEDICATED TO THE GLORY OF GOD AND IN MEMORY OF CHARLES ROGER JACSON BY A NUMBER OF THE TENANTRY ON THE BARTON ESTATE, EASTER, 1894.

COLLINSON MEMORIAL

A third tablet on the opposite side of the archway, commemorating Reverend Collinson, who was vicar at Broughton from 1886 to 1923, is inscribed:

TO THE GLORY OF GOD AND IN LOVING MEMORY OF THE REV. SAMUEL EDWARD COLLINSON, WHO SERVED THIS CHURCH AS P.P. FOR 37 YEARS AND DIED AT PORT ST MARY, ISLE OF MAN, 18TH DECEMBER IN HIS 72ND YEAR.
THE EAST WINDOW AND THIS TABLET HAVE BEEN ERECTED BY HIS FRIENDS AND PARISHIONERS TO WHOM HIS CHEERFUL BEARING IN ADVERSITY AND HIS ENTHUSIASM FOR HIS CHURCH, ITS LITURGY AND TEACHING, WERE A CONSTANT SOURCE OF INSPIRATION.
REQUIESCAT IN PACE

THE NORTH CHANCEL MEMORIAL WINDOW

This window, the oldest stained glass in the church, is probably also the least prominent. It is probably only ever noticed by the majority of the congregation when the late evening summer sun projects its rich colours onto the rear sanctuary wall. The window was installed in 1901 and is dedicated:

TO THE GLORY OF GOD AND IN LOVING MEMORY OF JOHN PALMOUR M.A., PRIEST WHO DIED 20 JULY 1901 AGED 68. ERECTED BY HIS WIDOW.

John Palmour was the Vicar of Christ Church in Fulwood during the last quarter of the nineteenth century, his name appearing in the parish registers from 1873 to1900, a year before his death.

The window depicts a somewhat asymmetrical image of two angels and Roman soldiers at the Resurrection.

THE OAK REREDOS

Perhaps the most immediately striking architectural feature of the chancel is the oak reredos behind the altar. It was presented to the church in 1907, a year after the new chancel was completed, by Miss Lucy Wilson, of The Cottage, Broughton, in memory of her godson and nephew, Cecil Edward Wilson, who died while a pupil at Charterhouse School.

The reredos was designed by Austen and Paley, the same firm which had designed the new chancel. The actual work was carried out by Hatch & Sons of Lancaster, with Mr Caleb Allen carving the figures. The theme of the design was explained by Reverend Collinson, the vicar at the time of the restoration: *Our Blessed Lord commissioned the Apostles equally to go out and preach the Gospel to the whole world. The branch of the Holy Catholic Church to which we belong, which has striven to preserve the Faith once delivered to the Saints in its primitive freedom and purity, can trace her origin, not to one individual Apostle, but to several Apostles. The endeavour in the design and selection of figures is*

126

to show the various sources from which we can claim our Catholicity. In explaining the choice of figures incorporated into the reredos, he goes on to say we should rejoice in the *Multiple Apostolic origin of the Church in these Islands.*

Four Apostles are included in the design.

St John the Evangelist founded the Church at Ephesus and it was from there that the first missionaries came to Britain.

St Mark the Evangelist was the founder and Patriarch of the Church in Alexandria, from where came the first missionaries to Ireland. Though their initial preaching and teaching were not especially successful, they did pave the way for St Patrick.

Saint Paul, it is claimed, did preach a mission in Britain. Clemens Romanus, writing in AD 96, asserts that *St Paul preached as far as the utmost bounds of the West*; Saint

Jerome, some three hundred years later, says *Saint Paul laboured unto the Western parts* and Theodoret in AD 420 further claims that *Saint Paul brought salvation to the isles of the ocean.*

Saint Peter's role in the conversion of these islands comes indirectly, through the mission of St Augustine at the end of the sixth century to the *Heathen Saxons.* At the end of the sixth century, the face of Christianity in Britain was forever changed by the Gregorian Mission. In this endeavour, Pope Gregory sent a group of clerics headed by the monk Augustine to convert the Saxons to Christianity and to establish new churches and dioceses in their territory.

The choice of these four figures clarifies the theme that Christianity in Britain does not have its origin in any one Apostolic source but from four at least.

If the central figures symbolise Christian conversion on a national, even international scale, then the side pillars symbolise a more local perspective. Here four Bishops are represented as being influential in the conversion of Lancashire.

Saint Aidan, Bishop of Lindisfarne in AD 632, and St Cuthbert, Bishop in AD 687, both visited Lancashire on their missionary journeys.

Saint Kentigern, Bishop of Glasgow in AD 601, presided over a diocese which at that time included the whole of the West coast from the Clyde to the Mersey.

The last bishop represented is Saint Patrick, Bishop in AD 465, who visited Lancashire during his missionary journeys.

The lives of all four of these enormously influential men are woven into the very fabric of the history of Christianity in Lancashire

The two figures at the top represent Saint Cecilia and Saint Lucia. Saint Cecilia, the patron saint of musicians and church music, is a most apposite choice for a church such as St John's, given its rich history of music. Saint Lucia or Lucy, whose feast day is the 13th December, is the patron saint of the blind. Refusing to marry a pagan husband and denounced by her spurned suitor as a Christian, she consecrated her virginity to God. In one version of her story her would-be husband is said to have admired her eyes, whereupon she tore them out and gave them to him, saying: *Now let me live to God.*

In the small canopy, are the figures of Moses holding the stone tablets bearing the Decalogue and representing the Law; Elijah, carrying scrolls, symbolising the Prophets, and the patron saint of Broughton Church itself, Saint John the Baptist. The positioning of these three figures, above the cross, representing Christ's death, and below the stained glass window depicting his Resurrection and Ascension, illustrates the way in which each of them prefigures the coming of Jesus, the fulfilment of their prophecy and teaching.

The window, a powerful and evocative backdrop to the reredos, was funded by public subscription in recognition of the thirty-year ministry of Reverend S.E. Collinson (1884 – 1923). It was largely through his efforts that the chancel, vestries and organ chamber were built.

Its three sections depict the Ascension and seem dominated by blue tones which are perhaps most conducive to contemplation and reflection. The imagery exists in three planes: the strong, dark colours of the crowd of disciples; the pearly tints of the ascending Jesus and attendant angels; the deep, rich gold and greens of Heaven, the Upper Glory, with two seraphs with folded wings, the cherubim and the rainbow about the Throne.

The artist has created a wonderful mosaic of glittering colour, best seen perhaps in the early morning light from the cross aisle towards the west end of the nave.

THE BISHOP'S CHAIR

The oak chair sits against the north wall of the sanctuary. It was funded as a result of an appeal begun before the Second World War but not completed until 1950. The appeal sought funds for a memorial to Miss Lucy Wilson (see page 42).

The chair was designed and carved by Stanley Davies of Windermere at a cost of £65. After its completion in 1950, it was exhibited at the Whitworth Art Gallery in Manchester, before being dedicated at the Carol Service on the 24th December 1950. It is inscribed:

IN MEMORY OF LUCY JANE WILSON. PRESENTED BY HER FRIENDS IN THE PARISH.

THE THREE SOUTH CHANCEL WINDOWS

The primary purpose of these three windows is to admit as much light as possible to the chancel and sanctuary but they also form a stained glass triptych, depicting the Holy Trinity. In addition, each window is dedicated to one of three of the Wilson sisters.

The first window, on the left, is dedicated :

TO THE GLORY OF GOD AND IN LOVING MEMORY OF FRANCES MARY WILSON 1847 - 1925

The predominant colour of the window is gold, symbolic of God the Holy Ghost. The principal figures depicted are St John the Baptist, on the left, and Saint Stephen, the first Christian martyr.
Below them are depicted two groups, a mother figure and her children on

130

the left, and on the right, the Virgin Mary sitting down with the lion and the lamb, images symbolic of the duality of her son Jesus, who was both the Lion of Judah and the Lamb of God.

The whole window represents the fruits of the Spirit, Love and Peace.

It bears the especially apt inscriptions:

HE SHALL BE FILLED WITH THE HOLY GHOST EVEN FROM HIS MOTHER'S WOMB.
(Luke 1:15 – speaking of John the Baptist)

and

A MAN FULL OF FAITH AND THE HOLY GHOST
(Acts 6:5 - spoken of Stephen)

The middle window is dedicated to Margaret Wilson (1850 – 1934) and bears the inscriptions:

BROUGHT UP IN THE CITY AND THE FEET OF GAMALIEL
(Acts 22:3)

and

IF IT BE OF GOD YE CANNOT OVERCOME IT
(Gamaliel's own words in Acts 5:39)

The prevailing colour of blue symbolises God the Son. One of the two main figures is Gamaliel, the great Jewish law-giver, who, in Acts, successfully advises his fellow members of the Sanhedrin not to have St Peter put to death. He was also the teacher of St Paul, who as the great Church organiser, is the second main figure depicted.

The emblems in the top lights represent Jesus and the four evangelists. The bottom of each light depicts Our Lord teaching the people. The whole window illustrates the works of the mind and the redemptive potency of the Gospel.

131

The third, right-hand window is predominantly green in colour, symbolic of earthly things. The top lights, bearing the Greek letters Alpha and Omega, the Beginning and the End, symbolise God the Father.

The central figures are Adam, the first man, and Solomon, the temple builder. Below them are depicted the work of man's hands: Adam shaping a yoke and Eve spinning, and in the second light, Solomon's Temple.

Here are portrayed the works of the body and creative power, echoed in the inscriptions:

IN THE SWEAT OF THY FACE
SHALT THOU EAT BREAD
(Genesis 3:19)

and

I HAVE SURELY BUILT THEE AN
HOUSE TO DWELL IN
(1 Kings 8:13)

This window is dedicated to Lucy Jane Wilson (1854 – 1937)

Two memorial plaques can also be found on this south chancel wall.

The first is dedicated to Charles Roger Jacson, *the last holder of the Manor of Barton*. It commemorates *the historical association of that Manor with the ancient Chapelry of Broughton* and records too the building of the south chantry by Charles Jacson's wife, Mrs C.R. Jacson, in memory of her husband.

Charles Jacson, the second son of George and Charlotte Jacson, followed his father into the textile business. He completed his education at Rugby School, under the headship of the celebrated Dr Arnold, and is described by Hewitson as *an active, cultured gentleman.* In 1846 he married Catherine Greenhalgh-Formby: their marriage was without issue.

He inherited the Barton estate after his father's death, and like his father, he became Mayor of Preston in 1865. Two years later he was elected an Alderman of Preston.

He was one of the first Patrons of the Broughton living and, as Chairman of the Board of Guardians and trustee of the Harris Legacies, had much to do with the building of several landmark buildings: the workhouse on Watling Street Road, where the *Jacson Wing* for elderly, infirm gentlemen and infectious cases, was named in his honour; the Harris Library; the Harris Institute and the Harris Orphanage, where a memorial plaque can still be seen in the hall. A window depicting the Transfiguration and gifted by Charles Jacson, can also be found at the west end of Preston Parish Church. It bears the inscription:

SOLI NATALIS REVERMO SECUNDATUM MEMOR IN DEI GLORIAM
AEDE REPARATA, P.C.: CAROLUS R. JACSON, 1854

In 1894 his widow left Barton Hall for Lytham. The whole of the Jacson property, some 2,600 acres along with the Hall, farm houses, corn mill, inns, cottages etc. was offered for sale en bloc. A sum of £100,000 was bid but deemed insufficient: and the property was withdrawn. Subsequently in 1899, the estate was divided into 72 lots and sold by auction. Mr W. Smith of Newsham House purchased the principal lot of Barton Hall and three farms totalling some 395 acres, for £25,000. The entire estate raised some £141,652, some of which was used a few years later to fund the building of the south chapel or *chantry* as the plaque describes it, in the new chancel of Broughton Church.

The second plaque (pictured opposite) is a memorial to Robert Meredith Wilson, the son of Edward Thomas Wilson.

As a lieutenant in the 6th Battalion, Loyal North Lancashire Regiment, he was killed in action at Chunuk Bair, Gallipoli, on the 10th August 1915, aged only twenty-three.

His valour and death are also recorded on the Helles Memorial on the Gallipoli peninsula.

133

THE ALTAR FURNITURE

The altar cross (pictured below) was dedicated at Christmas 1896 in memory of Alfred Neville Rolfe, the husband of Ada Wilson. The altar candles were

presented by members of the Wilson family and the altar vases by Bertha Redmayne in memory of her husband William Darbyshire Redmayne, who was organist and choirmaster at the church from 1928 to 1955, and of her son John G. Redmayne F.R.C.O.

The processional cross was presented by the Peake family in 1945 and dedicated:

IN LOVING MEMORY OF HENRY
PEAKE
DEC.15 1889 TO FEB 3 1945

THE CHURCH PLATE

In 1732 the then Vicar of Preston, Samuel Peploe, presented altar vessels to Broughton Church. These consisted of a pewter flagon, two silver chalices, seven and a quarter inches tall, and a silver paten. The chalices were inscribed *Capella de Broughton Sacrum 1732* and the base of each is inscribed:

THE GIFT OF REVEREND SAMUEL PEPLOE, ARCHDEACON OF
RICHMOND &VIC. OF PRESTON.

In 1851 additional vessels were purchased by subscription and the flagon, chalice and paten were all inscribed: *BROUGHTON PAROCHIAL CHAPEL, PURCHASED BY SUBSCRIPTION. MDCCCLI.*

The flagon or silver ewer, assayed at London in 1850, stands just over twelve inches tall, with a flat handle and hinged lid. It bears a central inscription: *IN THEE O LORD I PUT MY TRUST.*

The ciborium was donated *IN MEMORY OF KATHLEEN BROOK.*

The wafer box inscription reads:

DEDICATED BY M.E.D. & E.T. FOR USE IN THE CHURCH OF ST JOHN THE BAPTIST, BROUGHTON

A shell used at baptisms was presented in 1976 in memory of Ernest Ashwell and his wife. The churchwardens' staves, engraved *St John the Baptist, Broughton,* were bought with funds from a financial legacy. A silver salver to hold the cruets was donated by George and Doreen Thompson.

THE ORGAN

The organ, housed in the side chapel, but now no longer used, was built in 1906 by Mr Henry Ainscough of Preston and cost some £800. It is a three-manual organ, with approximately 1400 pipes and was constructed to the specifications of Dr T.H. Collinson, the organist of Edinburgh Cathedral and brother of the then vicar, Rev. S.E. Collinson.

Mr Ainscough regarded his creation as one of the finest organs in Lancashire. Originally it consisted of a pedal organ of thirty notes and a choir organ, great organ and swell organ, each offering 58 notes.

The Vicar, writing in 1928, was however less than impressed with *the constant thudding sound proceeding from the neighbourhood of the organ.*

This was not the drumming feet of bored choristers but due to the faulty motor, which powered the bellows and which would have to be replaced.

A further overhaul took place in 1967, at a cost of £910, the money largely being raised through gifts and individual loans of £100 from parishioners. A new electric blowing plant was installed as well as two new stops on the great organ, a mixture stop and a fifteenth stop.

Twelve years later, in 1979, an appeal was launched seeking to raise the capital needed to fund a further significant overhaul to be carried out by Rushworth and Dreaper Ltd of Liverpool. Mr Roger Houghton, the son of Major Arthur Theodore Houghton, was the driving force behind the successful appeal. Bishop Anthony Hoskyns-Abrahall rededicated the organ at Evensong on March 1st 1981.

The detail from the front of the organ illustrated opposite, bears the inscription Soli Deo Gloria, which translates as **Glory to God alone***. It was one of five solas propounded to summarise Protestant beliefs during the Reformation. The initials SDG were appended by both Handel and Bach to their musical manuscripts, illustrating the aptness of such a sentiment being carved into the organ casing. This epithet is repeated in the stained glass of the memorial window in the south wall of the nave.*

A new Phoenix organ was installed in 2005. This state-of-the-art instrument, pictured below, has four manuals and one hundred stops.

136

This window was created in memory of George Duckworth (1852 – 1926) and, appropriately given its location, depicts angels singing.

It looks down on what was once a side chapel. The once curtained opening, which faces the nave, is framed by carved oak beams, of grape and vine design, completed in the early 1930s by Miss Joan Wilson of *The Cottage*, Broughton. She carved them from timbers salvaged when an ancient barn at nearby Bank Hall was demolished by Mr B. Sykes. The chapel also housed the Jacobean table now to be found in the north-east corner of the nave.

THE LECTERN

The lectern, made of solid brass and in the form of an eagle with outstretched wings, is inscribed:

The flying eagle is the symbol of John the Evangelist (see Revelation, Ch 4, v 7) who proclaims Christ as 'the Word of God' at the beginning of his Gospel. The flying eagle is thus a suitable emblem from which God's word is read, reaching one hope the ends of the earth. The eagle is also thought of as the bird which

flies nearest to heaven. It was not until the Reformation that the lectern became prominent in ordinary parish churches of the reformed tradition, carrying the open bible.

There is a belief too that the eagle symbol actually dates back at least as far as the early medieval use of astrological symbols in church design. The eagle, an alternative symbol for Scorpio, is one of the four fixed signs of the zodiac, which represented stability and endurance. The Golden Eagle has been regarded from ancient times as a symbol of courage and power and appropriately represents clear vision, intelligence, and power.

The four fixed signs were appropriated to symbolise the four Apostles who were considered to be the firm and lasting foundation of the Church. Leo was given to Mark, Scorpio to John, Taurus to Luke and Aquarius to Matthew. In esoteric astrology the eagle replaces the scorpion as a sign of Scorpio's ability to be spiritually reborn, rising above earthly desires; divine inspiration is ascribed to Leo and the potential divinity of mankind to Aquarius. Taurus represents the voice of God and so was often omitted from the design, as it was left to the preacher to fulfil this role.

The lectern bible was itself presented by Mrs Hetty Dowden in September 1962, in memory of her husband Jack Dowden, who was killed in a motor-cycle accident on Whittingham Lane involving a drunk driver. The New English Bible was presented in memory of Stanley Griggs and was presented by his colleagues at the then British Aircraft Corporation factory at Warton and his family.

In the south east corner of the nave, near the entrance to the choir vestry, can be found this ancient oak chest, which once held church documents such as the baptism, marriage and burial records.

This window, depicting the baptism of Christ by St John the Baptist, in the River Jordan, is one of the most recent additions to the church's stained glass. It was financed by private, anonymous donors and dedicated on the 17th November 1985 by the Bishop of Lancaster.

It was designed and painted by Mrs Jane Gray of Uxbridge. Its inscription *Soli Deo Gloria* – Glory to God alone - repeats that on the front of the organ, and the musical association, is echoed, not only in the inscription's association with Bach and Handel, but also through the Anglo-Saxon musical instruments, the two robed choristers and the musical notation included in the design.

The choristers and the children, positioned outside an image of the church itself, emphasise not only its musical traditions but also how young people are central to its mission.

The flowers and foliage at the centre of the design illustrate a theme of growing and harvest, and the beauty of God's creation.

139

At the apex of the arch is a Maltese Cross, a symbol of St John and of the Venerable Order of the Hospital of St John in Jerusalem.

A little further along the south wall of the nave is a memorial plaque to:

IN REMEMBRANCE OF
JESSIE, BELOVED WIFE OF GEORGE HUNT OF THE GRANGE,
BROUGHTON. DIED DECEMBER 25TH 1846 AGED 33 YEARS
ALSO OF JESSIE BORTHWICK THEIR INFANT DAUGHTER, DIED
DECEMBER 28TH 1846, AGED 15 DAYS
AND THE ABOVE GEORGE HUNT
DIED APRIL 29TH 1887, AGED 77 YEARS.

It seems clear the Jessie Hunt died only a couple of weeks after giving birth to their daughter Jessie Borthwick Hunt. The couple had been married in Glendale, Northumberland in December 1844. Their first child, Frederick Goodricke Hunt, was born 6th August 1845, and baptised at Broughton Church on the 24th September.

George Hunt was a native of Durham and worked as a land agent. At the time of the 1851 Census, he was still living at *The Grange*, along with two servants. Their home, *The Grange*, still occupies an elevated position at the top of Church Hill on D'Urton Lane.

George was remarried to Sarah Jane Teebay, some twelve years his junior, in March 1855. Six years later the couple, their own two young children and George's eldest child from his first marriage, Frederick Goodrick, were living at Frenchwood House, along with three servants.

THE 'COMMUNITY' MILLENNIUM WINDOW

This window at the western end of the south nave wall is the most recent addition to the church's stained glass. Of contemporary design, it was created and constructed by local artist Ian McCormick and was dedicated by Rev David Jenkins on Sunday the 5th December 1999.

The window was commissioned, at a cost of £2,500, for the Millennium and depicts various aspects of parish life. These are illustrated within five circles, hanging like fruit from a serpentine tree or vine perhaps. Certainly each seems to flow from the image of the dove at the apex of the design. The lowest circle contains a sepia image of the south prospect of the church itself. Ascending from this are images of the old school hall of Broughton Primary School; St Peter's Primary School; emblems of the Scout and Guide movements; emblems of St Peter and St Martin, the church's satellite chapels.

Light and Hope were the themes of the Dedication Service, a Service full of optimism and inspiration, celebrated in drama and song. The young people at the heart of the celebration used light in various ways -in scientific and Biblical contexts – culminating in the Lighting of the Window when the exterior floodlighting was switched on.

It was created in the belief that: *In all that we do we are enfolded in the love of God, from whom all our blessings flow. The glowing streams descending from the Dove remind us of the power of His love, and encourage us to follow Him to its source.*

The congregation was reassured that through the young people of the Parish, God's light would guide them along the true path into the future as the Millennium dawned.

The book, inaugurated when the Garden of Remembrance was created, lies in its own case on a table adjacent to the window near the south door.

THE WEST WALL

THE DIXON MEMORIAL

The tablet is dedicated to the memory of Rev. William Dixon, Broughton's Vicar for some 55 years, from 1817 to 1872. He died on the 23rd March 1872, aged eighty-three. The plaque, pictured below, celebrates his *faithful ministry* and is inscribed:

IN TESTIMONY OF RESPECT FOR THE HOLY SIMPLICITY OF HIS LIFE AND IN AFFECTIONATE REMEMBRANCE OF HAPPY PASTORAL RELATIONS, HIS FRIENDS AND PARISHIONERS RAISED THIS TABLET TO HIS MEMORY.

NEAR THIS PLACE
LIE THE MORTAL REMAINS OF
THE REV: WILLIAM DIXON;
WHO, AFTER FIFTY-FIVE YEARS OF FAITHFUL MINISTRY
IN THIS CHURCH AND PARISH,
CALMLY AND THANKFULLY PASSED AWAY TO HIS REST
ON THE 23RD DAY OF MARCH, 1872;
IN THE 83RD YEAR OF HIS AGE.

IN TESTIMONY OF RESPECT
FOR THE HOLY SIMPLICITY OF HIS LIFE;
AND IN AFFECTIONATE REMEMBRANCE
OF HAPPY PASTORAL RELATIONS;
HIS FRIENDS AND PARISHIONERS
RAISED THIS TABLET TO HIS MEMORY.

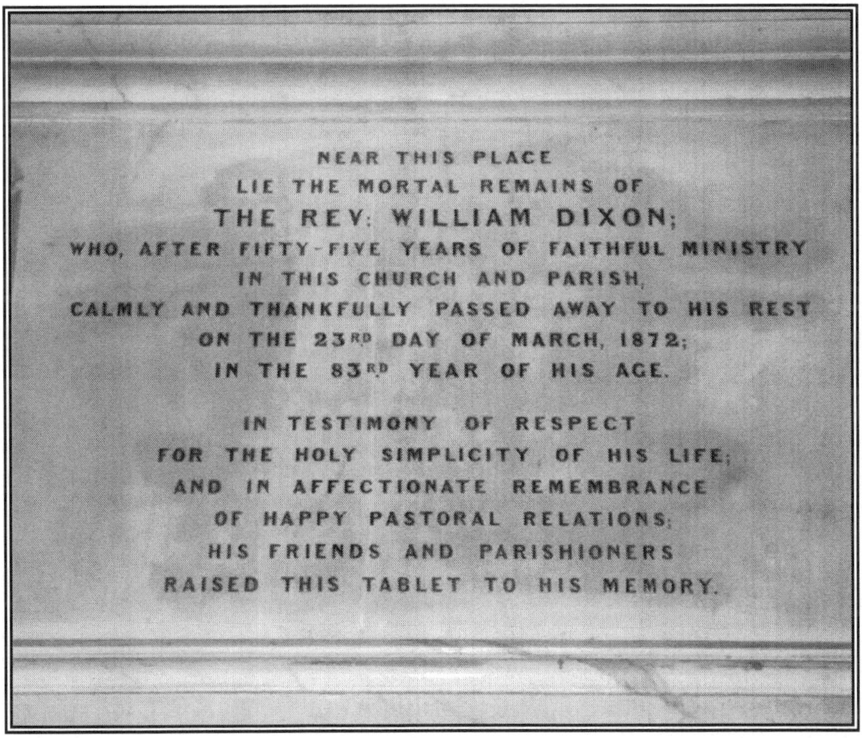

Below the Dixon plaque is the most recently installed memorial in the church, dedicated on Sunday 10th June 2012. Funded by their family, in memory of Brian and Eileen Worswick, the oak board records all the thirty-six -identifiable incumbents of Broughton Church over the six hundred and fifty years since 1353, and replaces the one previously displayed on the other side of the west wall.

INCUMBENTS of BROUGHTON in AMOUNDERNESS

Nicholas de Broughton	1353 -	John Winkley	1661 -
John le Clerk	1358 -	William Wood	1674 - 1714
William le Prestgate	1368 - 1396	Thomas Ryhe	1683 -
Geoffrey	1377 -	William Charnley	1721 -
Barry de Broughton	1441 -	John Starkie	1727 -
Edward Wall	1515 -	Joseph Cowper	1731 - 1761
Henry Halme	1530 -	John Hunter	1761 - 1774
Dominus V.E. Banester	1554 -	Randal Andrews	1774 - 1780
Roger Sharnocke	1548 - 1565	George Charnley	1780 - 1809
John Martin	1597 -	Hugh Hodgson	1810 - 1817
John Wilson	1604 - 1610	William Dixon	1817 - 1872
John Lawson	1622 -	William Bretherton	1872 - 1885
Peter Addison	1626 -	Samuel E. Collinson	1886 - 1923
Roger Farrand	1625 -	David R. Davies	1923 - 1940
James Aino	1650 -	Charles M.S. Clarke	1940 - 1946

Norman C. Outridge	1946 - 1968
John M.W. Adam	1969 - 1974
William G. Armstrong	1975 - 1983
Stanley J. Finch	1984 - 1998
David H. Jenkins	1999 - 2004
Sidney Fox	2005 -

In memory of Brian & Eileen Worswick

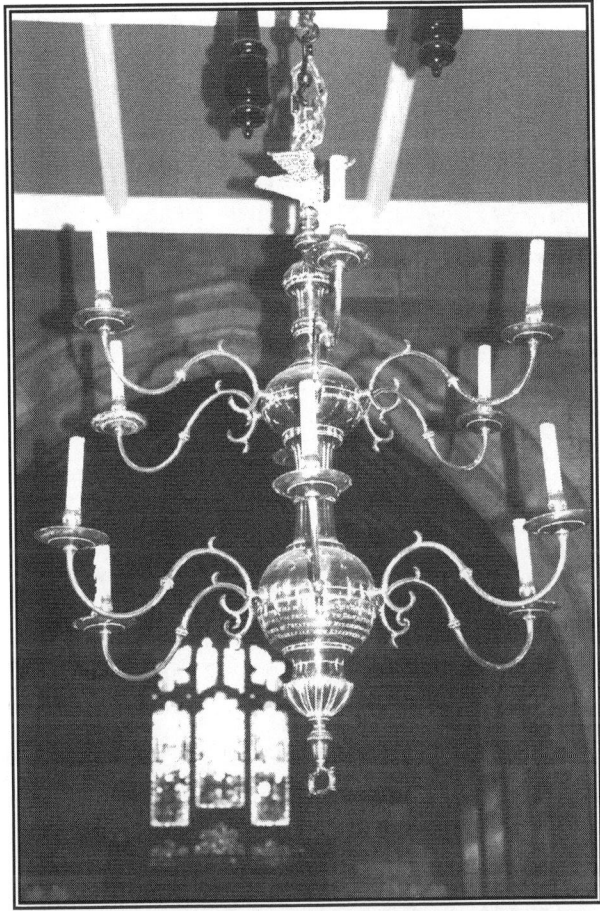

Looking back from the tower towards the chancel, the chandelier can be seen hanging by a chain from the ceiling over the central aisle. It was designed to hold twelve candles, representing the twelve apostles.

The inscription on its spherical base reads:

AGREEABLE TO THE WILL OF THE LATE ANN ROBINSON OF SALWICK, THIS CHANDELIER WAS PRESENTED TO BROUGHTON CHURCH BY JOHN SMITH OF PRESTON, JOHN MYERSCOUGH OF PLUMPTON AND RICHARD THRELFALL, HER EXECUTORS, 1817.

It was clearly then an item of church furniture before the present nave was built in 1826 and has survived for almost two hundred years, despite the many accidental blows from careless cubs and scouts as they carry their banners along the central aisle at the beginning and end of the Parade Day Service. Detailed opposite is the ceiling boss and lion's head supporting the chandelier.

In 1952 members of the Ashwell family provided money for the chandelier to be lacquered.

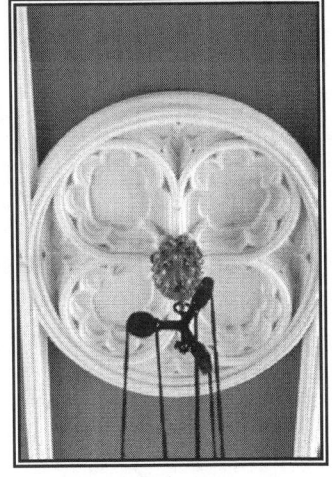

The tower, the oldest part of the church, is some 13 feet 3 inches square inside and built of millstone grit.

The base of the tower, some two and a half feet lower than the newly-built nave, is almost exclusively the preserve of the bell-ringers, but also provides an impressive processional entrance through the imposing west door.

The area is adorned with photographs of past generations of ringers: a plaque commemorates perhaps the most renowned of them all. John Jolleys (see pages 153-54), who, along with his wife and family lived for some years, in Church Cottage, devoted almost half a century to ringing in the church.

IN MEMORY OF
JOHN JOLLEYS
5 APRIL 1906 – 10 FEBRUARY 1967
FOR 47 YEARS A DEVOTED
RINGER IN THIS TOWER
AND CAPTAIN FOR MORE
THAN 33 YEARS

The window was dedicated by Archdeacon Hornby on Sunday, September 17th 1933. The work was carried out by Powell & Sons of Whitefriars and the gift of Miss Helen Duckworth, in memory of her two sisters. In her will she bequeathed £300 to the Vicar and Churchwardens for a memorial window. The three lights depict The Annunciation, The Incarnation and The Adoration. A decision was made that the subject matter would be confined to the two centre panels of each light so that as much light as possible from the setting sun would flood in through the only west window in the church.

It bears the inscription:
TO THE GLORY OF GOD, AND IN MEMORY OF HER TWO SISTERS ANN AND MARGARET, THIS WINDOW WAS DEDICATED IN ACCORDANCE WITH A BEQUEST IN THE WILL OF ELLEN DUCKWORTH, WHO DIED 9TH JANUARY, 1932.

146

The font was restored in 1889, largely through the efforts of the then churchwarden, Richard Hardman. When the church was rebuilt in 1826, it had been discarded and replaced by an alabaster font. During the intervening sixty years the original, ancient font had been used as a planter in the Cross family garden in Barton until it was rediscovered by the then vicar, Rev Collinson. It is roughly fashioned, from a single sandstone boulder, in a style known as *hatchet* or *hatched work*, a stone-cutting technique used in Saxon times, prior to the advent of the chisel. The font measures 81 cm in diameter, with an inside diameter of 62cm and a depth of 28cm.

Originally the font would have had a cover, it being the custom in many English churches to allow holy water to remain in the font. It was occasionally stolen being a valuable commodity, particularly in black magic rituals. In 1326, Edmund Rich, the Archbishop of Canterbury, ordered all fonts to be kept under locked cover at the expense of parishes. There are two holes on the rim, pictured opposite, where staples were let into the font to which the cover was attached. At the bottom is a hole as a water outlet.

During the Middle Ages the ceremony of Baptism was a major rite of passage. It took place within days of the birth: the child being carried to church by the parents and godparents. The priest met the group in the porch and having ascertained the sex of the baby, placed a boy to the right and a girl to the left. The parents would have brought salt with them for the first exorcism, when some was placed in the infant's mouth and prayers said. The child's forehead was then blessed twice with the sign of the cross. After spitting into his left hand (the *sinister* hand and seat of the devil), the priest moistened the child's nostrils and ears, mirroring Christ's actions in healing the deaf and dumb man. The sign of the cross was then made on the child's right hand, accompanied by the words: *May you remain in the Catholic faith and have eternal life for ever and ever. Amen.*

The baptismal party now entered the church and gathered round the font. The godparents, on behalf of the baby, renounced the Devil, before the priest signed the child on his chest and back with holy oil. The naked baby was then rotated three times, each time being completely immersed in the holy water of the font as the priest intoned: *God the Father; God the Son and the Holy Spirit.* Once lifted from the font by one of the godparents, the infant was again signed with chrism on the top of his head before being wrapped in its *chrisom*, a piece of cloth or hooded robe. The child wore this garment until his mother attended her *churching* ceremony, forty days after the birth of a boy or eighty days after that of a girl, and returned the clothing to the priest. Finally a lighted candle was placed in the child's right hand: *a burning and inextinguishable light.*

The font too played a key role in the rite of Confirmation, which could be undergone at any age.

In the early part of the C18th, when the font was sited in the south west corner of the nave, it was the custom for people living in Preston to bring any children suffering from scrofula, the *King's Evil*, to be dipped in the font at Broughton, when the water in it overflowed. This overflowing water was supposed to have magical, curative power. This superstition was exploded however, when it was discovered that the water only overflowed when Blundell Brook was in spate and the rush of water was too great to escape through the then small archway and backed up through the outlet pipe of the font.

THE DANIEL MEMORIAL

All the old memorial plaques were removed when the church was rebuilt in 1826: one however was replaced in the new church and could once be found on the inside wall of the tower. It had suffered considerable damage over the years but was inscribed now somewhat enigmatically:

> *William Daniel*
> *Broughton one*
> *Four and twen*
> *And feofie: for: t*
> *Urch: school: and*
> *Ore: who; died: th*
> *Of: April:167*

On 3rd November 1656, a legacy from a local yeoman, one William Daniel, was added to the endowment of Broughton Grammar School, and became known as Daniel's Charity. He left several parcels of land in Broughton, including Highest Fields, which consisted of three acres, and Little Meadow, to the trustees, to raise a *yearly sum of twenty shillings lawful money of England'* to be paid to the churchwardens in two equal portions at Whitsuntide and Martinmas. These several 'closes' were to be held for one thousand years after the death of William Daniel and his wife.

Again this money was intended for the;

Maintenance of a Grammar School at Broughton or for want thereof, towards the Repair of the Church & the Church Bridges.

William Daniel died without issue, and his widow Margaret, by an indenture dated 29th July 1690, granted £20 to be paid after her death to the trustees for use in helping the poor of Broughton.

The reference in the third line refers to his being one of the *Four and Twenty, the Select Vestry* established at the Parish Church in the mid C17th. The final line records his death during the 1670s.

THE LANGTON MEMORIAL

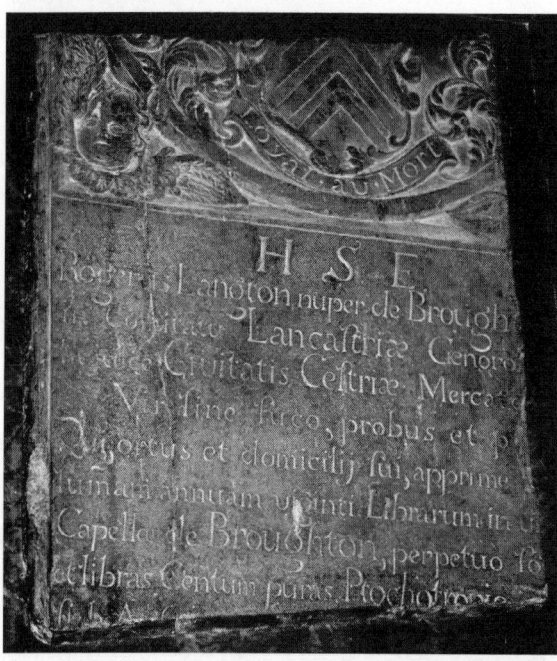

Roger Langton (1559-1644) purchased the Manor of Broughton, including Broughton Tower, from the Singleton family in 1615 (see page 18). The tablet on the west wall is inscribed:

THE MEMORIAL OF ROGER LANGTON OF BROUGHTON IN THIS PARISH, WHO DIED AND WAS BURIED AT CHESTER SEPTEMBER, 1714, WAS CAST ASIDE WHEN THE OLD CHURCH OF ST. BRIDGET, WHERE THE INTERNMENT TOOK PLACE, WAS PULLED DOWN.

The Latin inscription beneath, records the £20 he paid annually from his estate towards the stipend of the incumbent at Broughton Church.

These fragments were discovered by workmen involved in the demolition of St Bridget's: members of the family of William Langton of Manchester, one of Roger's descendants, had them removed and relocated to Broughton.

149

CHAPTER 13

BELLS AND BELL RINGERS

In country churches old and pale
I hear the changes smoothly rung
And watch the coloured sallies fly
From rugged hands to rafters high
As round and back the bells are swung.

(Church of England thoughts…John Betjeman)

The ring at Broughton Church is now made up of six bells, which have, in Betjeman's phrase, *pealed the centuries out with Evensong*, but originally it consisted of only three, which were especially noteworthy as they were said to date from pre-Reformation times and believed to be among the oldest in the county. Between them they had survived some 800 years.

The Old Tenor Bell bore the inscription:

> *Jesus be our spede. 1632.*

The founder's mark is P.H. probably Paul Hutton of Congleton.

The Old Second Bell was inscribed with the initials:

> *CW, W.W., I.C. 1681, Gloria in excelsis deo.*

The initials W.W. refer to the then curate William Wood: the founder's mark is W.S., probably William Seller of York. C.W. and I.C. were probably the initials of the contemporary Churchwardens.

The Old Treble Bell, probably the oldest bell, carried the rather cryptic inscription:

> *Sce   petre   o   p   n*

which decoded gives us: *Sancte   Petre   ora   pro   nobis*

and which in turn translates as*; Saint Peter pray for us.*

The lettering style on this bell suggested it was cast in the early part of the C15th. The founder's mark is T.B. probably for the most aptly named Thomas Bell of Leicester, who is likely to have cast the bell for the rebuilt tower of 1533.

In 1554 Queen Mary issued an enquiry regarding bells, which under the commission of her predecessor, Edward VI, should have been taken down and surrendered but which had in fact been retained in their chapels. The results of this enquiry revealed that Broughton Church still had two bells and two little bells, which had never been handed over, another indication perhaps of the local, Catholic resistance to the demands of Reformation statutes and edicts.

In 1587, Roger Langton was signatory to a document prescribing the use of bells at Preston Parish Church, rules also adhered to by the Broughton ringers.

- Three peals for a dead person: one for passing; one for entry to the church; one for the procession to the grave. A child or poor person was to have no more than three bells; for others, four bells; and for a gentleman or yeoman or honest householder, five bells
- No peals of pleasure were to be used except at the request of a worshipful man or gentleman of the parish
- So many peals of bells to be rung for a Member of Parliament as is customary
- On Queen's Day and all triumphs of joy for Her Majesty, Elizabeth I, or good success of the realm and commonwealth, all the said bells to be rung and for the entertainment of the nobility as is usual.
- Before every sermon the great bell is to be rung and also for any person in extremity of sickness
- If the clerk and church wardens permit bells to be rung otherwise than is set down, then they shall be fined twelve pence every time. It was later agreed that peals of pleasure could be rung one night in the week during winter from eight to ten p.m.

Though the practice at Broughton is unknown, Dearmer's *The Parson's Handbook*, makes the following comment on tolling:

The old usage at the time of death, known as the Passing Bell, was to toll a certain number of strokes, with Tellers at the beginning and end, usually three times three for a male, three times two for a woman. Some parishes use three single strokes in the case of a child, others distinguish children or infants by the use of one of the smaller bells in place of the tenor, which is ordinarily used. It is comparatively rare to denote the age by the number of strokes tolled.

The three old bells were recast in 1884 by *Mears and Stainbank* of Whitechapel, London and three smaller bells added, the funding having come from public subscription and *a generous donation by Daniel Arkwright Esq. of Preston*, who contributed £340. A subscription notebook was kept by the Churchwardens, which indicates that forty-four other people made donations of various amounts, ranging from 2s 6d to £25, giving a total of £179 9s 0d.

The six bells of this 'new' peal varied in diameter from 72 cm to 99 cm, and weighed a total of 2031 kilograms: the Tenor bell being the heaviest at 506 kg and the treble being the lightest at 239 kg. The old bells had been considerably lighter, totalling a mere 1260 kg.

In his book *Country Chapels*, Hewitson, writing in 1870, commented:

The tower contains three bells, somewhat unmelodious in tone, but pretty strong in noise. They do a great stroke of business and when the ringers get enthusiastic, the old pile fairly shakes again. The ringers had a fit of enthusiasm when John Rawcliffe of Prospect House, Broughton, was made Mayor of Preston in 1869. In celebrating that event, they nearly tore the bells out of the steeple, broke one of the clappers and drove on for a while most gleefully, 'two in hand'. To one of the ringers whom we met the other day, we said, 'You were doing it stiff when that bell broke', and he rejoined fervidly, 'Aye, we did rive it on that occogen (occasion).'

Perhaps the *unmelodious* tone had more to do with the style of the ringers than the quality of the bells. Certainly Broughton bell-ringers have, in the past, been a somewhat unruly and occasionally inebriated lot. On Guy Fawkes Day 1823 for example the ringers consumed twenty pints of home-brewed beer and devoured twelve dinners at a cost of 2s 3d per head. We have a hint of what such excesses might lead to in the Select Vestry Minutes for Preston Parish Church. Fifty years earlier in 1770 all the ringers there were discharged on account *of their irregular ringing, disobedience and insolent behaviour to the late mayor and present churchwardens.* The latter were then charged with the task of appointing *eight sober, well-behaved men, qualified men, to ring.*

While there is no suggestion that matters reached such a crisis at Broughton, probably in response to their boisterous behaviour, *rules* for the ringers of Broughton Church were drawn up. They were discovered by Mr Jolleys and printed in the January 1952 edition of the parish magazine, *Broughton Outlook*. The rules themselves are undated but the language and writing style, as well as the exclusively male orientation, suggest they were originally devised as early as the C18th and have influenced the conduct of many generations of ringers.

❖ *That all ringers of this Tower are to be a respectful body of men, and to give no occasion by their conduct for any person to speak evil against us, and not to bring disgrace on the Church to which we are connected by our office. Neither do we desire to take into our company any persons who are of low life and character, idle, drunken, or Sabbath breaker, for we acknowledge that the belfry is part of the Church, and that the ringers, being officers of the Church, should bear a good character.*

❖ *That all ringers should be in the Belfry before the clock strikes (the appointed time for the bell to commence to ring) either at divine service, or at any practice, or at any special occasion. Should he break this rule to be fined (one penny). And if not there in the Tower by ten minutes past the appointed time to start, he pays the fine of two pence, and if he misses the whole of the service, he pays the fine of four pence for every offence this rule is broken.*

A 1942 photograph of the lady bell ringers. From left to right: Kath Clarkson, Edna Hardman, Eunice Hardman, John Jolleys, Canon C.M.S. Clarke, Ted Woodburn, Margaret Catterall, Gabriel Singleton, Alice Hargreaves, Florrie Birchall

THE JOLLEYS FAMILY

Perhaps the one man however who epitomises the diligence and dedication of Broughton bell-ringers is Mr John Jolleys. Mr Jolleys, an ingenious handyman, was Captain of the bell-ringers at Broughton Church for many years. His obituary in the parish magazine of 1967 shows just how important he had become to the life of the parish, and how much he was admired and respected.

The churchyard will not be the same again. There are some who remember a time before Mr Jolleys lived at Church Cottages but to those of us who have come in recent years he seemed to have been there always. Calm and happy he went about his work, rarely far from home though his knowledge of the roads and the houses and the people ran wide through the district. He cared for the bells, spiced the ropes, adjusted them for the short and the tall, led and taught generations of ringers and, Sunday after Sunday, pulled rhythmically at the tenor.

His fellow ringers came in strength to the funeral, forty of them. Afterwards a team rang a quarter peal. We shall miss the man who lived by the church, whom we met often and never without a quiet, friendly word, some offer of help, some practical advice or pointed comment on the weather and the country

153

scene, a good man to meet on one's first visit to Broughton Church, and a good man to go on meeting, a good invincible character.

Mr and Mrs Jolleys are pictured here sometime during the late 1950s. They moved into the rented Church Cottage (pictured below) when they married, at a rent of three shillings per week. This was later doubled to six shillings when an inside flushing toilet was added to the property. The rent remained at that modest sum until the mid - 1980s when Mrs Jolleys died. They and their family of three children lived there for over fifty years.

The photograph reproduced on the previous page, was first published in the *Guardian*, marking the occasion when the boys' team, under the Captaincy of Mr Jolleys (pictured centre), rang for the first time in the late 1930s

A GHOSTLY PRESENCE

Mrs Jolleys was the last person to live at Church Cottages and according to her the building was haunted. She claimed that there was a spirit, which would knock at the door before passing through it, an occurrence which caused the dog's hair to stand on end. At a time when the front door of the cottage was sheltered by a porchway, her son vividly recalls hearing a knocking on the inside door of the house one night. He went out to see who it was, only to find that not only was there no-one there but that the porch door was firmly locked so that no-one could possibly have reached the inner door knocker!

This ghost could well be that of Edward Bamber, who was born at *The Moor* in Poulton-le-Fylde. He was the son of Richard Bamber, a staunch Catholic and rich landowner, and was smuggled to the continent by his father before training as a Roman Catholic priest at Valladolid in Spain in 1625. Following his ordination on the 6th June 1628 at the Abbey of Santa Maria in Cadiz, and after a severe illness from which he recuperated at Douai in Flanders, he returned to England. On landing at Dover, his first action was to kneel and thank God for a safe voyage. The Governor of Dover Castle noticed this gesture and at once suspected that this kneeling man was a priest. Bamber was immediately arrested but despite close questioning at Dover Castle, he insisted that he had not been on English soil long enough for the relevant statute to be enforceable. Even though he was banished, by 1631 he was back in England and working in Lancashire, perhaps under the assumed name of Reding or Reading and became chaplain at Standish Hall the following year.

As a catholic priest practising in England, his very presence was treason and he was duly arrested at Standish and brought north under escort to Lancaster Castle. En route, his captors are thought to have lodged at Church Inn (Church Cottages) and to ensure he did not escape, secured him in an upper room and took away all his clothing except his nightshirt. While his captors lay drunk however, Bamber, sparsely dressed as he was, made his escape.

Meanwhile in a room at Broughton Tower, a mile or so away from the inn, Edward Singleton, then head of the Singleton family, was enduring a nightmare in which he encountered a bedraggled figure in a field near the Tower. So powerful was this dream, that Singleton felt he must investigate and, despite the late hour, he wandered into the fields he had recognised in that dream and duly met with the fugitive Bamber, whom he took back to Broughton Tower.

Eventually Bamber was recaptured, arrested for a third time and taken to Lancaster, where, on the 7th August 1646 after three years imprisonment and now aged 46, he was hanged and 'drawn' or disembowelled, along with two other priests, John Woodcock of Clayton-le-Woods and Thomas Whitaker of Burnley. His spirit's unrest may well be due to the fact that his stoic and evangelical conduct immediately before his execution so enraged his captors, that the executioner was told to make his death even more cruel and painful than usual. He was therefore hanged only for a short time before being butchered while still alive.

Edward Bamber, acknowledged as one of the Forty English Martyrs, was beatified, becoming Blessed Edward Bamber, by Pope John Paul II in November 1987. It may well be the restless spirit of this determined man, which haunted, or perhaps still haunts, Church Cottage.

MODERN BELLS

The bells were recast again in 1905, when the new chancel was added and the west gallery demolished. Prior to this the bells had been rung from the gallery floor; now obviously the ringers took their enthusiasm to the floor of the tower itself. The three new bells bear the names of W. Bretherton, Vicar; J. Waddington, Warden; and W. Hoole, Warden.

In February 1930, following an inspection, the bells were found to be unsafe and in need of a complete overhaul. The bells would need to be rehung and the bell fittings replaced. A Bell Repair fund was created in April that year, and by May all the money needed, something in excess of £135, had been raised. The surplus money was used to place guards around the clock weight, which had recently fallen twice!

During the years of World War II, many of the ringers were called up for service but they were assured: *that even though the sound of their bells may be temporarily silenced, we will still assemble and will not forget them where'er they may be, on land or on the sea.*

Following a successful Appeal Fund launched in October 1982, the bells and fittings were removed after Christmas, in December that year and retuned by John Taylor's Bell Foundry in Loughborough. The firm also provided new, modern headstocks. The bells were re-hung and rededicated on Sunday 5th June, 1983. Much of the initial manual work involved in removing the bells, was undertaken by the ringers and parishioners in order to keep costs down, though it still amounted to some £8,000.

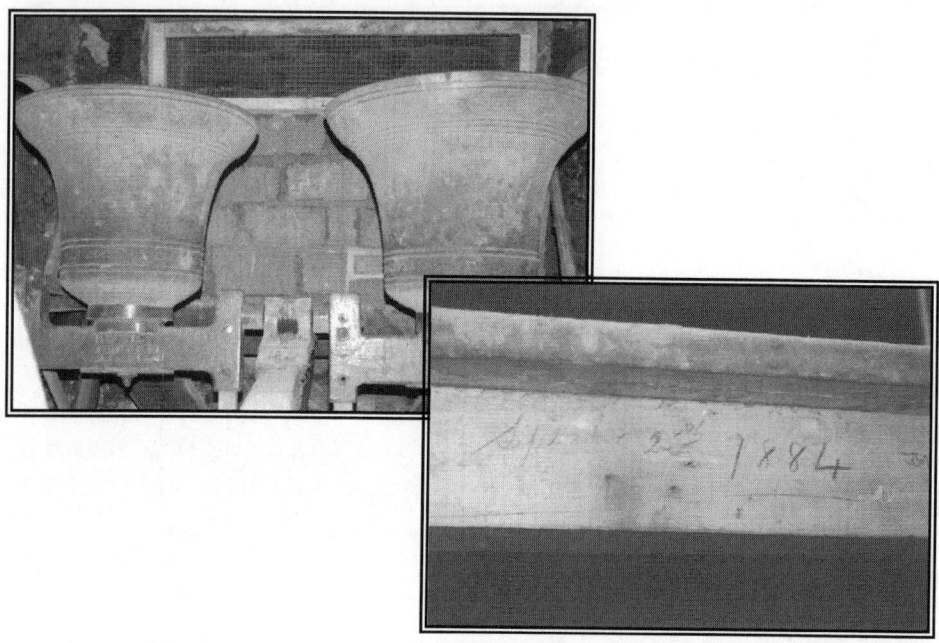

Incidentally other notable peals include one on the 19th February 1910: 5,040 changes in three hours, and one on the 3rd January 1932: 5,040 Minor changes in two hours forty-two minutes. The latter was rung by members of the Lancashire Association of Change Ringers. This was the first peal on the bells after they had been rehung on ball-bearings. Mr Jolleys claimed that there was a time when all six ringers were blacksmiths, of whom one, Bill Smith, was the Captain.

CHAPTER 14

THE CHURCH EXTERIOR

An anti-clockwise circuit of the building from the new porch reveals many interesting features of the church's history.

THE THRELFALL MEMORIALS

Where the west wall of the nave meets the north wall of the tower, the memorials lie within a small garden separated from the path by gated black metal railings. The two memorials commemorate members of the Threlfall family.

Richard, the second son of James Threlfall, married Elizabeth Parkinson, and in 1720 purchased the northern half of the Bank Hall property. The family of farmers and tanners remained in the property throughout the 18th century. The Richard Threlfall commemorated in the memorial, the son of another

James, was born there in 1799 and baptised at Broughton Church on the 27th October the same year.

He married Margaret, his first wife, on the 13th February 1823. Sadly she died, aged only 33, on the 18th November 1834. The memorial records her death and those of several of their children: Harriet, Elizabeth, Margaret, Alice and James Humphreys, all of whom died between 1834 and 1852. Richard himself died on the 19th October 1874, aged 75, having built up a very successful business and having found the time to father eleven children, five of whom sadly predeceased him.

In 1841, Richard, as a forty-one year-old widower, was living in the select and fashionable Ribblesdale Place, in a house sitting in a fine elevated position on the escarpment overlooking the riparian meadows that would, in the 1860s, become Avenham Park. Five of his surviving children shared the home: Alice, aged 17; Margaret, aged 15; James aged 11; nine year-old Amelia and Richard aged 7. Richard senior was described as a cotton spinner.

In September 1848, he was remarried in Lancaster to Dorothy Gardner, twenty-one years his junior. Three years later, they were living on Moor Park Avenue. James, Amelia and Richard remained in the family home, while two younger children had been born to Richard and Dorothy. John was aged one and his sister Frances, just 6 months. At some point Richard's father, James, had abandoned agriculture and tanning in favour of cotton. In 1857 he set up a spinning factory, Shelley Road Mills, and Richard joined the family business.

By 1861 the family had returned to the idyllic setting of Ribblesdale Place where they would remain for the next twenty years.

In the Census of 1871, Richard, aged 71, was described as a cotton manufacturer employing 200 people. His son, Richard junior, aged 38, was also involved in the family business. Four children from his second marriage remained in the family home: John; Frances Elizabeth; Charles, a solicitor's clerk, aged 18, and Louisa aged 16.

All the family's success was however to disappear almost overnight following a fire at the mill on October 16th 1874. The report in the Preston Herald the following day reads:

About half-past six o'clock yesterday morning a fire broke out among the cotton in the mixing-room of the Shelley Road Mill in the occupation of Messrs Threlfall & Co., cotton spinners and manufacturers. The mill is one of very large dimensions, 13 windows long and 5 storeys high, and when the fire was reported the greatest alarm prevailed among the residents in the district. Fortunately however the portion of the building in which the mixing-room was situated was fireproof and there was no cause for immediate alarm. Immediately the fire was reported, a number of the workmen obtained buckets and with a plentiful supply of water at their disposal, they set to work vigorously to quench the burning cotton and to remove that portion that had not caught fire.

Though a large quantity of cotton was destroyed or damaged by water, the building itself remained almost untouched. There was no loss of life – apparently the only person in any kind of danger was a William Bateson, who was in the store-room above the seat of the fire but who *was rescued by means of an improvised fire-escape, consisting of two long ladders fastened together.*

The fire was apparently the result of the spontaneous combustion of the cotton but only caused damage, described as *relatively trifling* and which was in any case covered by insurance. The real damage occurred at a much more human level. The shock of the fire and an acute awareness of what the consequences might have been, had a tragic personal impact: three days later Richard himself was dead.

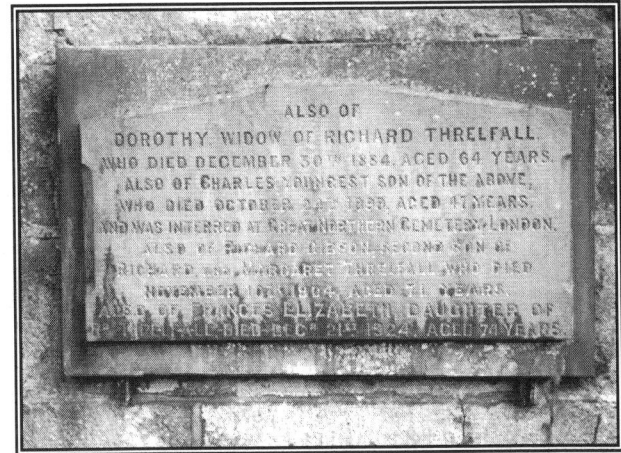

The second, smaller memorial commemorates the deaths of Richard's second wife Dorothy in 1884, aged 64; Charles, Richard and Dorothy's youngest son, in 1899, aged 47; Richard junior in 1904, aged 71, and Frances Elizabeth in 1924, aged 74, children from Richard's first marriage.

THE TOWER

Perhaps the most striking architectural feature of the church exterior is its sixteenth century tower.

Built of millstone grit, allegedly quarried in Longridge, the tower is constructed in the perpendicular style, with diagonal buttresses in seven stages. Internally it measures some 13 feet 3 inches square.

On the string course below the parapet on the south side, a four-leaved flower, the date 1533 and the initials R.T., probably those of the builder, can be seen.

There is a projecting vice in the south-east corner and the string course bears the letters B.G. There are belfry windows at the top of the tower, each of which has three lights under a pointed head without tracery.

The window above the west door was at one time partly built up but was restored in 1905, to enhance the imposing entrance. It has three lights and a traceried head.

On the north-west buttress are the initials T.B. along with the Barton escutcheon of three boars' heads on a shield, while on the south-west buttress are carved the arms of the Singleton and Barton families. The top of the tower has an embattled parapet added in 1733.

Atticus, writing in 1872, described the tower as:

Heavy, slightly out of perpendicular, smooth, clockless and rigid…there are at the corners of the tower vestiges of old armorial bearings – rudely carved specimens of heraldry, nearly worn out and undecipherable. Many odd iron arrangements are there in the front of the tower; seven curved bits of iron, like the letter S out of balance, are fastened up on the western side, whilst on the eastern side there are two or three similar articles. They are not intended as decorative ornaments but as strengtheners of the tower, yet the old pile is strong enough without them. In front and at the base of the tower is an old doorway; but it has been partially walled up, and surmounted in the archway by a window. Directly above it there is a window of similar proportions. At the western end there are the Royal Arms – full in size, the lion having a very savage look, and put up when George the Third was King.

These arms must have been located inside the church over the walled up west door and would have been removed when access to the tower was restored in 1905.

The tower is described as *clockless* because the clock, built by J.W. Benson of Ludgate Hill, London, was not installed until 1884. It cost some £80 and has a 54 inch copper dial. This clock is probably the second one housed in the tower: in 1773, the Select Vestry informed the vicar that a clock was needed and one was ordered from a Mr Warburton of Chorley. Clearly this original clock, if ever actually installed, had fallen into disrepair and been removed by 1872 when Atticus wrote his description.

The original flagpole, replaced in the 2010 restoration, was donated by Mr Rawcliffe in 1856.

THE SOUTH DOORWAY

Now reduced to an occasional emergency exit, the south doorway was originally the principal church entrance, as the diagram of the pre-1823 building on page 11 illustrates. It was protected by the church porch, an important parish meeting and information point. A church porch is a singular space, neither wholly inside nor outside, and without being too fanciful, a point of transition between the secular and spiritual worlds.

Nowadays often merely the repository of lost umbrellas and the home of the parish billboard, in the past, this south entrance was an essential element of church ritual, in baptisms for example. These porches were also working areas of the church. Until not so very long ago, churches were not only the hub of the community but they were often the only formal public building in the area and as such hosted and carried out many of the functions of today's local Council. Public notices would have been displayed and matters of business would have been conducted there:

executors of wills made payments of legacies, and coroners sometimes held their courts in the porch.

THE CHOIR VESTRY

The Choir Vestry was built in 1976, largely through the efforts of Denis and Roger Houghton, the sons of Major Houghton, about whom much has already been written. They secured funding for the building from the Tyson Trust, inaugurated by Mr John James Tyson, a bachelor and bank official, who lived on Garstang Road. When he died in 1935, he left his estate for charitable purposes carried out within a five miles radius of Preston.

In order to accommodate the new building, forty-five graves had to be excavated, the gravestones being used to pave the new terrace outside the vestry. The extension's architect was Kevin Fletcher and the vestry was dedicated on the 12th November 1976, by the former Bishop of Lancaster, Rt Rev.A.E.L. Hoskyns-Abrahall

Outside the vestry, as can be seen in the photograph opposite, is an ornamental sundial. It stands on the base of an old Calvary cross and was erected in 1818. Interestingly, for planning purposes, it is regarded as a *listed building*.

The cross base was initialled *J.B. 1550* and used to display commemorative plaques bearing the inscriptions:

SACRED TO THE MEMORY OF REV. HUGH HODGSON, MINISTER OF THIS CHURCH, WHO DEPARTED THIS LIFE MAY 4ᵀᴴ, 1817 IN HIS 76ᵀᴴ YEAR, MUCH RESPECTED.

163

ALSO MARY HODGSON, HIS NIECE, WHO DIED FEBRUARY 28TH, 1816, AGED 44 YEARS. ALSO ANN HODGSON, WHO DEPARTED THIS LIFE THE 26TH DAY OF MARCH, 1829, AGED 88 YEARS.

and

HERE LIE THE REMAINS OF THE REV. GEORGE CHARNLEY, LATE MINISTER OF THIS CHURCH, WHO DIED DECEMBER 15TH, 1809, AGED 58 YEARS. ALSO ALICE, RELICT OF THE ABOVE, WHO DEPARTED THIS LIFE ON THE 17TH MARCH, 1839, AGED 84 YEARS. IN MEMORY OF GEORGE, SON OF WILLIAM AND ANN CHARNLEY, DESCENDANT OF THE ABOVE, WHO DEPARTED THIS LIFE ON THE 19TH APRIL, 1832 AGED 15 YEARS. ALSO SARAH, SISTER OF ABOVE, WHO DIED SEPTEMBER 23RD, 1832, AGED 26 YEARS. ALSO DOROTHY, HER SISTER WHO DIED THE 29TH JANUARY, 1839 AGED 21 YEARS. ALSO ANN CHARNLEY, WHO DIED APRIL 15TH, 1862 AGED 78 YEARS.

The bench, which can also be found outside the choir vestry, was the gift of Mrs Kennedy in memory of her husband Bert Kennedy, who died in 1963 and who had been a member of the Choir for some thirty years.

Pictured below are some of the carved stones of the pre-1826 church, which were rescued when it was rebuilt. They were then embedded into the south wall of the new building and can be seen above roof of the choir vestry.

The top photograph shows centrally, the christogram **IHS**, representing the word **Jesus** and based on the first three letters of the name in Greek, ΙΗΣΟΥΣ.

To the right are the initials RS and the Singleton coat-of-arms.

In the lower photograph is a clawed foot and ivy leaf.

CHAPTER 15

THE CHURCHYARD

Superficially there is nothing at all remarkable about Broughton churchyard, surrounding the church as it does on all four sides, running down to Blundel Brook in the south and to the A6 to the west. This western area was the most recent to be opened, and the northern part of it, the Garden of Remembrance alongside Church Lane, was dedicated on the 28th September 1969.

Every grave is special, even sacred, to the family whose members are interred there. Two things however make Broughton graveyard especially interesting to anyone who might simply stroll there and enjoy its tranquillity: the stories revealed by some of the graves and memorials found there, and perhaps even more intriguingly, the graves that are no longer there!

Extant Broughton parish burial records go back to the middle of the C17th, the first volume covering the thirty-seven years between 1653 and 1690. Some of the interments of that period reveal much about the population and social climate of the times. For example, during that time there were seventy-four infant mortalities, including six bastard children and nine who were stillborn. Other burials included:

John Osbaldeston – *a traveller* – **24.6.1668**

A wandering beggar's child – **9.2.1678**

Grace Singleton – *a wandring beggar* – **6.3.1678**

A poore beggar man – **12.12.1678**

Ould Allins – *a traveller* – **29.10.1669**

Robert Willasie – *a wandring poor boy* – **9.8.1684**

Robert Tomson – *a poor child* – **30.6.1690**

Perhaps one of the most noticeable graves in the churchyard is that of one Lachlan Black, lying as it does immediately to the left of the pathway leading from the church gates to the west doorway in the base of the tower. The position and size of the memorial would lead one to believe that it marked the grave of a prominent Broughton parishioner. In fact Lachlan Black, as his name might suggest, was a native of Scotland and a humble gardener and nurseryman.

He was born in Kilninian and KIlmore, Argyll in 1833, the son of Neil and Janet Black, and made his way south sometime between 1861 and 1868, when he married Margaret Marsden, the daughter of a Goosnargh farmer, at Broughton Church on the 1st of January.

Early in their married life the couple lived in Farrington, where their first child John was born in 1871. Later they moved to Fulwood and made their home at 27 Watling Street Road. Two further children completed the family: Elizabeth born in 1874 and Mary born in 1877. In 1911 all three children remained in the family home. John, aged 40, worked as a solicitor's clerk and Elizabeth, aged 37, as a dressmaker. The Census does not record Mary's occupation but it seems likely that she played a domestic role, caring for her parents, both in their seventies.

Lachlan Black, as his grave reveals, died on the 31st December 1911, aged 78, and his wife eight years later on the 19th March 1919, aged 84. The base of the memorial records the death of their daughter Elizabeth, who never married, on the 9th February, 1950, aged 76.

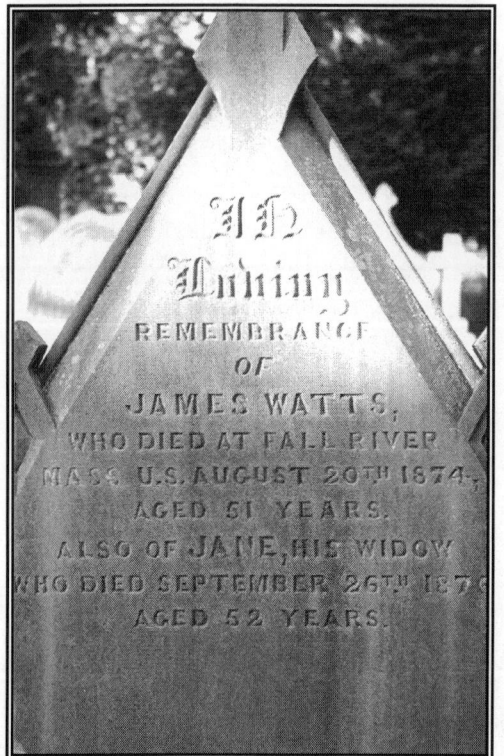

In
Loving
REMEMBRANCE
OF
JAMES WATTS,
WHO DIED AT FALL RIVER
MASS U.S. AUGUST 20TH 1874,
AGED 51 YEARS.
ALSO OF JANE, HIS WIDOW
WHO DIED SEPTEMBER 26TH 1876
AGED 52 YEARS.

This intriguing gravestone, facing the choir vestry, lies near to the south doorway. James Watts, the son of James and Mary Watts, aged 29, married Jane Thompson at St John's, Preston on the 23rd October 1852. In 1869 he was recorded as the landlord of the *Hesketh Arms* on Lancaster Road in Preston

At some point after that the couple emigrated to the United States. James, a spinner by trade, clearly attracted by the new life and opportunities offered by the rapidly developing textile industry in Fall River, Massachusetts, joined the thousands of people drawn to its cotton mills. .

Fall River, some 53 miles south of Boston, on the eastern shore of Mount Hope Bay at the mouth of the Taunton River, became the leading textile manufacturing centre in the USA during the C19th. Between 1871 and 1872 for example, the years of the city's most dramatic expansion, its population grew by some twenty thousand and twenty-two new mills were built.

The immigrant couple lived on Daughty Street in the city but sadly neither James nor his wife was destined to enjoy their new life for very long. James died of cholera on the 20th August 1874. The disease spread rapidly through the hastily erected, wooden, three-storey, multi-family tenements built to house all the new workers. His death record is illustrated on the following page and gives a vivid picture of the crowded and insanitary living conditions, which resulted in so many deaths, not only from cholera but also from those other nineteenth century killers, consumption and dysentery. Interestingly he was certainly 51 not 41 years old when he died. This may of course have been a simple clerical error or perhaps James lied about his age in order to ensure his application to enter the USA was approved at a time when immigration restrictions were becoming more stringent.

167

The death register at the top of the page is handwritten and largely illegible; it records "DEATHS REGISTERED IN THE City of [...] for the Year eighteen hundred and seventy-[...]"

A LONG WAY FROM HOME

A number of memorial stones, designed and funded by the then Imperial War Graves Commission, honouring individuals who died in both World Wars, can be found in the churchyard. One of the most enigmatic and poignant is that pictured opposite, which records the death of Second Lieutenant William Dering Stainbank of the Royal Field Artillery, on the 8th April 1916, aged 24. His death was registered in Preston, where he died only thirty-six hours after contracting cerebro-spinal meningitis during his training, and he was interred in Broughton churchyard.

At its base it further records the death, a year later, of his younger brother, Second Lieutenant Arthur Reeve Stainbank, also of the Royal Field Artillery and also aged 24. He was killed in action at Passchendaele on the 20th July 1917. His grave is unknown but his name is recorded on the Menin Gate memorial at Ypres.

A simple white stone in a country churchyard can only offer a small if poignant intimation of the family's anguish at the tragic loss of two sons. However what makes this memorial particularly interesting is the fact that both brothers were born in, and prior to the war, lived in South Africa. After service in German West Africa and perhaps in response to the Durban Recruitment Committee's exhortations, both brothers had arrived in London aboard the *Llandovery Castle* on the 19th December 1915, as the Passenger List illustrated below indicates. In William's war record his mother's address, as next of kin, (his father had died in 1907) is given as: Coedmore, Bellair, Natal. Indeed his first military service was as a private in the *Natal Mounted Rifles.*

Almost sixty years earlier in 1857, their father, Dering Lee Warner Stainbank, aged 16, had made the reverse journey from Surrey to Natal to begin work as a coffee planter. He sailed from Gravesend on the 21st April 1857, aboard the *Lady of the Lake,* a ship owned by his father and grandfather. He completed the three month voyage on the 24th July as he sailed into Durban Bay to be met by his brother, who had been in the colony for some two years.

After his marriage to Ethel Lyne, a native South African, he took over the isolated farm at Coedmore. The couple had five children: the two eldest as we have seen perished in the Great War.

Their younger sister, Mary Agnes Stainbank, (1899-1996) became a well-known South African sculptress, embodying in her work *the Spirit of Africa.* She studied in Durban but also at the Royal College of Art in London, where among her fellow students were Barbara Hepworth and Henry Moore. Their younger brothers Christopher (1897-1978) and Kenneth also remained in South Africa to run the family estate at Coedmore Castle, now an exclusive hotel and Nature Reserve.

How then did a memorial stone to two native South African soldiers come to be erected in Broughton churchyard, six thousand miles from their home? Although there appears to be no family connection with the Church, it seems highly likely that as members of the Royal Field Artillery, the brothers were stationed at Fulwood Barracks before being posted overseas, and during that time worshipped not at the barrack's chapel but at Broughton Church, where the congregation welcomed two young men so far from home. Indeed so warmly welcomed were these two young men and so strong the affection they felt for the Church and its congregation, that their mother, who visited England in 1920, decided it would be appropriate and meaningful if their respective grave and memorial stone was placed in its churchyard. The current stone replaces the one commissioned by the family at the time. However it may be that the Army itself selected William's burial place and Broughton was the nearest Anglican graveyard.

A LIFE CUT SHORT AND A LIFE FULFILLED

An identical memorial stone near to the pathway leading to the church's south door, commemorates the death in action of Anthony Chambre Dickson. Captain Dickson, of the 88th Field Regiment of the Royal Artillery, lost his life at the Battle of Gurun in Malaya on the 15th December, 1941, eight days after the Japanese attack on Pearl Harbour. Aged only twenty-five, he was interred at Taiping War Cemetery.

His younger brother, Edward Chambre Dickson, who remains a Broughton parishioner, was to survive the war and live a full and fascinating life.

Known to all as Teddy, he was born on July 29th 1918 in Lytham, the second son of a family of four boys and one girl. His father, a chartered surveyor, worked in a Manchester-based firm.

His early childhood was spent playing on the Green and the beach, watching the ships moves along the Ribble Estuary. His education was undertaken initially by a governess, until at the age of eight, he went as a boarder to Bigshotte School in Berkshire. Two years later the family moved from Lytham to Broughton House (now the Marriott Hotel) and so began his link with Broughton Church.

In 1932, at the age of 13, his education continued at Marlborough College in Wiltshire, where he remained for the next five years, before taking up a place at St John's College, Cambridge to read Law. After only a year however, he came down to be articled to his uncle's firm of *Buck and Dicksons* in Winckley Street, Preston, offices which the firm occupied for over a 150 years.

Just before the outbreak of World War II, Teddy joined the Territorial Army, the 88th Field Regiment Royal Artillery, the Preston Gunners. At the outbreak of war he was commissioned and in September 1939, found himself en route to France as a member of the British Expeditionary Force. Some eight months later he was among the thousands of men being driven back to the Channel to be evacuated from Dunkirk in Operation Dynamo.

Fifteen months later the Regiment saw action again, this time in Malaya. By February 1942 the Japanese had forced the surrender of the Allied Armies in Singapore and Teddy became a prisoner of war. His captivity began in Singapore but continued in several camps along the infamous Siam-Burma Railway. Many died but Teddy viewed the experience a positive one, one which brought out the very best in the men who were his comrades. In a Parish Magazine article in 1989, he says:

It was a great experience. I learned to live with men. We learned to love and trust each other. It was a great revelation to me. We tried to help each other all the time. We were glad to be alive and we made sure we said our prayers and stayed in touch with God, and expressed our thanks to Him.

This spirituality and dialogue with God continued when he returned to civilian life and qualified as a solicitor, and has done so throughout his life. He married his first wife, Joyce May Houghton, sister of Roger and Denis, in 1951. They began married life at Fairholme, before moving to Townley Lodge in Goosnargh, which incidentally was to become the venue for Choir Sports for many years. Sadly his wife, Pip, as she was known, died suddenly while the family was on holiday in France in 1964. Once again his faith was tested and once again it prevailed: his communion with God brought him through the dark, traumatic days of loss and grief. In 1965 he was remarried to his second wife Isabella Healey.

Teddy sang bass in the Church Choir for over thirty years; served on the PCC for many years and has acted as a Parish Patron during the selection of four vicars – John Adam, Gerald Armstrong, Stanley Finch and David Jenkins. For over thirty years he was a member of Broughton Parish Council, and from 1948 was a member of the Council of the Lancashire Youth Clubs Association. Teddy was instrumental in the purchase of Borwick Hall near Carnforth, as a training and outdoor centre for young people. One of his proudest moments was his selection as High Sheriff of Lancashire in 1986.

His life of commitment and dedication, and his involvement in so many aspects of local life, have for some eighty years been founded on his spiritual life and worship at St John's Church.

171

Of all the sad stories hidden beneath the churchyard gravestones, none can be more poignant than that of Mary Ann Yates, whose gravestone had vanished by the 1980s. The only daughter of James Yates, an agricultural labourer, and his wife Ellen, she was baptised at Broughton Church on the 12th April 1863. Eight years later the family was living at Tower Cottage in Broughton, before moving to another cottage on Black Bull Lane.

Later, just after her twelfth birthday, she entered domestic service, employed in the home of Mr Knagg, a schoolteacher, of Grosvenor Terrace. She proved a kind, reliable and hard-working servant and attended the St Peter's Church Bible class, run by Mr Knagg. There, during 1880, she met a young trainee solicitor's clerk, James Brocklebank Proctor, who was employed by Mr John Catterall of Preston. James lived with his parents on Brook Street and was reputedly an eighteen year-old of *sober and regular habits*.

Three years later the couple was contemplating marriage, though it would appear that Mary was much more enthusiastic about this than her boyfriend. Some seven months before her death, Mary Yates left Mr Knagg's employment with the intention of getting married, Mr Knagg tried to dissuade her but she was determined. For whatever reason however, the marriage did not take place and so Mary found another post as domestic servant to a Mr Wilding, of Sunny Bank in Fulwood.

On the evening of Sunday, 27th May 1883, the couple met and walked around the streets of Fulwood. Witnesses later told how the couple seemed to be having some kind of argument but no-one was prepared for what happened shortly after 9 o'clock that evening. As the couple walked along Albert Road in Fulwood, James Proctor produced a revolver and shot Mary Ann before turning the gun on himself. His dead body crumpled into the hedge; Mary Ann lay on the pavement.

She was still alive and as luck would have it, one of the first people on the scene was Dr Charles Moore Jessop the brigade surgeon stationed at Fulwood Barracks, who gave what medical help he could. Using a sheet as a stretcher, Mary was taken to the nearby workhouse hospital on Watling Street Road, where Dr Jessop continued to treat her. Her father was informed and came from his cottage on Black Bull Lane to be at her bedside. Unfortunately she never regained consciousness and died at 1.30 the following morning.

The tragedy was reported in both the *Preston Guardian* and the *Preston Herald* on Wednesday, 30th May, the day of her funeral. The former offered a detailed, factual account of the murder and the subsequent inquest, and was mildly critical of those who showed a morbid interest in the crime:

Large crowds have visited the spot where the tragedy took place and last night particularly, numbers of young people, impelled by a morbid curiosity, lingered about the locality and discussed the details of the murder.

The Herald however reported the events in a somewhat more emotive and sensational style. Mary Yates was it declared: *cut off by the hand of an assassin in the prime of youth and on the border of womanhood.*

Though there was little in their relationship to suggest such a tragic ending, it transpired at the inquest, that Proctor had bought the revolver from a local pawnbroker, Mr Baines, a few months earlier, on the 16th April.

He had taken other girls to the theatre and, despite all his promises, seemed very unwilling to marry Mary. She apparently had had enough of his procrastination and had decided to end their engagement if he did not keep his word. Significantly perhaps, he had never told his parents of their engagement. These facts and the arguments described by witnesses who saw the couple at different times on that Sunday evening, led the inquest jury to verdicts of premeditated murder and suicide.

Proctor was given a Christian burial in Preston Cemetery. An Act of Parliament the previous year had made this possible. However the crowds gathered outside Preston Prison, where they assumed his body had been taken and from where they thought it would be removed at midnight for interment in unhallowed ground, were clearly unaware of the change in the law, and stood there in disappointment.

Albert Road, with Christ Church in the background.

A morbid curiosity brought crowds of visitors and, according to the Preston Herald, they created a deep hole in the ground where the head of the murderer had lain, presumably as they scraped away earth taken as some kind of strange souvenir.

173

The *Preston Herald* of June 2nd, 1883 published a letter from Mr Knagg, Mary's former employer. He described her as: *warm-hearted, strictly honest and faithful.* He added however that she had a stubborn disposition and that despite opposition from her parents and her employer, she persisted in the belief that Proctor had a good salary and prospects.

Even after her death and in typical Victorian style perhaps, Mr Knagg was anxious to maintain Mary's moral reputation – *she was not in an unfortunate condition.*

He was determined too to draw a moral from her murder:

May the unhappy event prove a warning to other girls not to act in opposition to those who have their best interests at heart and thereby misplace their affections.

On the following pages is a copy of the *Preston Herald* article, also published on the 2nd June, describing in more measured tones than it often used, the funeral of Mary Yates.

FUNERAL OF MISS YATES.

The body of Miss Yates was removed from the home of her parents in Black Bull-lane, Broughton, for burial on Tuesday. The house is one of a short row of cottages about a quarter of a mile down the lane, and, like the others, it has a garden in front and a patch of land at the rear, within tall, well kept, and, at this season, beautifully green hedgerows. The spot was, till a few days ago, very seldom frequented, as it is out of the main road, but since the tragic event it has acquired a melancholy interest. A morbid curiosity drew large crowds on Tuesday night to view the house which had been from childhood the abode of the murdered girl, and this interest did not lessen on Wednesday, when it was known when the funeral would take place. An hour or two before the time when it was understood the funeral *cortège* should start people from the surrounding hamlets and villages, and a large number from Preston, found their way to the house, where they were in most cases allowed to view the body. A carriage had brought out a few of the friends of the deceased girl from Preston, and shortly after two o'clock a hearse with two coaches arrived, and took up their position at the gate. The spectators had by this time become very numerous, and in the interval which ensued, before the coffin was borne from the house, they waited in the roadway discussing in low tones the one theme possible there. Intense sympathy was felt for the mother of the poor girl, who, apparently half crazed with grief, threw herself back into a corner of the first carriage and sobbed aloud, and for the silent father, who with more fortitude bore his sorrow. The other two vehicles contained relatives and the most intimate friends of the bereaved family, and another friend attended, according to country custom, in his trap. The mournful procession left the house about three o'clock, *en route* for the churchyard, a distance of considerably over one mile. The main road, the highway to Garstang, was by this time crowded with people, who poured in a continuous stream towards the scene of the interment. The graveyard speedily became alive with moving figures, who clustered thickly on all available spots, waiting the arrival of the funeral party. Others found their way into the church, and there awaited the service. The party having reached the church, the coffin was removed from the hearse and covered with wreaths, placed on a bier, to be borne by the relatives. At the church gates it was met by the vicar of Broughton, the Rev. W. Bretherton, who preceded it into the church, as he advanced up the pathway quoting with solemn accent the hopeful opening words of the office for the burial of the dead, "I am the resurection and the life." Behind the coffin came the mourners, the poor mother in advance, leaning for support on a friend on each side, and amongst the others was Mr. Knagg, of Preston, whose school the girl attended, and with whom she was so long a servant. The coffin was deposited at the bottom of the middle aisle, and the crowd, anxious to see the most of the ceremony, crushed into all parts of the church, and it was some time before the service could be proceeded with. That part of the service to be said within the church ended, the bearers resumed their burthen, and the concluding part of the ceremonial was performed at the graveside. There were many tear-dimmed eyes in the crowd when, above the hum of life and rustle of the green foliage on the trees in which the churchyard is embowered, were heard the words " Ashes to ashes, dust to dust," and the dull sound of the earth rattling on the coffin. The floral offerings which had been on the coffin were laid on the graveside, and were very numerous, consisting principally of wreaths sent by friends. A beautiful wreath was left at the house that morning by Mrs. John Humber, of Oak House, and wreaths had also been sent by Mrs. Wilding, the girl's last employer, and by Mr. Knagg, a former employer. When all had ended the spectators withdrew, and thus terminated the last scene but one in this singularly strange but painfully eventful drama.

On this and the following page are photographs of the graves of several Broughton Vicars, who between them served Broughton parishioners throughout the whole of Queen Victoria's reign: William Dixon (1817-1872); William Bretherton (1872-1885) and Samuel Collinson (1886-1923)

It was common practice in the C17th for the sexton when digging graves, to begin at one end of the churchyard and, over time, continue to the other. Having done so, he would then return to the beginning and start digging new graves. Consequently as these new graves were dug, where old ones already existed, human remains, normally bones, appeared on the surface. As commonly none but the graves of the wealthiest families, were marked, unless by a simple wooden cross, there was little to inhibit this process, except the gruesome unsightliness the process created.

The 1674 Vestry Minute Book for Preston Parish Church contains an interesting comment on the state of the churchyard:

Whereas thers many bones of the dead which lye scattered up and downe in the church and churchyard, which is looked upon as an undecent and uncomely thinge & which 'twere convenient yf they were from time to time gathered and laied together untill, as a full heap or number of them being gathered together, they might be conveniently buried.

While this C17th description of the problem of human remains littering a church and churchyard is somewhat more restrained and far less outraged than would be our reaction today, the solution was typically pragmatic – build a charnel house in which to keep the bones, and when this is filled, rebury them in a communal pit, the sexton being paid an extra penny per funeral for this additional work.

At Broughton, parish records began in October 1653, and over the next forty-seven years, up to the year 1700, there were 1378 burials recorded there. Throughout the following one hundred years there was an average of some 267 burials per decade, giving a total of approximately 2670 for the century. So during the years 1653 to 1800, over four thousand souls were interred in Broughton churchyard. A survey completed in 1982, a year before the churchyard was closed to new burials except for those in existing graves, revealed only one extant grave from the whole of the C17th (dated 1696) and only three from the C18th. Indeed there are very few before 1826, the year the church was rebuilt. While the construction work on the new building may account for the loss of some graves and gravestones, there has to be another explanation for what happened to those four thousand bodies interred before 1800.

One obvious explanation is that, as noted earlier, many graves during that period were not marked with any permanent headstone or plaque. Coupled with this and much more intriguing however, is the fact that, like Preston Parish Church, Broughton had its own charnel house. An extract from the Churchwardens' accounts for 1729, reproduced below, confirms that this was indeed the case and records that the sexton was to be paid additional monies for clearing the *Bone house*.

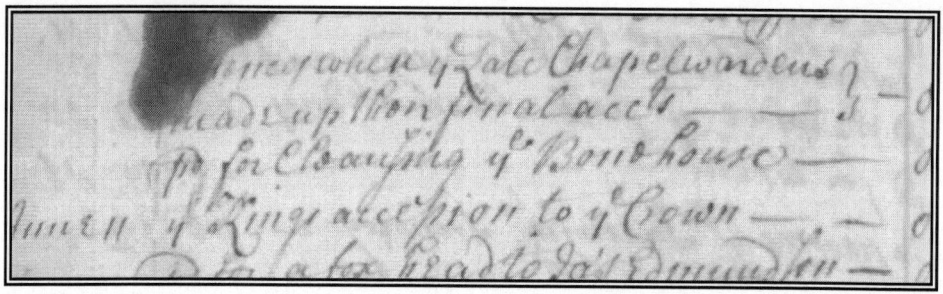

Almost a hundred years later, in 1821, the work of clearing bones remained essential and now needed a week's work, costing 19s 10d.

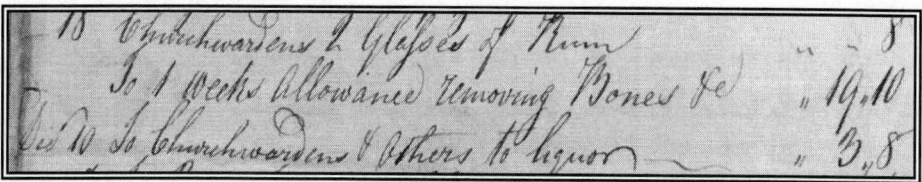

Although exactly where the bone house was located is not known with absolute certainty, it clearly must have been close to the church itself, within the churchyard as it existed in the first decades of the C19th, most probably discretely located in the south eastern corner. Indeed a detailed map of the area, dated 1839, reveals a highly likely location for the ossuary, one which future archaeology may perhaps be able to confirm.

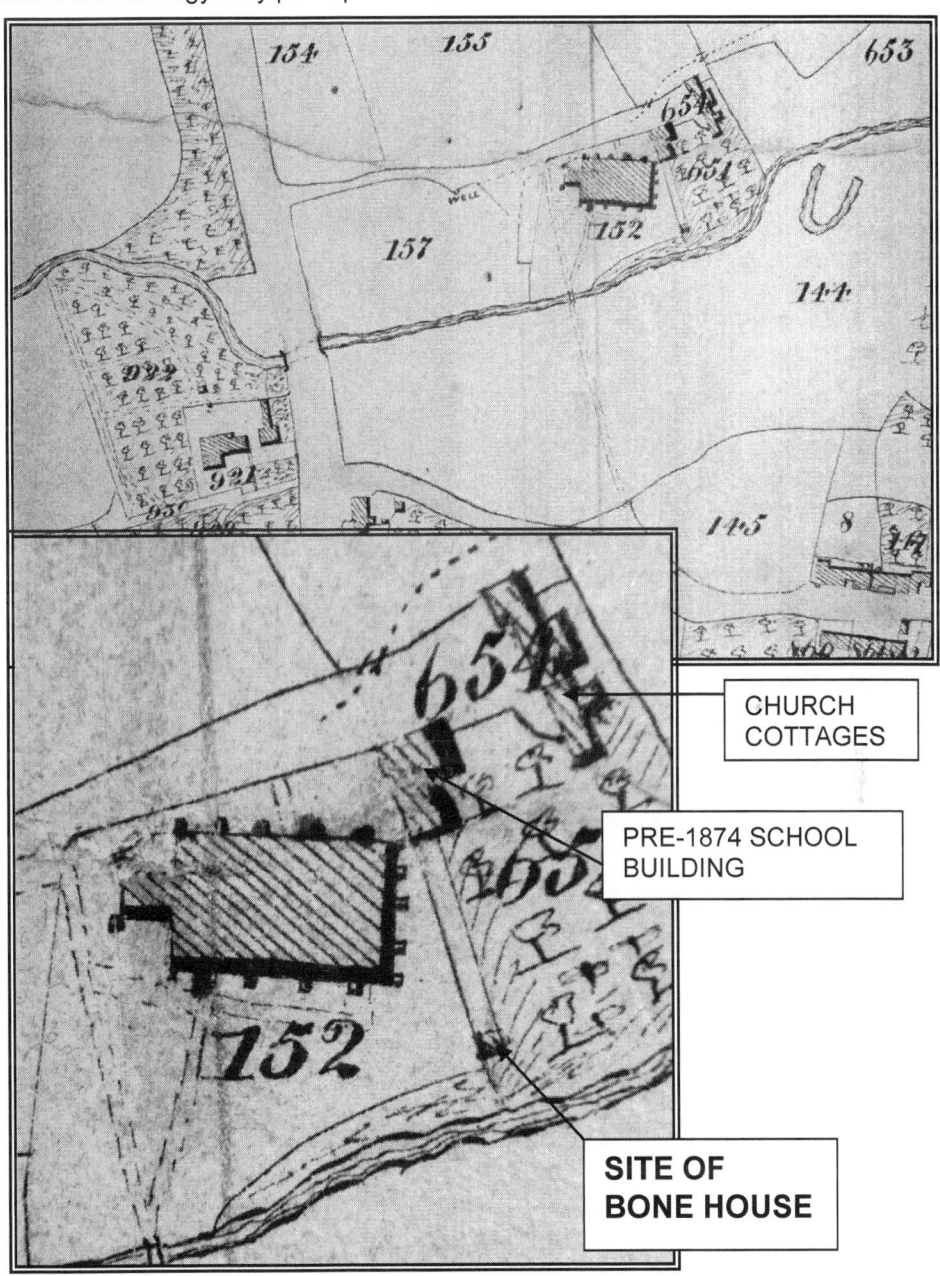

CHURCH COTTAGES

PRE-1874 SCHOOL BUILDING

SITE OF BONE HOUSE

The photograph above of the recently restored charnel or bone house in the corner of the graveyard at St Helen's Church in Cliffe, Kent, gives an excellent impression of the size, shape and design of the one that existed at Broughton Church.

CHAPTER 16

BROUGHTON CHURCH MUSIC

At the time of the Reformation, music and singing were almost exclusively confined to the chapels royal and cathedrals. Only the singing of psalms was a feature of parish churches and even this was felt to smack of Puritanism: the *Directory* of 1645 had declared:

It is the duty of Christians to praise God publicly, by singing of psalms together in the congregation, and also privately in the family.

A love of music was however inherent in the Lancashire character and found an outlet in many services and festivals in every parish church. Feudal lords had in the past set up endowments based on the revenues of land set aside or the purpose, to pay parish musicians. Music figured at rush-bearings and other public festivals, as well as christenings, weddings and funerals, but as early as 1590, clergymen of a Puritan leaning, complained bitterly of brides and bridegrooms entering and leaving church accompanied by *piping*. During the period of the *Commonwealth*, music was silenced in Lancashire churches. Organs were destroyed and any choirs in existence were disbanded.

Following the Restoration in 1660, psalm singing again became part of parish worship though through the somewhat tedious and ponderous method of *lining out*, in which, at a time of general illiteracy, the minister would read out a line and the congregation would then sing it. One musician at the time lamented the discordant effect and the musical mayhem of this process: *it was sad to hear what whining, toting, yelling or screeching there is in many country congregations*. It was however surprisingly popular among church-goers and attempts to change it proved difficult. Then as now perhaps, people preferred the tunes they knew, which at the time, were those published by Sternhold and Hopkins a century earlier, in 1562. At least now though pipes and fiddles could be heard once more at village fairs and gatherings.

A year before the death of Charles II, Warden Stratford of Manchester Collegiate Church, in the face of bitter opposition, re-established the choir, built an organ and restored the old services of Mattins and Evensong.

Only towards the end of the seventeenth century however did thoughts of a modest church choir, singing sacred music, begin to emerge in other churches: *It would be a commendable thing if six, eight or more sober young men that have good voices, would associate and form themselves into a choir. Moreover, a few such in a congregation might in a little time bring into the church better singing than is common, and more variety of good tunes.*

Thomas Webster's painting of 1847, *The Village Choir*, now displayed in the Victoria and Albert Museum, illustrates perfectly the musicians, instruments and singers that formed these early church choirs.

Such choirs required the assistance of singing teachers, who often came from London and toured the country, teaching parish clerks, who in turn led their parish singers. By the middle of the eighteenth century, instruments, such as the bassoon and cello also began to appear in church music, replacing simple pitch pipes. At some time after 1770, village bands began to accompany choirs, standing together in a designated pew or sometimes in a music gallery, such as the one at Broughton, at the west end of the church.

Inevitably choirs grew more ambitious, keen to sing more complex anthems. There was resentment in some congregations as the singers' role in the liturgy grew and the people's psalm singing diminished and eventually disappeared. Not surprisingly, choirs were however extremely popular among those who sang in them, a group Roy Strong describes as: *a motley array of shopkeepers, landowners and domestics taking part in a community activity that came to be seen as the peak of village life.*

By the end of the eighteenth century hymns began to appear in Church of England services. Originating with the Methodists and further inspired by the giants of hymn writing, Charles Wesley and Isaac Watts, their use in church after 1820, led to a deluge of hymnals, especially in the Victorian era. They were seen by ministry and laity alike, as adding a spiritual and emotional depth to what otherwise could become a rather dry liturgy. More especially, like the psalm singing before them, they allowed the congregation once more to participate actively in services.

183

The first specific reference to music and singing at Broughton Church comes in the Churchwardens' accounts for 1823-4, when it was recorded that twenty-three year-old Betty Blacow, christened at Broughton in 1800, was paid 3 shillings, her annual fee, for singing,

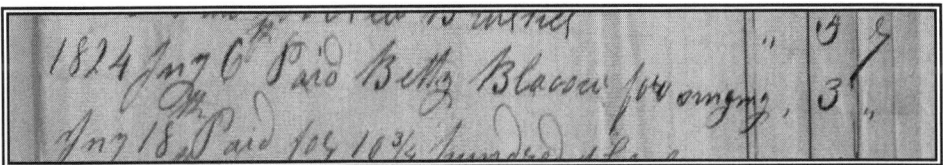

and her father and local Barton farmer, Cuthbert Blacow, was paid 8s 8d for the provision of or more likely, for the repair of musical instruments.

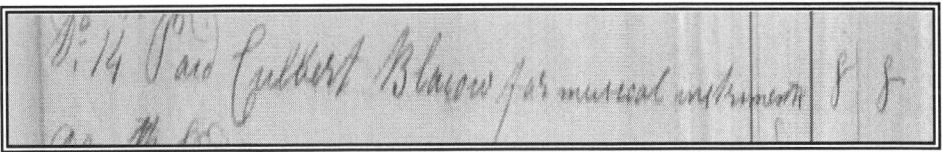

In 1813, the churchwardens' accounts show that Thomas Parkinson was paid two shillings for repairing a fiddle and 8 shillings for repairs to the bass viol.

The earliest known singing master at Broughton was one James Molyneux, who in 1814 published a list of donations made by parishioners to raise money for the purchase of new instruments. These included a violin, a violin cello, bass viol, a clarinet and a bassoon.

In total some £9 12s was collected from thirty-six people. This enabled Mr Molyneux to buy a new clarinet for £2 12s 6d, an additional mouthpiece for 4s 6d and a new bassoon at a cost of six guineas, which, following repairs by Mr Denis Houghton, is still in the church's possession. The list of subscribers, the monies collected and details of expenditure is illustrated overleaf.

'The Bass Viol Lesson' by Caspar Netscher, a seventeenth century oil on canvas now exhibited in the Louvre.

A List of Subscribers to the Musical instruments belonging Broughton Church. 18...

Some other instruments were borrowed: in 1814 one such instrument, a clarinet, had to be repaired at a cost of seven shillings. In 1820 new violin cello strings and a new bow were purchased, costing 4s 6d and 1s 6d respectively.

This small orchestra accompanied the singing in church for many years until an organ was installed in 1826, when the church was rebuilt. *Atticus*, writing in 1872, observed, rather scathingly, that::...*the choir sit in the western gallery. They are spirited but rather weak numerically, are quite musical and show signs of fair precision, but require force. The addition of a few clear-ringing, energetic voices would cure the rheumatic pain sometimes apparent in their melody. An organ, respectably blown and played, assists them; but being thirty-three years old it is getting dull and eccentric.*

It is not known for how long Mr Molyneux remained in post but the next recorded reference to an organist came in 1876, when an annual payment of £8 2s 0d, was recorded as being made to Miss Robinson.

By 1912 there were some twelve village boys in the front rows of the Choir, all dressed in black cassocks and sporting Eton collars and black, clip-on bow ties, a fashion which persisted into the 1930s. Behind them sat a few older men singing lustily and a few ladies (not robed) near the organ, who added their contralto voices. The organ bellows still had to be pumped by hand, the older choirboys taking turns to do this. From time to time, perhaps when exhaustion set in, the pumping faltered and the singing ground to a halt. Occasionally during the sermon, the choirboy operating the bellows might nod off and would need to be hurriedly wakened when the next hymn was announced.

In 1931 the Choir was still a rather modest group, consisting of ten men, eight women and nine boys. Four years earlier. In 1927, Sir Sydney Nicholson had founded the School of English Church Music. He made a visit to Preston in the early 1930s and Broughton was one of the first choirs he heard. Soon after this visit, in April 1934, Broughton Church Choir, under the guidance of organist and choirmaster William Darbyshire Redmayne, became one of the first Lancashire choirs to be affiliated to the S.E.C.M.

Mr Redmayne, *Willie*, as he was affectionately nick-named, came to Broughton from St Paul's Church, Preston to replace Mr Jackson. The choir made rapid progress under his leadership and he engendered a new spirit among the choristers. The number of boys grew from an original twelve to over twenty. At that time the Cathedral Psalter was used in church and had been for many years. The choir and congregation had become accustomed to its long, drawn-out phrases of the Canticles and Psalms, with an emphasis apparently on all the wrong words. Mr Redmayne, working closely with the vicar Reverend Davis, and Sydney Nicholson, sought to change all that, and in the early 1930s the R.S.C.M. Parish Psalter was introduced, the object of which was to present Psalms and Canticles in normal speech rhythms. This meant a natural emphasis on the words, in which the length and accentuation of each note in the chant was governed entirely by the words and not the reverse.

From the 1930s a highlight of the choirboys' year was the annual outing to Blackpool. Even the Vicar was sensitive to the growing excitement. Writing in the parish magazine he explains:

As soon as the month of June comes in a very anxious look comes to the faces of the choirboys. They peer up at me so long and so earnestly in the vestry, both before and after the service, that I begin to think I am improperly robed or something, until I remember that they are waiting for a pronouncement as to the date of their annual Blackpool outing.

The excursion was funded partly by an allowance from the Churchwardens and partly through gifts from parishioners. The adult section of the choir had a choice of destination for their annual outing. A *Choir Sunday*, often held in June, became another annual event, at which parishioners could donate to funds and show their appreciation of the Choir's huge contribution to Church worship.

Mr Redmayne also introduced the robing of the ladies, the 'ruffing' of the boys, and an admission service for new boys. During the 1930s the choir sang for the first time at Chester Cathedral and York Minster.

THE CHOIR IN 1934

No registers exist prior to 1946 so the photograph above is the only record of the choir in the 1930s. The names of individuals are unknown but the ladies include Mrs Charlotte Jolleys, and her sister-in-law, Emily Jolleys, Ethel Hodgson, Miss Yates and Miss Binfield.

Among the men are John Jolleys (bass), Arthur Holden (tenor), Fred Moffatt (bass), Cyril Watson (tenor), Bert Kennedy (bass).

The boys include Tom Smith, Bobby Blackhurst, Ronald Buckley, Tom Burrow, John Law, the Laraway brothers, Sidney Kitchen and Tony Marks

In 1949 and 1950 Mr Redmayne took a party of boys to sing in Westminster Abbey. He was, according to Roger Houghton, writing in a 1951 parish magazine in celebration of Mr Redmayne's 25 years at Broughton:

A hard worker and a patient and tireless one, and he will not hesitate, when he sees the need, to hold extra practices...

THE CHOIR IN 1949

Back row: Miss A.Hesketh, Miss N.M.Hodgson, Miss M.C.Travis, Mrs D.A.S.Houghton, Miss J.M.Houghton, Miss E.T. Nixon, Miss J.Pilkington

Third row: J.R.Crofts, R.Fitch, J.A.Kennedy, R.D.Houghton, A.J.Holden, D.A.S.Houghton, F.Moffatt, J.A.Hodgson, G.H.Smithies, J.Pilkington

Second row: W.D.Coupe, M.S.Whitwell, D.H.Meyler, J.H.Thornton (warden), W.D.Redmayne (choirmaster), Rev. Oatridge (vicar), A.T.R. Houghton (warden), J.N.Rogerson, D.M.Piercy, M.F.Thorn

Front row: J.M.C.Smithies, P.H.Calvert, P.B.Smith, A.J.Shepherd, J.V.C.Parker, J.E.Meyler, W.A.Davidson, D.H.Stanley, W.G.Smithies

His efforts were reflected in the 1951 report of the R.S.C.M. Chief Commissioner, Mr Hubert Crook:

188

A very good choir, and all the principles are very sound indeed. Work like this must be a great asset to the worshippers at Broughton.

Mr Redmayne died in 1955 and was succeeded in January 1956, by Mr Alan Tranah, a young but highly qualified organist, who at the time of his appointment was Music Master at Preston Grammar School. He served at Broughton, at a salary of £80 per annum, for just over a year until March 1957, when he moved to St Silas' Church in Blackburn, his local parish.

THE CHOIR IN 1958

Back row: E.Livingstone, C.Broadbent, J.R.Broadbent, D.M.Piercy, R.Fitch, P.Arnold, W.G.Smithies, M.J.Breakall

Third row: Mrs J.M.Dickson, Miss B.Dawson, P.B. Smith, D.Coupe, F. Matthews, J.A.Kennedy, F.Moffatt, R.D.Houghton, G.H.Smithies, E.C.Dickson, A.Shepherd, D.Pope, Miss A. Hesketh, Mrs T. Wilcock

Second row: W.S.Breakell, W.G.Hudson, D.Chiverton, J.F.Shaw, J.S.Jolleys, J.B.Hargreaves (warden), W.J.Reynolds (warden), Rev. Oatridge (vicar), G.Dawson (organist/choirmaster), C.Broadbent (treasurer), J.M.Ross, D.B.Livingstone, R.E.Critch, P.A.N.Syms, M.C.Hey, W.A.Brown

Front row: P.J.Knowles, J,Shaw, J.C.Marsden, F.D.Taylor, P.J.Cooper, J.P.Dandy, N.W.Cooper, J.M.Law, D.T.Wilkinson, W.I.Clarkson, M.Barnes, M.A.Kennedy

Mr G. Dawson took over as Organist and Choirmaster. For the previous eleven years he had held a similar position at Penwortham Parish Church and was already well-known to many members of the choir, who had taken part in Festivals of Church Music. He made an excellent start as Mr Hubert Crook's Royal School of Church Music report pictured below, indicates:

"A VERY GOOD CHOIR"

On February 26th, Mr. Hubert Crook, Chief Commissioner of the Royal School of Church Music, attended Mattins at Broughton Church, and made the following report on his impressions.

Note: A = "Good"; B = "Moderate"; C = "Poor."

+ or — may be added to these signs.

Tone:

Boys: B+. Clear, steady tone. Quite well produced and effective.

Women: B+. Voices used effectively.

Men: B+. Some good voices here, and they are used very well.

Blend: B. Occasionally a voice "comes through," but in the main it is good blend.

Pitch and chording: B+. Pitch generally very good. Chording generally good; one or two lapses.

Balance: A. Balance was extraordinarily good throughout.

Attack, release and unanimity: B+. Good alert work, this—team-work good.

Diction: B+. Words carry very well, though more finish would help—better contrast in vowels and better consonants. +

Emphasis: B—. A weak spot! You ought to distinguish much more between important and less important words and syllables. You do in conversation, you know!

Responses: A. Very good work. I liked particularly the restraint—they are usually sung far too loudly.

Chanting (Parish Psalter used): B+. Very good work. Well-controlled and with some flexibility. I **don't** like your " Gloria "!

Hymn singing, 92: B—. Started too slowly and got slower still. **You must learn to keep slow, quiet music moving.**

Goss Anthem: B+. Very good work, and, except for some forcing among the trebles, the climax built up well.

Interpretation: Your Creed is much too fast, in my view, and the words become a jumble!

Phrasing: B. Moderate work.

Breath Control: B. Breathing might be better—deeper and less frequent.

Demeanour: A. Excellent.

Special Notes

A **very** good Choir, and all the principles are very sound indeed.

Work like this must be a great asset to the worshippers at Broughton.

Under his guidance a reorganised 'hierarchy' among the twenty-six choirboys, familiar to the choristers of today, began to emerge. Boys were formally appointed *Choristers* and distinguishing ribbons were awarded. The rest were termed *singing boys* or *probationers*, the latter term applying to those boys not formally admitted to the choir. All of this fostered a keen sense of competition among the boys. Perhaps as a consequence of this fresh impetus, the choir began to grow: by 1959 there were 28 boys and 27 adults, 12 of whom had graduated from the boys' section. Additional seating was required and twelve chairs were provided by Mr and Mrs A.E. Dickson. 1959 also saw the inaugural hot-pot and prize-giving supper for choristers and parents.

Mr Hubert Crook, Chief Commissioner of the R.S.C.M., died on September 13th 1960. This brilliant musician had devoted his life to improving the standard of Church Music throughout the country and was a regular visitor to Broughton Church. He was also the Principal of the Choirboys' Course held at Rossall School every Easter, in which many Broughton choristers over the previous fifteen years, had taken part. A Memorial Fund was set up by the R.S.C.M. the income from which it was hoped, would assist those needing help in order to study Church Music. The *Hubert Crook Choirboys' Cup* was first presented at Broughton in January 1961 to the choirboy, who during the past year, has shown merit in: endeavour, singing ability, sight-reading, good behaviour, regular attendance, reverence, loyalty, willingness to help and in setting set an example to younger boys. It has been presented annually ever since.

Mr Dawson left in February 1964, after seven years in charge. His successor was Mr Brian Cryer G.R.S.M., L.R.A.M., A.R.C.M. the Music Master at Preston Grammar School, who took up his post in March. He inherited a strong choir with potential for even greater development, praised by Dr Gerald Knight, Director of the Royal School of Church Music:

The work of this choir is quite impressive and reflects credit on those who have trained it on R.S.C.M. lines. The spirit of the choir is admirable and with such fine materials available, the future promises well.

Despite these accolades however, during 1964 and 1965, there was an urgent need for new choirboys to come forward. Roger Houghton, son of Major Houghton and himself a long-standing member of the choir and regular contributor to the Parish Magazine, made an eloquent plea for volunteers, which is reproduced overleaf.

CHOIR-BOYS WANTED

An Urgent Appeal to Parents

We are desperately in need of at least six boys between the ages of 8 and 11 to fill our fast depleting ranks. The only conditions are that the boys are:

(a) Baptized in the Church of England;

(b) Able to sing and to pitch notes accurately (i.e., are not tone deaf);

(c) Able and willing to attend practices at 6-30 p.m. to 8-30 p.m. each Wednesday evening and Matins and Evensong on Sundays, plus occasional Weddings and Funerals.

The boys are paid 2d. per practice and attendance, provided they attain an 80 per cent. attendance over the year, and in addition they are paid for weddings and funerals.

We have an absolutely first-class Choirmaster and Trainer in Mr. Brian Cryer (the Music Master at Preston Grammar School), and being a choir-boy is quite one of the best forms of service which a boy can give to his church and which the parents, by encouraging the boy to join, can do for their church.

It is felt that no one in Broughton would wish to see our front choir-stalls devoid of boys, but that is what is going to happen if the present state of affairs is not quickly remedied.

A boy can be a choir-boy as well as a Scout or Cub, and the interests of the two seldom clash, owing to excellent co-operation with " Doc " Livingstone and the Scoutmasters.

Boys who join the choir learn to think quickly, and they obtain excellent practical musical knowledge as well as training in team spirit and leadership. They make friendships which can last a lifetime, and they get wonderful opportunities to benefit from residential courses organized by the Royal School of Church Music, as well as occasional visits to massed choir festivals at the Royal Albert Hall and elsewhere. Last year one of our boys was in the R.S.C.M. Choir for the Anglican Conference in Canada.

Being a member of the choir helps a boy with his school work, as it gives him much training in the ability to concentrate, and a high proportion of our present boys have already passed the 11-plus examination.

Being a choir-boy is a thoroughly worthwhile " hobby," full of fun, full of interest, and really satisfying.

On the social side, there is the boys' Choir Outing on the first Saturday in September each year, and the Parents' Evening in early January each year, at which attendance and merit prizes are presented to various boys. On this latter occasion the " Hubert Crook " Choir-boys' Cup is also presented to the boy who is considered to have made the most progress during the previous year.

For many years now our front choir-stalls have always been full of boys, and while it is recognized that TV and other counter attractions are always present, this appeal should not go unheeded in Broughton—where there are scores of potential choir-boys—if everyone who reads it makes a real effort to help us by finding some boys.

Parents wishing their boys to join are asked to bring them to see Mr. Cryer at Broughton Church, at 6-30 on any Wednesday evening, or alternatively on any Sunday after Matins or Evensong.

R. D. H.

Mr Cryer did not remain long. After only a year in charge, he left on July 31st 1965 to take up a school appointment in Glossop. His successor Mr John Catterall M.B.E. was appointed organist and choir master in September the same year, and has remained in post ever since.

For many years choirboys enjoyed the annual treasure hunts in the garden of Roger Houghton's home.

Mr John Catterall came from St Christopher's Church in Lea, where he had been choirmaster for the previous five years, and organist since the age of fourteen. He trained as a teacher at Chester College, where he was College Organist and gained a distinction in Music. In addition, he undertook part-time study with the deputy organist at Chester Cathedral and gained his L.R.A.M. (Organ) diploma in April 1964. At the time of his appointment he was completing a course of advanced organ study with Mr John Bertalot at Blackburn Cathedral as well as working as assistant Music Teacher at the newly opened William Temple Church of England School in Preston. In 1971 he returned to his *alma mater*, Kirkham Grammar School, as Head of Music.

When he took over the Choir at St John's, it consisted of about 13 boys and a dozen adults (including several women). By 1990, after twenty-five years of hard work and dedication, Mr Catterall had doubled the size of the choir to some 34 boys and 16 adults. At the time of writing, 2011, the Choir was made up of 36 boys and some 25 men, many of the latter being *graduates* from the treble stalls. Not only did the Choir grow in size however but also in its reputation for excellence, a reputation which travelled well beyond Preston and Lancashire to all parts of this country and to the Isle of Man and France.

In 1966 the R.S.C.M. introduced a new training scheme for choirboys, one instantly recognisable to the choristers of today. Intended to encourage both competition and loyalty, under the scheme every choir would have a Head Chorister and Team Leaders, each responsible for four or five other boys. Points would be awarded for attendance and work, and each boy's progress would be recorded on different coloured cards. A system of promotion, indicated by different coloured ribbons and badges, would indicate a boy's seniority.

193

By May 1966 this *Choirboys' Training and Incentive Scheme* was being fully used at Broughton, the twenty-eight boys having been divided in to teams. In June, the Choir was admitted to the Guild of St Nicholas, a fellowship within the R.S.C.M. for those choirs with an independent boys' section and which had adopted the training scheme principles. With its definition of ranks among the boys, common agreement of the ability needed to attain those levels, and identifying ribbons and badges, it was, as Roger Houghton explained, *a sort of scouting movement for Choirboys*.

THE CHOIR IN 1966

Back row: (left to right) E.C.Dickson, J.Cox, G.H.Smithies, D.A.S.Houghton, D.M.Piercy, R.D.Houghton, T.Burton, C.Oglesby

Third row: Miss A.Hesketh, Mrs T.Wilcocks, A.Sherratt, M.Birch, Joseph Shaw, S.Grundy, M.Barnes, Jon Shaw, Mrs D.M.Piercy

Second row: B.Chiverton, G.Billington, J.Syms, J.Shaw (warden), Rev. Fielding (curate), Rev. Oatridge (vicar), J.Catterall (choirmaster/organist), F.Benson (warden), C.Broadbent (treasurer), R.Cavanagh, N.Hibell, J.Allen

Front row: J.Sunter, P.Wilkinson, M.Anson, K. Taylor, K.Oglesby, R.Syms, M.Bonnick, M.Harwood, D.Jones, C.Cockerham, M.Cockerham, K.Hatton, R.Dean, J.Turner

Demonstrating that being a chorister wasn't just about singing, the senior boys, perhaps inspired by England's World Cup victory, formed a Choirboys' Football League team in September 1966. By August 1969 the choir was able to regularly field three teams, one of which topped Division 1!

194

20 years of making music

● *Mr John Catterall, choirmaster at Broughton Parish Church and his choristers.* **Picture: Neil Cross.**

CHORISTERS at Broughton Parish Church are familiar with songs of praise ... and now they are singing the praises of their own choirmaster, Mr John Catterall.

For he has just completed 20 years as choirmaster and organist at the church.

At a time when churches are faced with dwindling numbers of choristers and accomplished choirmasters are in short supply, Mr Catterall's achievement is remarkable.

While other churches launch major recruiting drives, St John's, Broughton, boasts a choir comprising 33 boys and 15 adults, figures which bear testimony to Mr Catterall's efforts.

He took over as choirmaster at the church in 1965 when he was just 22. Previously he had been organist at St Christopher's, Lea. He'd been appointed there at the tender age of 16.

At Broughton he took over from Mr Brian Cryer and admits he inherited a "good choral foundation". However, there were only 14 boys in the choir, and he concentrated on building up the trebles section by launching a recruitment drive.

Standards

Twenty years later the success of those efforts is clear to see – a large choir which has maintained consistently high standards.

● Twice the choir has had boys in the last 16 of the Rediffusion Chorister of the Year awards.

● Twice the choir has sung at the Royal Albert Hall – at a Festival of Remembrance and at a Royal School of Church Music Festival.

THE latest member of Broughton Parish Church choir to win top honours is 12-year-old Stuart Stratford (right). He has become a Bishop's Chorister after being successful in the examination at Blackburn Cathedral.

Stuart is a second year pupil at Broughton High School and lives in Marina Drive, Fulwood. He is also a member of Northern Cathedral Singers and, during the summer, was invited to attend a cathedral course at York Minster.

His singing prowess is shared by his two older brothers. Andrew, aged 16, is a former head chorister at Broughton, and is a holder of the coveted St Nicolas award; Ian, aged 14, is currently a team leader in the Broughton choir.

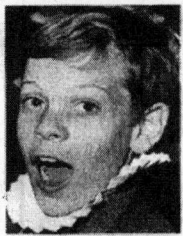

● In the past nine years, since the choir members started auditioning, 40 Broughton boys have been selected for the Northern Cathedral Singers, a showpiece choir which makes appearances in cathedrals and major churches in the North of England.

● Nine Broughton choristers in the past nine years have gained the St Nicolas Award, the highest honour any treble can achieve from the Royal School of Church Music.

● The choir receive regular invitations to sing in cathedrals and major churches. This year Chester Cathedral and Cartmel Priory invited them back.

Faith

Mr Catterall lives in Thornpark Drive, Lea, and is Head of Music at Kirkham Grammar School. He is conscious of the choristers' role in parish life. "Our aim is to foster the boys' Christian faith, not just create musical machines," he says. "The boys gain a sense of purpose and a sense of responsibility and, of course, they enhance the worship in church."

He stresses the commitment which young choristers have to make – a practice every Wednesday night; two services every Sunday; extra preparation for special services, solos, awards and auditions. Favourite diversions are weddings, for there's a small incentive here ... 90p per boy.

Members of the choir have also been invited to sing with local opera groups at wedding receptions, and at Christmas there is a big demand for their services.

The choirmaster himself gets just three weeks off a year ... and they have to be taken in July and August.

The choir receives staunch support from the parish's primary schools, Broughton CE Primary and St Peter's. There is a steady supply of young voices emanating from the schools. "Without that support we would be finished," he says.

Learning

"The process is self-perpetuating. The whole philosophy of the choir is geared to younger boys learning from older boys. As voices break you have constantly changing faces among the trebles. I find myself working with different people and promoting new talents, having been a choirboy myself I enjoy the job."

Many ex-trebles have retained choir membership by moving up into the thriving adults section.

There is a parental commitment too. "Families give up their Sundays completely for several years so that their boys can sing in the choir, and the parental encouragement given to the boys is a big help in maintaining enthusiasm," he says.

One of Mr Catterall's most successful innovations was a week-long holiday course for the choristers in the Isle of Man. That has been held annually since 1973.

"It's a training course and a holiday," he says. "So much of the success the boys have gained has stemmed from what they have learned there."

Tribute

He also tries to promote activities outside music. The choristers have an annual sports day, play soccer and cricket matches and visit places of interest.

There is a family atmosphere about the whole organisation.

One parent paid tribute to Mr Catterall's efforts: "His enthusiasm is infectious. The boys have respect for him as a musician and as a person. There is a lot of hard work but also a lot of fun in being a chorister at Broughton. Mr Catterall is the constant factor that fosters and promotes that atmosphere; this is why Broughton Parish Church choir has prospered and endured."

The choirmaster himself is predictably modest about this kind of praise. "I just love hearing people make music," he says.

The Lancashire Evening Post's 1985 article celebrating Mr Catterall's twenty year career at Broughton and some of the Choir's achievements under his guidance and leadership.

Three years later, thanks to the generosity of Mrs L.B. Flewitt in making a bequest to the Church, the choir was able to buy new cassocks and surplices, to replace those which had been in use since the turn of the century, as well as additional music shelving and robing space in the vestry.

The new cassocks were red, to tone with the Chancel, and were first worn in November 1969. Under Mr Catterall's inspired and inspirational leadership, the choir has flourished. In 1971 it took part in the British Legion Festival of Remembrance at the Albert Hall. Choirboys attended courses at Rossall School and, from April 1973 to the present day, have attended an annual Easter Holiday Course on the Isle of Man.

In 1990 Mr Catterall celebrated twenty-five years in charge of the Choir and the PCC organised a presentation to him to mark what Jack Chiverton, the PCC Secretary, described as his *excellent and devoted service.*

CHOIR GUILD

In 1981 Roger Houghton made an appeal to the ladies of the Parish for a group to form a Choir Guild who would look after and repair the fifty sets of Choir Robes on a regular basis. Several ladies offered their services, among them Mrs Dryland, Mrs Armstrong, Mrs Taylor, Mrs Stratford and Mrs Cronkshaw.

GOLDEN JUBILEE

On the 16th September 1984, the choir celebrated fifty years of affiliation to the R.S.C.M., a milestone marked by two services of Praise and Thanksgiving. The preacher at the Evensong service was Dr Lionel Dakers, the Director of the R.S.C.M.. The service was attended by over ninety past and present singers, forty of whom had been Head or Deputy Head choristers. The celebrations concluded with a celebratory dinner at Broughton Park Hotel.

NEW CHOIR DESKS

The new desks fitted in the choir stalls were dedicated on December 17th 1989, by Canon John Adam, as a memorial to the late Roger Houghton. He was working on plans to design and raise money for the desks when he died. The wrought iron work was carried out by John Hale of Leyland, and the woodwork by Ken Stafford.

DEDICATED CHORISTERS

Many choristers have given dedicated service to the church. Arthur Theodore Houghton was a choir member for forty years, as was George Smithies,

Headteacher at Broughton Primary School. Ted Cavanagh and Frank McLaughlin also completed forty years as choristers though some of this time was spent singing with other choirs. Bert Kennedy sang for some thirty years: a seat outside the choir vestry door, is dedicated to his memory. Roger, the son of Arthur Houghton, was for many years a member of the R.S.C.M. Council, and he too received an award for forty years service in 1973 (see pages 82-83). He in fact completed over fifty-five years service and music desks in the choir stalls were donated in his memory. Few however are likely to rival the longevity of Mr Richard Hardman, who, before his death in 1939, had been for fifty-three years the People's Churchwarden and, for seventy years, a member of the choir. Of the current gentlemen Choristers, Michael Anson has completed forty years as a member of Broughton Choir.

A MOST PARTICULAR FRIEND

One special *friend* of the choir, a warm and generous lady, was Miss A.M. (*Andy*) Anderton. Both her parents died in 1911, within months of each other, and she had to leave her home in Ellen Street, Preston. She was taken into care at the Harris Orphanage at just four years of age. Each Sunday for some eleven years, she would make the three-mile round trip from there to Broughton Church and back, a ritual that whatever the weather, she always enjoyed. After leaving the orphanage at the age of fifteen, she spent some time in Canada before eventually settling in Bamford, near Rochdale, with her niece Eileen.

However a chance visit to Broughton Church in 1977, her first in fifty-five years, brought back many happy childhood memories as she sat in her old pew. She began to correspond with the choirmaster and some of the boys, following the choir's activities closely. She sent hand-made soft toys to be raffled in aid of the Choirboys' Outings Fund.

In 1982 she invited all the boys to a mammoth barbecue at her house, which was to become an annual event for the next five years. She claimed the choir had given her, *the most wonderful moments of my life.* Of the boys themselves, she confessed that she had *grown to love them all*.

Miss Anderton died in September 1986. A section of the choir sang at her funeral service, held at St Michael's Church, Bamford and a memorial service was held at St John's a couple of months later, on Sunday, November 16th.

The A.M. Anderton Cup was first presented in January 1988 to the choirboy with the best attendance during the previous year.

RECENT TIMES

On Sunday 14th June 2009 the Choir celebrated 75 years membership of the RSCM, and as they had done twenty-five years earlier, former Choristers came together to mark the occasion.

Lindsay Gray, the Director of the RSCM was the Guest of Honour, and having met the boys before Evensong, was hugely impressed by their maturity, confidence and of course, their singing.

Gordon Appleton, Director of the *Northern Cathedral Singers*, also commented in his letter to Mr Catterall following the celebration:

The Choral Evensong was splendid: I doubt there is any other Parish Church in the UK (or perhaps the world?) that could boast so many boys, and what is more, boys and men who sing so well!

Not surprisingly, given such praise, The Choir has been invited in recent years, to sing Services at St Paul's Cathedral and, more locally, in both Liverpool Cathedrals for example.

Over the past 20 years the Choir has also undertaken tours to France. Following successful approaches to the Parish Priest at Arzon by Chorister Mr David Ratcliffe during his summer holidays in the Morbihan district of Brittany, the first tour took place in 1991 and a new Broughton Choir tradition was born.

As the Choir increased in number (currently 36 boys and 25 gentlemen) it became clear that a second member of the music staff was needed. This post has been held successively by Paul Dean, Ian Seddon and David Scott-Thomas, the present organist (pictured left).

Mr Catterall (pictured right), for over forty years the inspiration of Broughton Choir and the architect of its success, was awarded the M.B.E. in 2001 in recognition of his *Services to Music in Lancashire.*

In 2010 he was created an Associate of the Royal School of Church Music, receiving the honorary award at a special Service in Durham Cathedral.

CHAPTER 17
A CHURCH RESTORED

The 2006 quinquennial review of the state of repair of the Church buildings at Broughton revealed some worrying problems in both the nave and the tower. The roof of the nave required urgent attention if the interior damp issues were to be resolved: this was to become **Phase 1** of the restoration programme.

The photograph opposite illustrates not only the damp problems in the nave interior but also highlights the urgency of the repair work on its exterior and on the roof.

The Restoration Appeal was launched in 2006. The following year work on the exterior of the nave was completed under the supervision of architect, Michael Rayner, and Church Project Manager, Chris Couper. Before any work on the interior could be attempted however, the rubble-filled walls needed to dry out, a process which took over a year. The work itself, at a cost of £22,777, was carried out by *J C Holden Ltd* of Goosnargh, reflecting the Appeal Committee's stated intention of using local companies for all the work wherever this was possible.

The tower, a Grade 2* Listed Building, required extensive repair work on the roof and considerable specialist restoration work on its stonework. These elements would form **Phase 2** of the programme. This Phase would prove not only the most expensive but also the most demanding in terms of construction specialisms and the specific detail demanded by the sensitive restoration of a C16th building.

The work on the tower attracted a grant of some £60,000 from *English Heritage* and *Heritage Lottery Funding* but this in turn meant the involvement of a second, specialist architect, Mr Steve Burke. The work was carried out by *Bullen Conservation Ltd* of Oldham, at a total cost of £148,688.

The tower almost hidden under its network of scaffolding, shows just how extensive was the restoration work.

Pictured opposite is the roof of the tower and the old flagpole, before repair work. The repaired roof and parapet stonework as well as the new flagpole are illustrated below.

The photograph on the left illustrates the extent to which the stonework had deteriorated over the years. The one below shows how newly carved stone blocks had to be used in some places, as well as the re-pointing required extensively. In order to retain the architectural integrity of the tower, this had to be completed in lime mortar, a notoriously difficult material to work with.

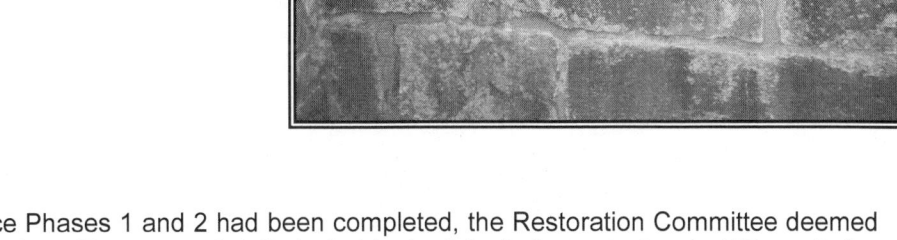

Once Phases 1 and 2 had been completed, the Restoration Committee deemed it prudent, if not essential, that what had originally been designated Phase 5, the repair and redecoration of the nave, be brought forward.

The extensive re-plastering was carried out by *Mark Hull Plastering Ltd* of Fulwood: the redecoration and repainting, following a design scheme approved by parishioners, was undertaken by *Norman J Burke Decorating Services* of Broughton and Joseph Cebrero of Fulwood. The total cost of this Phase was £24,495.

Phase 4, the resurfacing of the footpaths around the church, was carried out by Jim Ramsbottom of Haighton at a cost of £23,867. **Phase 3**, work on the perimeter walls and fences, at an estimated cost of £7,500, is planned for 2012.

The Restoration Appeal ran for some five years, from 2006 to 2011. During that time, through individual donations, fund-raising events, Gift Aid, the sale of recipe books and calendars as well as several grants, it raised an impressive £207,290. On Sunday the 30th January, 2011, the Parish held its *Big Sing,* a choral celebration that marked the formal end of the Restoration Appeal. The congregation expressed its thanks to all the contractors who had done so much to restore and refresh the church building and its surroundings. A special presentation of an album of photographs detailing the restoration work, was presented to Chris Couper. He had acted as unpaid clerk of works for the whole project as well as spending many hours completing the various forms and presentations necessary for the work to proceed.

Over eight hundred years after the original building of a simple wooden chapel on a slightly elevated site on the banks of Blundel Brook, the people who had inherited this sacred space and assumed its stewardship, had ensured that it would continue as a place of worship for many future generations.

The Damaris Dixon Charity

This Charity, the history of which is explored on pages 107-108, was created to assist people living within the Ecclesiastical Parish of Broughton. Although the income only amounts to a few hundred pounds annually, grants can be made where there are cases of need, hardship or distress. The Trustees are able to consider 'one-off' applications rather than regular or recurring grants.

If you know of any person in the Ecclesiastical Parish of Broughton who may be eligible, please advise him or her of this Charity and invite that person to contact the vicar for further information. All applications are treated in the strictest confidence.

Charity number: 222925

Daniel's and Houghton's Charity

This Charity is available to residents of Preston and the local area, and awards grants or provisions in cases of need. It is an amalgamation of the William Daniel Charity of 1656 and the Thomas Houghton Charity of 1649, both histories of which can be found on pages 102-107.

The Trustees meet twice a year to consider applications, although there is provision to assist with emergencies. Grants maybe given for household appliances and repairs, recuperative holidays, special payments to reduce distress and the general relief of need. Further details can be obtained from: Brabners Chaffe Street Solicitors, 7-8 Chapel Street, Preston. PR1 8AN, to whom applications should be made and marked: *For the attention of HR*.

Charity number: 1074762

BIBLIOGRAPHY

A History of Preston: Anthony Hewitson (1883)

A History of Preston in Amounderness: H.W. Clemsha (1912)

A History of Preston: David Hunt (1992)

A History of Lancashire: Baines (1825)

A Little History of the English Country Church: Roy Strong (2008)

An Account of Broughton Parish Church: Rev D.R. Davies

A Short History of Broughton Parish Church: F.E. Wilson and R.D. Houghton (1971)

Broughton Outlook: past editions

Broughton Roundabout: George Jackson (1979)

History of the Parish of Preston: Fishwick (1900)

History of the Borough of Preston and its environs…: Charles Hardwick (1857)

Lancashire Martyrs and Confessors: John Myerscough (1958)

Northward: Anthony Hewitson (1900)

Reformation and Resistance in Tudor Lancashire: Christopher Haigh (1975)

The History of the Parish of St. John Baptist, Broughton: Joyce Rawlinson (1995)